PENGUIN BOOKS
THE LAZY MAN'S WAY TO RICHES

RICHARD GILLY NIXON is a man with a passion about purpose. That was the catalyst of this book, based on the million-plus-copy seller by self-made millionaire Joe Karbo. In keeping with the tone of the book, Richard states with enthusiasm, "You've got to have a purpose to get anywhere in this life." Mr. Nixon is inspired by the throngs of people who have let him know how much the original book helped them achieve self-discovery and success.

Richard achieved early success in the field of real estate, with his own real estate investment firm, and in the consumer products industry with International Playtex Corporation. As an executive with K-Tel International, Inc., he pioneered the television promotion industry in the early 1970s by promoting such products as The Miracle Brush®, The Kitchen Magician®, Wham-O Toys®, and K-Tel's most famous products, Compilation Records ("22 original hits by the original stars" — and "the best of . . ."). Richard founded Radiographic Development Corporation (RDC), a medical X-Ray manufacturing company, which he took public in 1980. He is now the President of F. P. Publishing Co., Inc., a publisher of books, audio and video tapes, and seminars.

Richard has personally achieved both success and failure, enabling him to learn compelling lessons from both experiences. He has dedicated the past three years to working on this updated version of the book, combining his work with the original text plus utilizing Joe Karbo's unpublished notes and manuscripts, as well as gathering additional material from other noted sources.

In addition to being a gifted public speaker, seminar leader, and business consultant, Richard is the proud parent of three children and the grandparent of three. He lives in El Morro Beach, California.

JOE KARBO was the author of the original *The Lazy Man's Way to Riches*, first published in 1973, right after he gained a net worth in excess of a million dollars. Quite an achievement for a man from humble beginnings. In 1945, at 20, he was discharged from the service with a wife and child, no money, and only a high school education. He forwent college to get on with making his fortune, starting with minor success in the scrap paper business. He moved on to acting, then selling, followed by advertising, radio, and, finally, to the field he truly loved, television, with a show of his own with his wife, Betty. Their all-night show, airing live from midnight to 8 A.M. from Hollywood, was the first in the country. Sponsors for such a new venture were scarce, so to keep the show on the air the Karbos started a direct-mail business selling a diversity of products, the most memorable being the Super Spy, which "lets you see through walls, fences and locked doors." Joe became a master of advertising and copywriting, and his formulas and teaching are still taught and used today in the direct-mail business.

Joe was ahead of his time also in the area of personal development, in which he developed his Dyna-Psyc psychology, whose principles are in the forefront of what is being taught today. As a result of all his experiences and success, Joe wrote *The Lazy Man's Way to Riches* to share what he had learned and believed with others. Joe passed away in 1980, ironically, as Joe would have chosen to go, on camera. He is survived by his wife, Betty, and eight children.

*How to have
everything in the world
you really want*

THE LAZY MAN'S WAY TO RICHE$

COMPLETELY REVISED AND UPDATED BY

RICHARD GILLY NIXON

BASED ON THE BOOK BY

JOE KARBO

PENGUIN BOOKS

PENGUIN BOOKS
Published by the Penguin Group
Penguin Books USA Inc., 375 Hudson Street, New York, New York 10014, U.S.A.
Penguin Books Ltd, 27 Wrights Lane, London W8 5TZ, England
Penguin Books Australia Ltd, Ringwood, Victoria, Australia
Penguin Books Canada Ltd, 10 Alcorn Avenue, Toronto, Ontario, Canada M4V 3B2
Penguin Books (N.Z.) Ltd, 182–190 Wairau Road, Auckland 10, New Zealand

Penguin Books Ltd, Registered Offices: Harmondsworth, Middlesex, England

The Lazy Man's Way to Riches by Joe Karbo first published in the United States of America 1973
Revised and expanded edition by Richard G. Nixon published by F. P. Publishing Co., Inc. 1993
Published in Penguin Books 1995

1 3 5 7 9 10 8 6 4 2

ISBN 0 14 02.4936 2

Printed in the United States of America

THE LAZY MAN'S
WAY TO RICHE$

ON THIS DATE

_____

(Today's Date)

BEGINS THE PERSONAL JOURNEY OF

_____

(Your Name)

*This book is dedicated
to the memory of*
Joe Karbo

ACKNOWLEDGMENTS

Any major project involves the contribution of many people: *The Lazy Man's Way to Riches* is no exception.

The first debt of thanks must go to the thousands of people who inspired us by writing over the years to express their appreciation for the teachings in this book and to share their success stories with us. Many of you asked for an expanded and updated version. Your letters were the impetus for this revised, updated, and expanded book. You asked for it so here it is.

Deepest appreciation goes out to my friend Suzanne Edwards. When I first told her about this project she expressed a dislike for the title because she felt the word *lazy* carried a negative connotation. How could anything good come out of being lazy?

As she read the manuscript she began to understand Joe's connotation of "lazy," and that riches *could* come easily. She decided to jump aboard as the editor — editor extraordinaire! Her insightful and challenging input and editing magic enabled me to do the near impossible task of compiling Joe's original classic book with other notes and unpublished manuscripts of his, along with my extensive manuscript and portions of material published by Joe's Society of Partners. It was a task not unlike shuffling the pages of four or five books and having them end up reading like a single book; yet all the while keeping the original message and style of the true classic. Bravo! And thank you to Suzanne, who took time away from her own television production company and television shows to add so very much to this project.

Grateful appreciation to Jay Flanagan, who worked tirelessly on this entire project, especially the second part of this book. He made sure it was revised and updated correctly and accurately. Jay worked with and for Joe Karbo for more than twenty years, starting as a gofer, working his way up to general manager and ultimately to the presidency of Joe's companies. He remained in that position until joining me at Nixon • Karbo Publishing. Jay's personal knowledge and insights about Joe were invaluable and greatly appreciated.

Appreciation also to Chuck Abbott, who is a best-selling author, a leading speaker, and a top attorney. He is one of Joe's best students — some would even say surpassing Joe in the area of Direct Response Marketing. I'd like to thank Chuck for his assistance during the editing process and give special thanks for his help on Book Two. Chuck, himself a Mail Order Millionaire, is currently one of the most sought-after speakers on the subject of Direct Response Marketing in the country today. (Most of his material is currently available in his audio or video marketing courses.) In my opinion, Chuck is one of the glowing examples of how well the principles in this book work.

Thanks to Karl Wolfe of Creative Personal Communications for sharing his insight about the book with me, which guided me in making valuable course corrections for the book as well as for our company in general. He is a master fine tuner and a important friend for our projects.

This entire project was produced in-house using Macintosh computers, particularly the Ilci, Powerbook 170, and Quadra 800. A variety of software including Quark XPress, MSWord, Filemaker Pro, and Adobe Illustrator were utilized, all of it under the skillful direction of Charles R. Bouley II. Charles is a veteran of desktop publishing as well as a seasoned music industry journalist. His talents have led him to singing and nightclub performing. His recordings and videos are available from Orbik Productions under the name of Karel. He is a virtuoso of the musical, journalistic, and computer arts.

The highest compliment this book could have received over the years is to be constantly used by the current giants of the direct reponse industry. The continuing sales of this book are due in large measure to the fact that they not only use it but recommend it in their books, newsletters, and seminars. So a special thanks to Jay Abraham, E. Joseph Cossman, Carl Galetti, Gary Halbert, Tyler G. Hicks, Jim Kobs, Ted Nicholas, Dr. Gary North, Mac Ross, Tom and Marilyn Ross, Eugene M. Schwartz, Russ Von Hoelsher, and all else for their continued references and recommendations of *The Lazy Man's Way to Riches*.

Thanks also to: Shawn Edwards for the tedious job of transcribing and typing support; to Cheryl Johnson and Saundra Clark, who are working on a student workbook version of *The Lazy Man's Way to Riches* (under the working title, *Roadmap to Success*); to Bruce Haniford, C.P.A., my friend and business adviser, who makes sure that it all works the way we say it is supposed to. I owe a special debt of gratitude to Yvonne Lambie, who performed the initial proofreading and corrected multitudes of my spelling and grammatical errors, and Holly Novak, who not only did the final proofreading but diligently undertook the laborious task of cross-referencing the entire book.

Last, but certainly not least, I'd like to thank Betty Karbo for her faith in this project and her faith in me.

CONTENTS

BOOK ONE: THE JOURNEY

PART 1 – YOUR ITINERARY

PART 2 – ON THE ROAD

BOOK TWO: TURNING DYNA-PSYC INTO DOLLARS

BOOK ONE

THE JOURNEY

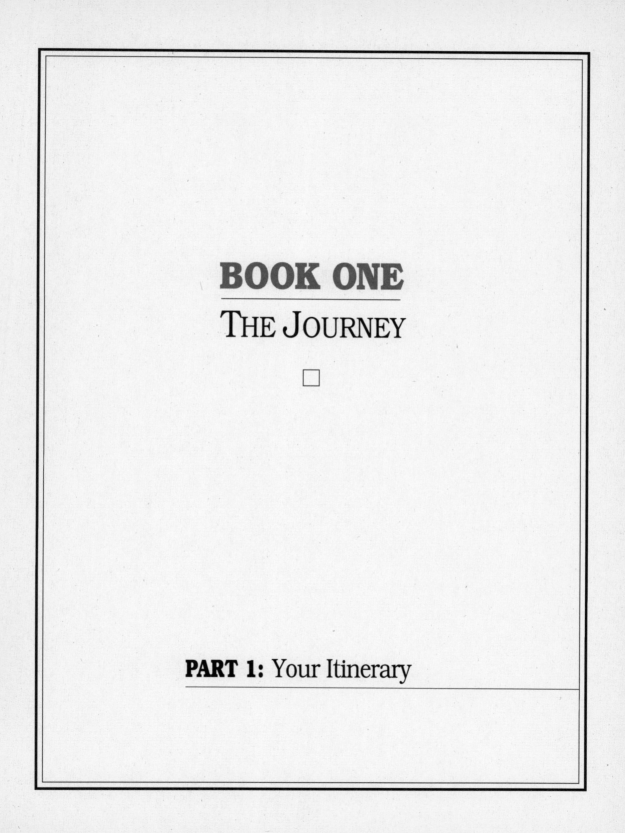

PART 1: Your Itinerary

THE SECRET OF SUCCESS

You are about to read an updated, expanded, and revised classic — a book that has sold more than three million copies. The author, Joe Karbo, sold this book from 1973 until his death in 1980 through the most powerful channels of sales in existence — Direct Response Advertising and word of mouth.

That is a good book which is opened with expectation and closed in profit.

AMOS BRONSON ALCOTT (1799–1888)
American author, educator, mystic

JOE KARBO

Joe Karbo was a uniquely amazing man, and both he and this remarkable book were the subjects of articles and stories in *Time, Money, Changing Times, Forbes*, and even *Consumer Reports*. Newspapers too numerous to mention also chronicled the story of Joe Karbo and the book that was changing the lives of those who utilized its secrets. Joe was most probably the very first, and possibly the only author of a book of this type, to write in the first person. Others tell you "how" to do what they themselves haven't done successfully based on some theory or principle, but Joe wrote from personal, practical experience. Joe was a self-made man — a lazy man by his own admission — and a rich man. Some people thought Joe made his fortune from the enormous sales of this book, but he had made millions prior to even thinking about writing a book. *The Lazy Man's Way to Riches* is Joe's philosophy on life and how to live it richly, successfully, lovingly, joyously, and lazily. It is also a detailed report on exactly how he made millions of dollars, and in it he reveals those secrets to you. In his masterful simplicity, Joe Karbo records some of the most dynamic principles ever penned regarding what it means to be truly rich and how to get there.

The man who writes about himself and his own time is the only man who writes about all people and about all time.

GEORGE BERNARD SHAW (1856–1950)
Irish playwright, critic, social reformer

TRUE WEALTH

The valuable and lasting lessons you will receive from

Books give not wisdom where none was before. But where some is, there reading makes it more.

JOHN HARINGTON (1516–1617)
English satirist, writer

this book will bring you the freedom to be, to do, and to have what you want. It will also bring you financial freedom, but more importantly it will bring you your idea of true success — *true wealth.* Success is best defined by one's own achievements, which may include excellent mental health, physical health, loving relationships — with both family members and friends — spiritual fulfillment, self-actualization, material wealth, and a rarely achieved peace of mind.

Bottom line? This book can help you attain all that's important to you, to become all that you were created to be and to do — to become that uniquely wonderful person that is hiding down deep inside — the real you.

No mind ever receives the truth until it's prepared to receive it. Remember the old adage, "When the student is ready, the teacher will appear." You're obviously ready to receive this new truth. Congratulations as you enter the world of freedom, success, and true wealth. So, let's get started now!

THE BEST OF YOUR LIFE

Welcome to the first day of the **Best** of your life. We are going to take you step by step down the road to Riches, success, and happiness. I'm Richard Gilly Nixon, and it is my pleasure to be your guide on your exciting journey to everything you have ever wanted. I am going to bring you Joe Karbo's personal advice, and together with some wonderful people who helped me on this project, I will tell you how to find within yourself the talents and resources to get everything you want out of life — The Lazy Man's Way.

No man is great enough or wise enough for any of us to surrender our destiny to. The only way in which anyone can lead us is to restore to us the belief in our own guidance.

HENRY MILLER (1891–1980)
American writer

In order to bring you this exciting new book, we have spent countless hours revising, expanding, and editing Joe's original book. We have added the lessons learned from the business and psychological communities in the past twenty years since its original printing and our own experience learned from *The Lazy Man's Way to Riches.*

To help you understand and appreciate the exciting metamorphosis of this book, we have set off all of Joe Karbo's original book, from the expanded revision, with a faint gray line running alongside Joe's text (illustrated next to this paragraph) so you will be able to identify and taste the unique flavor of Joe Karbo. When no line is present, you are reading new, expanded, and revised text of *The Lazy Man's Way to Riches.* We have taken the liberty of updating some of the figures in Joe's text so that they might be more easily understood in relation to today's economy and have made some minor changes to better fit the times. Other than that, it is pure Joe Karbo!

I first became aware of Joe Karbo in September 1973, while I was running a successful television promotion company. A very bright employee brought in an ad written for *The Lazy Man's Way to Riches.* She was so impressed with the ad that she sent for the book. When the book arrived, she read it over and over again, carefully highlighting key thoughts and ideas on each page, in a different color with each new reading. By the fifth reading, she had a virtual rainbow of colors throughout her treasured new book. She didn't simply read it; she studied, visualized, and consumed it. Instead of sharing her copy of *The Lazy Man's Way to Riches* with me, she bought me a copy of my own. Upon studying the book, Linda's self-esteem dramatically improved and her performance at the office skyrocketed. It was astonishing! She credited *The Lazy Man's Way to Riches* for it all. Linda went on to become successful and rich beyond her dreams, in the medical supply business and as an entrepreneur. Linda bought many copies of *The Lazy Man's Way to Riches* as gifts for her friends. She became a disciple of Joe Karbo and the lessons that brought her true Riches.

I read the book for myself and found, much to my

The books that help you most are those which make you think the most.

THEODORE PARKER (1810–1860)
Unitarian theologian, publicist

delight, that it lived up to its promises as expressed by Linda. Unfortunately, as a student, I wasn't ready for it yet. I was impressed because it rang true to my own life experiences, but because I was already successful beyond my limited dreams, I didn't pay much attention to it. After leaving the television promotion company, I helped establish a company that manufactured medical X-ray equipment. This company became enormously successful, through internal growth and the purchase of other companies, and was quickly listed on the stock exchange. Because of this success at that point in my life, no self-help book mattered to me. What more could there be for me to know?

At age 40, I retired. I felt I had worked long enough and had achieved all my goals. I decided I had enough money to last for the rest of my life; I could finally relax and play. But in my "success," I managed to destroy everything over the next four years — a lifetime of money went down the proverbial drain. This self-destruction culminated in a divorce and a bankruptcy. I was living proof that this book works — by diligently applying everything *backwards* — I went from wealth to poverty; from physical health to sickness; from mental health to stressed-out; from loving relationships to wrecked relationships — and certainly there was no inner peace.

When you hit bottom, there's no place to go but up. But because the human mind works in wonderful ways, I remembered the book. I dug it out. I read it for the second time — but studied it for the first time. The student was finally ready; I was prepared to learn.

Having applied the principles of *The Lazy Man's Way to Riches*, I have successfully rebuilt my life based upon what I really want to do with my life. I can personally testify that these principles work — often in spite of me. That's how powerful this book is. It helped me deactivate the self-destructive and self-limiting mechanisms and

I suggest that the only books that influence us are those for which we are ready, and which have gone a little further down our particular path than we have yet got ourselves.

E. M. FORSTER (1879–1970)
English novelist, short-story writer, essayist

begin to rebuild my positive self-images and my self-esteem. I now enjoy the Riches that have blossomed from the most revolutionary life-principles. My success story is a direct application of the powerful principles in *The Lazy Man's Way to Riches*. These principles have given me a way to effect long-lasting results and have put me on the road to permanent change.

THE POWER OF BELIEF — FOR YOU

The power of belief can be a destructive force or a dynamic, positive force for you. You decide which it will be. It has been said that "When one person believes he can and another person believes he can't, they are both right." The power of believing in your purpose or vision is at the core of performance, achievement, and Riches. Your beliefs create your reality. This book shows you a way to transform your belief system from a passive, destructive force into a positive, dynamic force. Some of the statements in this book may be argued; but every day these same principles are working for us as well as millions of others, and they will work for you, too.

TRY TO PROVE IT RIGHT.
DO IT.
DO IT NOW.
DO IT FOR YOU.

With this book you can have *everything* you want. Yes, I said everything. There is probably a good chance that you were drawn to this book primarily for the purpose of improving your life financially and that you relate to *everything* in terms of what only having more money can provide for you. I promise you that as you travel the road to success with *The Lazy Man's Way to Riches* you will discover that you can have *everything* in <u>all</u> areas of your life so that your life will be balanced; the stimulation of having a clear mind, the joy of feeling good about yourself,

A man only learns in two ways, one by reading, and the other by association with smarter people.

WILL ROGERS (1879–1935)
American actor, humorist

How many a man has dated a new era in his life from reading a book?

HENRY DAVID THOREAU (1817–1862)
American essayist, naturalist, poet

When one person believes he can and another person believes he can't, they are both right.

HENRY FORD (1863–1947)
American industrialist

One must live the way one thinks or end up thinking the way one has lived.

PAUL BOURGET (1852–1935)
French novelist, critic, poet

Insanity is doing the same thing in the same way and expecting a different outcome.

LESLIE CALVIN BROWN (B. 1945)
Lecturer, speaker, motivator, author

the satisfaction of relating effectively with your fellow man, the thrill of loving your vocational endeavor, the exhilaration of feeling physically fit and the comfort of finding your place in the universe and with the beliefs you hold dear. True Riches. Everything! You may say there has to be a limit to what you could be and do and have; but no one, not even you, knows what that limit is. So, break through the barriers. Remember, one person's floor is another person's ceiling. Break through that ceiling. It's time to educate yourself beyond your current education, because your current education only got you where you are now. Get yourself a "Ph.D." in who you can be, what you can have, what you can do, and how to get your success — your Riches. Just remember . . .

**"IF YOU KEEP DOING WHAT YOU'RE DOING,
YOU'LL JUST KEEP GETTING WHAT YOU'RE GETTING."**

Once you begin applying the Dyna/Psyc principles of *The Lazy Man's Way to Riches*, you'll make more progress in a very few months or even weeks than in all the preceding years of your life. In many ways, the older you are the better, because you already have a wealth of experience to build upon; and you already know what doesn't work for you.

THE KEYS TO SUCCESS AND RICHES

So, how has this book become one of the best-sellers of all time? Simple. It works. This book will not only show you how to have *anything* you want, but *everything* you want. I wish it were possible for you to read the thousands of letters written to us in praise of this book. They are such dramatic testimonials to the worth of a single book. For some people, it meant a drastic change of direction in their lives. For some, it meant a subtle fine-tuning of their thinking that opened new worlds. For others, it meant a new flow of wellness — including personal, mental, emotional, relational, and **financial wealth.** For most the story was pretty much the same — it was positively life-changing.

There is one thing these letters have in common. They are all "thank you" letters to Joe for writing this book. You may want to write us such a letter yourself after you achieve your Riches. There is no magic, no hocus-pocus, no mumbo-jumbo here; it's just uncommon thought presented in a common way. It's common sense.

What a sense of security in an old book which time has criticized for us.

JAMES RUSSELL LOWELL (1819–1891)
American poet, critic, editor, diplomat

TRUE RICHES

Joe's insight into how life works brought him true Riches in addition to the millions of dollars he earned: joy, love, fulfillment, satisfaction, and freedom in all its forms. He was free to do what he wanted to do, how he wanted to do it, where he wanted to do it, when he wanted to do it, and with whom. It also brought him the Riches of "freedom from": freedom from want, freedom from fear, freedom from jealousy, freedom from envy, and freedom from worry. Joe's insights can do the same for you. All you have to do is follow along and do the steps that will lead you to your life of Riches.

The secret point of money and power in America is neither the thing that money can buy nor power for power's sake . . . but absolute personal freedom, mobility, privacy. It is the instinct which drove Americans to the Pacific.

JOAN DIDION (B. 1934)
American writer

YOUR RICHES?

Different Riches await you — *your* Riches — when you dig into this book and find the treasures for yourself. It's knowing what courses to take in the "school of life" and having a teacher who cares. All of us who are enjoying a heartbeat right now are enrolled in this universal school.

The question is: What classes must you attend? What courses must you take in order to graduate to your Riches, to experience and enjoy life to its fullest? Here are just a few of the "courses" we are offering in this book:

PURPOSE 101

Purpose is the primary "course" necessary for growth and progress throughout your life. It's the answer to the question, Why am I here? Each of us has been uniquely created to be and do certain things — our purpose. It's a sense of destiny. This is the life course that drives all of the others. If your purpose is to be a teacher or coach, then stop kidding yourself about buying expensive new sports cars, a multimillion dollar oceanfront home, or anything else that demands big bucks. Follow your purpose and be that teacher or coach. You'll never be happy or find that inner peace and joy of life until you find and follow your own powerful purpose. It's been said, "If you do what you love — the money will follow." Note the order: Do what you love, then the money will follow. Following your purpose assures you the Riches you seek.

SUCCESS 101

Some say the real answer to enjoying life to its fullest is to have P.M.A. (Positive Mental Attitude): positive expectations, motivation, desire, and commitment to go along with the dynamic principles available through the "self-help" movement. But there are vital "missing links" that are most often overlooked. You need someone to walk you through the application of the great truths of life. You

Existence is a strange bargain. Life owes us little; we owe it everything. The only true happiness comes from squandering ourselves for a purpose.

WILLIAM COWPER (1731–1800)
English poet

There is only one success—to be able to live your life in your own way.

CHRISTOPHER MORLEY (1890–1957)
American novelist, journalist, essayist

need a mentor, a teacher, a tutor, or an assistant to help you process what you know to be true and incorporate that truth into your entire lifestyle — your purpose statement. Your mentor is exactly what this book is. Use it that way. When you purchased this book, you enrolled in one of the most exciting classes of your life — SUCCESS 101.

SELF-LOVE 101

A third course that shows you how to experience and enjoy life to its fullest is SELF-LOVE. One of the keys to self-loving is to permit yourself to *be* and *do* what you really love to be and to do. Being and doing what you love is vital to a highly successful life. There is an epidemic of toxic thought in our world today that goes like this:

**I MUST KEEP DOING ALL THE THINGS THAT I HATE DOING
IN ORDER TO GET AHEAD IN LIFE.**

It is true that you must learn to discipline yourself to do things that you don't necessarily love; but when you see that these things are going to give you what you want, you begin to see them as friends, not enemies. The best-selling author Dr. M. Scott Peck defines discipline as "love translated into action."

Some of us have easily become our own worst enemies. It's so easy to become toxic — poisonous to ourselves. Many of us learn to sabotage our lives by listening to the many "expert" voices out there rather than looking within ourselves; therefore, the masses of people just like us are living their lives to please everyone else — in order to simply get by. How sad. What a miserable existence that is. It is so important to trust your own inner voice, your own integrity, to be dependent upon only yourself and to be honest with yourself.

Be careful of the toxic people in your world. They are like weeds in your garden. They will inevitably choke the very life out of you. You want someone in your life who is

To love one's self is the beginning of a life-long romance.

OSCAR WILDE (1854–1900)
Irish-born English poet, playwright, novelist

What I must do is all that concerns me, not what the people think.

RALPH WALDO EMERSON (1803–1882)
American poet, essayist, philosopher

your best friend. Someone who will hang in there with you and support you no matter what. Someone who is always on your side, good times and bad, aware of your needs, willing to encourage you and to challenge you to do your best. Someone who is considerate, dependable, honest, and loving. Someone you can trust. Someone who really gives a rip whether you live or die. Who is that someone? It's *you*. When Jesus was asked to summarize the Law of Moses, He said, "Love God with all your heart, soul, and mind. And love your neighbor as yourself." In other words, if you don't love yourself, your neighbor is in a heap of trouble. In this book SELF-LOVE teaches you how to love yourself most effectively.

PERSONAL RIGHTS 101

You have the right to be happy. You have the right to be prosperous. You have the right to be productive. You have the right to be healthy in body, mind, and spirit. You have the right to be who you want to be.

The Constitution of the United States of America is set up to protect the rights of its citizens. Those who attack those rights within its borders are brought to justice by the constituted authorities. Those outside the borders who attack the rights of U.S. citizens are repelled by its armed forces. When our bodies are attacked by various diseases, our immune system fights back to keep us healthy. Most people are in the same way affected by "viruses" outside the body causing a "dis-ease" in financial, mental, career, physical, social, family, and spiritual areas of their lives. You have the right to fight that dis-ease. You can do that by learning WHO YOU REALLY ARE, WHAT YOU WANT IN LIFE AND HOW TO GET IT. This book helps you do just that.

They have rights who dare to maintain them.

JAMES RUSSELL LOWELL (1819–1891)
American poet, critic, editor, diplomat

GROWTH 101

Although change is constantly happening, it's natural to try to avoid it. People just don't like change; it's too uncomfortable. But in order to get what you want in life, it will require some changes. If you are not truly happy where you are, a lack of change will surely keep you where you are — dissatisfied and stuck. Master-Motivator Les Brown says that, "Insanity is doing the same thing in the same way and expecting a different result." So let's grow.

YOU HAVE THE RIGHT TO GROW.
YOU HAVE THE OPTION TO GROW.
YOU CAN ALLOW YOURSELF TO GROW.
YOU CAN ENCOURAGE YOURSELF TO GROW.

Growth comes in three opportunity packages:

First, growth by starting something new. As you read this book you will be motivated and challenged to make several decisions. It's your choice. You are in the driver's seat. You can *choose* to do new things and try new approaches.

Second, growth by stopping something you are presently doing. Remember, if you keep doing what you're doing, you will just keep getting what you're getting. Growth sometimes is easiest to affect by simply stopping the doing of that which isn't working for you. Growth doesn't have to mean doing something. If it isn't working for you, it can't propel you toward your personal Riches. It follows then that it would be wise to learn to stop doing what you're doing that's getting in your way. So, stop kidding yourself. Stop lying to yourself. Stop blaming others. Stop drinking, drugging, overeating, procrastinating or whatever it is that gets in your way. Stop doing those things that are not working for you, and your life will instantly and dramatically improve. You may be thinking, "Easy for you to say"; and it is. With Dyna/Psyc and the other principles you will learn in this book you can stop

The strongest principle of growth lies in human choice.

GEORGE ELIOT (Pen name of MARY ANN EVANS) (1819–1880)
English novelist

At the end of the next 20 years you can have 20 years experience — or you can have one year's experience 20 times. It's a matter of choice.

RICHARD GILLY NIXON (B. 1940)
American entrepreneur, publisher, author, speaker, seminar leader

The man who makes no mistakes does not usually make anything.

EDWARD J. PHELPS (1822–1900)
Lawyer, diplomat

As a man thinketh so is he, and as a man chooseth so is he.

RALPH WALDO EMERSON (1803–1882)
American poet, essayist, philosopher

In the case of good books, the point is not how many of them you can get through, but rather how many can get through to you.

MORTIMER JEROME ADLER (B. 1902)
American author, philosopher

putting speed bumps or roadblocks on your way to your Riches.

Third, growth through the mistakes we make. Mistakes offer you a major opportunity for personal growth, if you take advantage of them. Mistakes can be encouraged, even welcomed. That's how we learn and grow. They are course corrections in your life, *if* you know where you are headed. So, welcome your mistakes as friends that provide stepping stones and course corrections on your journey to your personal successes and Riches.

GROWTH REQUIRES MAKING CHOICES We live the way we have chosen to live, but seldom is it the way we *want* to live. Our choices are driven by our purpose (or our lack of a clear purpose) and emerge out of our beliefs, preferences, habits, tastes, and behaviors. What we want can only come to us through positive change. First we start doing what will work for us, then we stop doing what doesn't work for us.

What if someone else were to take your liberty from you? The authorities would arrest and punish that person. But aren't *you* the one who has taken away your liberty? And haven't you punished yourself by being unwilling to grow so that you can change those things that don't work for you?

Do you like where your life has been? Do you like where it is now? And where it's probably headed if you continue without change? Are you involved in worthwhile and meaningful pursuits of your own choosing? Are you satisfied with your job, your career? Do you like how you're living — your home, your neighborhood, your clothes, your furniture, your cars, vacations and recreation? Are you happy with your relationships and friends? You can answer "Yes" to all of these questions with the lessons you will learn in Growth 101. GROWTH IN ALL AREAS WILL BE YOURS!

ABOUT THIS PROGRAM

This program is organized in a special way for you to maximize your efforts learning everything you possibly can for yourself. There are three important components that make up the program:

BOOK ONE - PART ONE *Your Itinerary.* In this part you begin your journey on the road to Riches by looking at yourself and the tools necessary for the trip — putting things into perspective.

BOOK ONE - PART TWO *On the Road.* You're on your way: and in this part, you learn to deal with what you will find on your journey, as you choose the right paths to your destination — success and your Riches.

BOOK ONE - PART THREE *The Destination — Your Way!* This part moves you along the road to your personal Riches by showing you the application of the principles you have learned and how to take control of your life. It's a game plan for living your life on purpose.

BOOK TWO *Turning Dyna/Psyc into Dollars* — In this part of the book, we tell you all of the secrets that will enable you to make millions of dollars just as Joe Karbo did. He actually spells out the success formula for what many people call "the most exciting business in the world." This may be why you bought the book, but please read the books in order — one, then two; that is the only way to maximize the program's benefits.

As an added bonus throughout the book, we bring you quotations from all of recorded human history on the subjects we are discussing. The quotes serve to reinforce and amplify the text with the wisdom of the ages. You'll see that the ideas we present are solid, time-tested, accepted, and valued by scholars, writers, religious leaders, politicians, thinkers and just plain folks from all corners of the world, for over 2500 years. Quotes are mankind's way of "snapshoting" the truths of the ages. We use them to

When it is dark enough, you can see the stars.

CHARLES AUSTIN BEARD (1874–1948)
American historian

A fine quotation is a diamond in the hand of a man of wit and a pebble in the hand of a fool.

JOSEPH ROUX (1834–1905)
French priest, writer

provide you with food for thought as you ponder the concepts we are presenting that may be foreign or new to you. There is not a right way or wrong way to read these quotes. If you find it too distracting to read them as you are reading the text, then don't read them at that time. It may work better for you to come back and read the quotes separately. Some people have read the quotes along with the text and have enjoyed the experience as a nice set up for the material. You may find that you want to review the quotes as you finish reading each chapter. Experiment. See what works for you.

The Lazy Man's Way to Riches that you are holding in your hands contains everything — and much, much more — that the original (the best-selling "classic") contained. It contains virtually every word, every thought, every bit of wisdom that Joe originally penned. Yet it also contains the additional insights and expertise from myself, Tim Timmons, Jay Flanagan, Chuck Abbott, Dick Johnson, Suzanne Edwards, and others, making this, the new *Lazy Man's Way To Riches*, a more beneficial program than it was before.

One final thing. *The Lazy Man's Way to Riches* is not an ordinary program. It's an extraordinary program. It will tell you all you need to know to have everything you want. It should not be read like a novel or story. It should be read with thought about what you have just read, then digested, mulled over and questioned. (What does this mean? What does this mean to *me*? How can I apply this to my life? Could this be true?) Read it chapter by chapter, concept by concept; then read it again and again.

HOW TO READ THIS BOOK

Of course you know how to read but if you merely read this book as you have read other books, you are going to cheat yourself out of one of life's great experiences. So, let us help you — please.

You can't expect to hit the jackpot if you don't put a few nickels in the machine.

FLIP (CLEROW) WILSON (B. 1933)
American actor, comedian

As you read this book imagine that you are on a shopping tour. Take only those ideas that appeal to you now and use them only if they make sense to you. From my experience, I find that a book of this type is most beneficial when I withhold my natural or fear-driven skepticism. Read the following pages with an open mind. If something makes sense to you, try it. If it doesn't make sense to you or you feel it doesn't apply to you at this point in your life, feel free to discard it. In whatever you do, be a student, not merely a follower. Joe Karbo's suggestion to R.S.V.P. (read it, study it, visualize it, perform it) was most beneficial in making me a more effective student.

WRITE IN YOUR BOOK Write in the margins of your book. Yes, write in it. Why not? It's yours. Make notes about those things that you feel are most important to you. Underline in pencil or ink. Use a highlighter — whatever; use something. The first time I read *The Lazy Man's Way to Riches* I used a yellow highlighter. The second time, I used a pink highlighter and found I had highlighted passages and thoughts I had missed my first time through. The third time I read the book, I used a blue highlighter. This time I discovered new insights and principles that just didn't seem so important the first two times. Just as Linda had done years before, I was creating my own rainbow. I was highlighting ideas I repeatedly viewed as important. Each time I reviewed the book, it took much less time, because I simply reviewed the highlighted passages. With each successive review, I began to learn more about *me*, what I wanted, and how I could and would possess my Riches. The fourth time I used orange to highlight those parts that now jumped out at me. They were becoming keys to my success. The last color I used, on my fifth journey through *The Lazy Man's Way to Riches,* was red; it was too dark to read through with all the other colors layered under it. So then I bracketed the sentences or paragraphs (even whole pages) that now reinforce the way to my Riches.

On subsequent re-readings you could even use arrows or exclamation points in the margins to draw your attention. You do what you want with your book. After all, it's your life we are talking about, and it deserves to be understood, highlighted, underlined, and punctuated.

FINDING RICHES IN THE PAGES OF THIS BOOK

Imagine how different your life is from your parents' lives when they were the age you are now. Then consider how different your life is from your grandparents when they were the age you are now. Everything is different in the world today because of someone's thoughts resulting from their desires and beliefs. Everything. Thoughts created all of the inanimate things you see. Some human being thought of it, worked to bring it into existence; and we enjoy it today. Houses, X-rays, cars, airplanes, vaccines, appliances, televisions, contact lenses, computers, jet planes, skyscrapers, frozen food, plastic, running water, supermarkets, wristwatches, ballpoint pens, pantyhose, faxes, videos — everything is either new or radically different.

Imagine that! Everything was first just a thought that someone *made up* to improve something, solve a problem or simply because of the joy they received by bringing something that they loved into existence. Our modern buildings are just an improvement on the cave of ancient man. All of our modern appliances are nothing more than thoughts on how to solve various problems of performing some task in an easier manner. Some of what we enjoy is the result of pure creative thought for no purpose except the love of it: music, poetry, dance, and most of the arts. No one really "needs" the arts; they are pure manifestations of the love of their creators. Mozart created his music because he loved it. Picasso created his paintings because he loved to paint. Fred Astaire loved to

There are two kinds of success. One is the very rare kind that comes to the man who has the power to do what no one else has the power to do. That is genius. But the average man who wins what we call success is not a genius. He is a man who has merely the ordinary qualities that he shares with his fellows, but who has developed those ordinary qualities to a more than ordinary degree.

THEODORE ROOSEVELT (1858–1919)
26th President of the United States

dance. Walt Disney created several characters all for the sheer love of doing it and for the potential entertainment value they might offer. The United States of America was created from a vision of the love of freedom backed by a burning desire and a belief that it could be created. Your thoughts create your reality and your thoughts will create your future — *change your thoughts and you change your life now and for the Best of your life.*

GETTING EVERYTHING YOU WANT

That's what this book is all about — thoughts, self-love and creating your life the way you want it. That's what Riches are. This is not just another self-help book on the latest fad out of pop psychology. This book contains the proven best thinking from over 2500 years of human civilization upon which to build the foundation for your life. It is from this foundation that you can get *everything* you want out of your life.

In "computerese" the saying goes, "Garbage in; garbage out." Most of us are where we are now because of input fed to us and accepted by us during the course of growing up. This input was from role models: parents, teachers, mentors, and the myriad of other people who formed and guided our lives; who were probably not highly trained, well-educated, super-intelligent, or enormously successful. They were just average people. If you are looking today for your version of success as you know it to be in your heart, then you need to reprogram yourself using different input. Would Ross Perot use *your* role models as a way to further his success? Probably not. Then why should you? It is now up to you to accept responsibility for erasing inadequate old data and inserting new data that is being offered to you in this book. It is our job to supply that input — but it's your job to determine how it can best serve you and then apply it to your life.

Many of the thoughts that I will expose you to may be

Your life is an expression of all your thoughts.

MARCUS AURELIUS ANTONINUS (121–180) Roman emperor, Stoic philosopher

A thought is often original, though you have uttered it a hundred times. It has come to you over a new route, by a new and express train of associations.

OLIVER WENDELL HOLMES, SR. (1809–1894) American physician, professor, man of letters

*Knowledge of what is possible is
the beginning of happiness.*

GEORGE SANTAYANA (1863–1952)
Spanish-born American philosopher, poet,
novelist, critic

new to you, but they are not necessarily original. They are simply presented in new and easy ways so that you can apply them to your life.

This book was written for average people who are reasonably healthy in spirit, mind, and body. (If you are suffering from some addiction, abuse, or handicap, you may need to seek out professional assistance.) If you are the average person who is dissatisfied with where you are and where you are going, this is the right book for you. This book will help you get total control over your life and your destiny.

CAN YOU REALLY EXPECT TO FIND RICHES IN THE PAGES OF THIS BOOK? YOU BET YOU CAN!

IF RICHES MEAN HEALTH, YOU CAN IMPROVE YOUR HEALTH WITH THE TEACHINGS OF THIS BOOK.

IF RICHES MEAN HAVING BETTER RELATIONSHIPS, THIS BOOK CAN BRING YOU THOSE RICHES.

IF YOUR IDEA OF RICHES IS GETTING OUT OF POVERTY, THIS BOOK CAN SHOW YOU HOW TO ATTAIN THE WEALTH YOU WANT.

IF RICHES MEAN JOY AND HAPPINESS, THIS BOOK CAN EASILY SHOW YOU HOW TO ACHIEVE THOSE RICHES.

*Climb high. Climb far. Your
goal the sky, your aim the star.*

INSCRIPTION

No matter what your definition of Riches is, this book shows you how to get them. Is there a limit to what you can have? Perhaps — we don't know what that limit is for you — and neither do you. So, why not make it your goal to find out how high "up" is for you — *The Lazy Man's Way?*

Buckle up your seat belt because you are about to launch yourself on a major trip — an exciting adventure. The destination? Your success — your new life of Riches!

DO YOU HAVE WHAT IT TAKES?

CHAPTER 3 OF PART 1

Is *The Lazy Man's Way* really the best way? All of our lives we have been warned of the destructive results that will surely come our way if we are lazy. Maybe what we need is the "committed man's way" or the "disciplined man's way" or the "work-til-you-are-exhausted man's way." The primary difficulty with these and countless other, well-intended "ways" is that, for the most part, none of these "ways" work. The secondary difficulty with all other "ways" is that they are the "ways" of "experts" — the "ways" of "others!" They are not *your* way. Rather than living life your natural way, you are asked to "adopt" someone else's "way." *The Lazy Man's Way is living your life your way.* I truly believe that our discontent and "dis-ease" is our true self — our nature, our inner vision of our self — trying to get out; not only do we not act upon it, we don't seem to know that it even exists. When we learn to allow our inner visions to become the embodiment of all of our actions, we achieve a remarkable balance, a contentment which, in turn, frees us up to a full expression of what is really inside us — and it is beautiful. You can see this emergence of true self most clearly in people in the arts: writers, dancers, painters, singers, poets, sculptors, and composers. But the potential exists in all of us.

An inner vision allows you to be who you were meant to be.

- It is not just problem solving.
- It is not just "fixing" your life.
- It is not just "relief."
- It is not just programming your subconscious.
- It is not just changing your view or attitude.

It is the answer to the questions that all people ultimately ask themselves: Why am I here? And, What does

It is our less conscious thoughts and our less conscious actions which mainly mould our lives and the lives of those who spring from us.

SAMUEL BUTLER (1835–1902)
English novelist, scholar, translator

There is only one meaning of life; the act of living itself.

ERICH FROMM (1900–1980)
German-born American psychoanalyst, philosopher

my life stand for? IT'S YOUR PURPOSE IN LIFE. Purpose gives meaning, power, focus, and direction to your goals and therefore to your life. We will talk about purpose a great deal in later chapters.

EXPERTS — WHAT DO THEY KNOW ABOUT YOU?

All of the "experts" in the world are more than willing to show you "how," offer you "the" solutions, and guide you through the obstacles of life; there is no lack of advice for living out your life. The "experts" are everywhere. There are medical "experts," legal "experts," political "experts," economic "experts," psychological "experts," religious "experts," scientific "experts." They are most eager to squeeze you into their molds for working, parenting, marrying, dating, buying, selling, managing, dieting, exercising, feeling, being, doing and just plain living. Some of these "experts" have Ph.Ds or other prestigious degrees that move you to awe and respect. Others have positions of power that impress you. Still others have unusual testimonials that dazzle you. All of these experts want you to follow their advice for how you ought to live your life — their way — the way *they* think is best.

These "experts," for the most part, know plenty about their field of endeavor and definitely can be helpful — *to a point.* They can offer you helpful facts that can be verified. They can give you several helpful principles and observations related to their particular field. They can present to you the history of what does and doesn't generally work in a given area. But they don't know what you want. And they don't know your way of doing things. You see, your way is the best way for you. *You are the best and only expert on you that exists.*

WANTED — MY OWN PERSONAL EXPERT

You can take in all the rent-an-expert advice that you want; but let's face it, you are the captain of your ship.

An expert is one who knows more and more about less and less.

NICOLAS MURRAY BUTLER (1862–1948)
President of Columbia University

An expert is a man who has made all the mistakes which can be made in a very narrow field.

NIELS BOHR (1885–1962)
Danish physicist

Even if you work for someone else, you are actually *self-employed*. You go out into the marketplace and sell your services, whatever they may be, to the highest bidder, but you always work for the same boss — you. You are the Chief Executive Officer of your personal corporation, the President of your personal country, the Emperor of your world. In other words, you must call the shots about your life at every turn. We seem to jump on every opportunity to be responsible for everyone else. The fact is, we are only responsible for ourselves, and we are the only ones who know our own truths. It has been said that the true start of maturity is the realization that no one else is coming to our rescue. With *The Lazy Man's Way,* you will *want* to take responsibility for you.

Now let's get you started along the road to your Riches. Each chapter is a new idea right out of Joe's success story and the success stories of the many others who have followed his method to attain the Riches they desire. Each chapter brings a new message, or an expansion of a message, which you can use to develop attitudes and habits that guarantee success. Your success.

I'm going to ask you to do something — something simple and easy to do (after all, this is *The Lazy Man's Way*) but nonetheless something very important. I'm asking that you not skip any of the steps I ask you to do, even if they seem trivial to you. Each and every step is important and part of the total picture; miss one or two and you won't get the best results. I'll do everything I can to encourage you to do all that I ask of you.

The Lazy Man's Way to Riches is built around the development of success habits. About 90% — no, I believe it's closer to 99% — of what you do every day is habitual behavior. The difference between being successful and not being successful really depends on those habits. We have to change our failure habits into success habits and that takes time and constant reinforcement. Psychiatrists tell

Every man is the architect of his own future.

SALLUST (86–35 BC)
Roman historian

To learn new habits is everything, for it is to reach the substance of life. Life is but a tissue of habits.

HENRI FREDERIC AMIEL (1821–1881)
Swiss philosopher, poet

us it takes the average person about 30 repetitions of an activity to turn it into a habit. And the more of you that is involved, the quicker you will develop the new habit. That's why I'll ask you to write some things down. So take it from me, don't try to rush things, be patient, do your part in every chapter and step. Let *The Lazy Man's Way* do the rest.

WRITING IS THINKING

By the way, *don't even think about skipping the writing.* There is no better way to "think" than to write things down. If you are serious about getting the Riches you have not yet been able to attain, you must do things you are not used to doing. If writing is one of those things you never do, or haven't done for a long time, or have been afraid to do, relax. It's just talking on paper. But the impact on your thinking process is dynamic and, in some cases, it is the only way to reach the parts of the mind you haven't been exercising lately.

THE LAZY MAN'S WAY — EASY AS 1. 2. 3

At this point I would like to give you a general idea of what we are going to do together. It's my intention to help you answer the three most fundamental questions in your life.

1. Who are you?
2. Where are you going?
3. How are you going to get there?

I know that when you possess clearly defined answers to these three questions, nothing can stop you from attaining all the Riches you desire. I'm not talking just about money, although that is an important part, I'm talking fulfillment in every aspect of your life. After all, when you have all the money you want, you will find there are other facets that add Riches to your life.

How can I know what I think till I see what I say?

E. M. FORSTER (1879–1970)
English novelist, short-story writer, essayist

The greatest magnifying glasses in the world are a man's own eyes when they look upon his own person.

ALEXANDER POPE (1688–1744)
English poet, satirist

Since the way to Riches is what we are after, maybe we should start by asking what kind of qualities you actually need to be a candidate for a successful journey on this road. What is really necessary for success? Before we answer that, let's look at some things that are not necessary — a college degree, for instance. Many people think a college degree is essential for success, and some even go farther and believe that it must be from a particular school. Interestingly enough, it's usually people without a college degree who feel that way. Most of the people with a college degree know better. All a college degree does is train you to work for someone else, and nowadays, it doesn't even guarantee you a decent job, let alone success.

Or maybe you're one of those who thinks it takes money to make money. Obviously it doesn't hurt to have some capital. But for every person who started out with money and made a lot more, there are two who managed to lose what they started with and several more who started with nothing or — as in Joe Karbo's case — less than nothing and made it big.

And it's not brains, either — if by brains you mean the kind of intelligence that is indicated by getting good grades in school. The ranks of successful people are full of people whose report cards had more D's and C's than A's. Some of the most brilliant people are failures at almost every area of life, because they never learned that in this life **you get paid for what you do, not what you know!**

And it's not good looks, or where you live, or how old or young you are, or who your parents were, or who your contacts are. I could go on and on listing all the alibis, rationalizations, justifications and excuses people give for not getting out of life all the happiness and success they desire.

Recognize any excuses that you have used? You are not alone. We all find ways to excuse our lack of success.

Man is not the sum of what he has but the totality of what he does not yet have, or what he might have.

JEAN-PAUL SARTRE (1905–1980)
French existentialist, philosopher,
playwright, novelist, teacher

Success follows doing what you want to do. There is no other way to be successful.

MALCOLM STEVENSON FORBES
(1919–1990)
American publisher, billionaire,
sportsman

The thing is, we can't go any farther until we realize the painful truth: the lack of education, contacts, money, brains, or luck are the most common excuses that people give for not getting what they want out of life.

You should have heard Joe Karbo back in the days before he found out the truth. Since he was then focused on what he didn't have, he was fighting a constant, exhausting battle to overcome his limitations — a battle he could never win because his problem was with his own *attitudes* about himself, not his so-called limitations. Most of his time and energy went into trying to climb over and break down barriers that existed mostly in his own mind. It wasn't until he started building on what he had, instead of worrying about what he didn't have, that he was able to find *The Lazy Man's Way to Riches*. And that's where you are going to begin — by finding out just who and what you are, and what you have to offer. Are you ready for the first step? Evaluating yourself honestly?

Examine your personal assets, your qualities and abilities. Can you communicate with others, either verbally or in writing? Do you enjoy responsibility? What have you done in the past that shows determination, ambition, and persistence? Regardless of past positions, what would you really enjoy doing? Be truly honest with yourself in this step; but don't fall into the trap of giving away all your talents, while you cling to your problems. Most people have the attitude, "If I can do it, anyone can." That's not exactly the truth. The easier something is for us, the more likely we are to assume that it is easy for everyone.

Dick Johnson, an associate of Joe's, tells the following story that illustrates the point.

Since Joe started me on The Lazy Man's Way *to Riches I've taught many seminars on personal development. To break the ice in my classes I usually have the students stand, introduce themselves, and tell the class one interesting thing*

All glory comes from daring to begin.

ANONYMOUS

A journey of a thousand miles must begin with a single step.

CHINESE PROVERB

about themselves. One student, we'll call her Fritzi, introduced herself and said, "I can't think of one interesting thing about myself" and quickly sat down. Her friend Pat, who was sitting next to her, was astonished. "That's the most ridiculous thing I've ever heard," Pat said, and proceeded to list some of Fritzi's talents and accomplishments. These included sky diving, dancing (well enough to win contests), and a job as a fashion buyer at a large department store chain. "As I came to know Fritzi I realized she had many personal qualities as well, but she just couldn't see them in herself."

PLEASE NOTE!

Below is a paragraph from page 5 that you may have missed or skimmed over. I'm repeating it here just in case.

To help you understand and appreciate the exciting metamorphosis of this book, we have set off all of Joe Karbo's original book, from the expanded revision, with a faint gray line running alongside Joe's text (illustrated next to this paragraph) so you will be able to identify and taste the unique flavor of Joe Karbo. When no line is present, you are reading new, expanded, and revised text of *The Lazy Man's Way to Riches*. We have taken the liberty of updating some of the figures in Joe's portions so that they might be more easily understood in relation to today's economy and have made some minor changes to better fit the times. Other than that, it is pure Joe Karbo!

*As long as I have a want,
I have a reason for living.
Satisfaction is death.*

GEORGE BERNARD SHAW (1856–1950)
Irish playwright, critic, social reformer

*Men are not troubled by things
themselves, but by their
thoughts about them.*

EPICTETUS (55–135)
Greek Stoic philosopher

You are now on your way to having everything in the world you really want! Notice I say *"everything"* not *"anything."* There is an important difference!

If someone were to give you "anything" in the world for which you might wish, the gift would automatically be *limited.* And far more would be withheld than would be given. "Anything" really means "any one thing." If the world were someone's to give, you'd get a tiny fraction of it, and the giver would keep the rest.

But to have "everything" is a promise without limitation! And an important part of Dyna/Psyc practice is the need to detect and be free of *any limitation.* When you read the first sentence above, you may already have started to limit what this book can give you. It is important that you do not let this happen.

Let's look at that first sentence again!

**YOU ARE NOW ON YOUR WAY TO HAVING
EVERYTHING IN THE WORLD YOU WANT!**

What was your reaction when you read it? Did you start to reject the *possibility* of truth in that simple statement? Did your habit-conditioned mind automatically say, "Not me . . . No way," "Is he kidding?" The strong possibility that you did *just that* is the reason we're dwelling on this statement at length.

Only a fool would accept such a statement on absolute faith, without any evidence whatsoever. But, a wise man, free of deadly self-limitation, would merely ask, "How?"

Don't be guilty of self-limitation. Don't reject the Riches which can be yours by "knowing" or "fearing" you can't have them. Ask only, "How?"

How can you have everything in the world you really

want? Go with me through these pages, step by step, and you will KNOW! Can you forget self-limitation for the moment? Can you cast aside failure-oriented doubt long enough to *try to learn how?*

This is all that is required of you at this step. You don't have to believe anything, yet. But you must not disbelieve the possibility that Dyna/Psyc, *The Lazy Man's Way to Riches*, just might work for you.

WHAT IS DYNA/PSYC?

What is Dyna/Psyc? It is the "code word" I have found most fitting to use when referring to that collection of natural laws or truths that make up this fantastic success formula. Dyna . . . because it is indeed a dynamic concept, one that moves you forward with great energy to the achievement of any goal. It is a source of great power, like some giant dynamo creating endless energy. And Psyc . . . because of two sciences fundamental to the method. Psychology, about which we have learned so much in the last seventy-five years, and Psychic Research, those far less understood natural laws we are barely beginning to understand.

> **Dyna/Psyc: the programmed study and practice of achieving success by the planned application of important, but little understood, natural laws.**

There may be certain fundamental truths in this approach to Dyna/Psyc that you have heard before, but now you will see even these familiar facts in a new light and you will learn how to apply them to your problems. (You knew there were automobiles long before you were old enough or skilled enough to drive or repair them.)

Most of the things you will be learning, however, will be new and perhaps even a little *strange* to you. To help you rid yourself of disbelief, let me remind you of what

Knowledge and human power are synonymous.

SIR FRANCIS BACON (1561–1626)
English philosopher, statesman, essayist

Dyna/Psyc has done for me.

To put this in its proper perspective, you have to be aware of my situation 11 years ago.

I was out of a job. My wife and I and our eight children were renting a ramshackle house in a deteriorating neighborhood. We were driving an old Falcon we'd had to refinance. We were $50,000 in debt. Under those circumstances, can you imagine how I felt when I was told that with Dyna/Psyc I could have "everything I really wanted"? I didn't believe it, but I had to admit that I had very little to lose. And maybe that's what saved me; I was desperate enough to try anything, even if it seemed foolish and ridiculously easy.

So they were saying that I could have "everything I really wanted" . . . well, I'd put that theory to the test. I'd set goals that were beyond my *wildest* dreams.

As God is my witness, these are the goals I wrote out during those black days — and this is what happened:

Goal: "I own a house on the water."

Fact: Three years later I bought a home in a marina community. With the improvements we added, it's now worth over $1,000,000. I know, because I turned down an offer for that much.

Goal: "I drive a brand new black Thunderbird."

Fact: Within 30 days, I'd picked up an advertising account. It was a Ford agency. The manager said the Falcon I was driving was an embarrassment to the agency. He gave me a brand new black Thunderbird to drive. A few months later I bought it.

Goal: "I earn $100,000 a year."

Fact: The next year I made $216,000 and haven't made less than that since.

It is the disposition of the thought that altereth the nature of the thing.

JOHN LYLY (1554?-1606)
English prose writer, poet, playwright

Goal: "I own several small successful businesses. I leave the actual management to other capable people."

Fact: I do.

Goal: "I own a boat just like my neighbor Steve's!"

Fact: For a couple of years, I'd admired a boat that belonged to a friend of ours. Within 30 days, he phoned and told me he'd decided to sell it for a fraction of what he'd paid for it — and I could pay for it any way I wanted. It was so spooky that I accepted his offer. Now we have two boats — and we paid cash for them.

Goal: "My bills are paid."

Fact: That was really a tough one to say without feeling like an idiot. But, contrary to my lawyer's advice (who thought I should declare bankruptcy), I had a meeting with my creditors. I told them that I wanted to pay them back, but I couldn't concentrate on the effort with the fear that they'd attach my bank account every time I made a few bucks. They agreed to a repayment program that I felt I could live with. I never missed a payment and a few years later I paid off the balance in a lump sum.

Now, in case you are afraid the truths of Dyna/Psyc are somehow personal ones, producing rules that will work only for me, consider this:

Seven years ago I told a young man who sold me a boat dock about Dyna/Psyc. I did so because we had become friends, and he told me that the company he was working for was going broke and he'd be out of a job. His total assets were a half-interest in a motorcycle. He owed the bank for a loan. He'd never earned more than $10,000 a year.

He dropped by my office the other day, showed me his

Give me a stock clerk with a goal, and I will give you a man who will make history. Give me a man without a goal and I'll give you a stock clerk.

JAMES CASH PENNEY (1875–1971)
Founder JC Penney Co.

original goals and told me about his progress — every bit of which he credits to Dyna/Psyc. He not only reached but surpassed every one of his goals — and has set new ones.

Original goal: A salary of $18,000 a year.

Fact: He earns $40,000 a year and has stock options in the New York Stock Exchange-listed company he works for.

Original goal: Ownership of a vacation hideaway.

Fact: He owns a half-interest in a $100,000 ranch.

Original goal: To quit drinking.

Fact: He did.

Original goal: To own income property.

Fact: He does. Two duplexes.

Original goal: To own speculative and growth stocks.

Fact: He does — $30,000 worth.

And there are lots of other people who have rebuilt their lives with the information I'm going to give you here.

There's a widow in Chicago who's earned $25,000 a year for the past five years, using my methods. The 70-year-old woman who has traveled all over the world is making all the money she needs, doing only what I taught her. Another man who works a lot harder than I'm willing to do, who is using these same principles, made eleven million dollars in eight years.

Fact: It's worked, without exception, for everyone who's tried it! I'll admit, 'til now, I haven't shared the secret of Dyna/Psyc with too many people. Because most of the time, my only reward would be a patronizing smile. "After all," I can see them saying to themselves, "it couldn't be that easy."

But it is.

IT'S THAT EASY — IF YOU KNOW HOW

Perhaps you are wondering how so many people came to know of these natural laws and learned to take advantage of them. As long ago as the 1950s, key executives of highly successful, really big corporations, began to be "turned-on" to the very same truths you are to receive. No one knows, or at least I have been unable to determine with accuracy, the names of the very first researchers into what might be called the Scientific Basis of Success. But soon a number of costly but highly effective classes, seminars, and private sessions were being carried on by the various practitioners.

The price for such services was high. But the thousands of dollars that were paid by the blue-chip executives was a paltry fee for the *immediate and spectacular success stories* which resulted from the application of the secrets they had learned.

Needless to say, as is always the secret with power, the men who were fortunate enough to have gained it were in no hurry to broadcast the news of it. They wanted to keep the powerful advantage they had received.

So great was the desire for secrecy that most of these power sessions were carried on away from the executive towers of the corporate giants. Small groups journeyed to mountain or desert retreats for the closed meetings. The fees were so high that attendance was already limited to these top executives but, beyond that, only key people were even informed of the opportunity.

Since those early days, research has continued. The truths that evolved were the result of putting together facts from every phase of human development. And as the findings of this research were assembled, certain well-

To be conscious that you are ignorant is a great step to knowledge.

BENJAMIN DISRAELI (1804–1881)
English statesman, novelist

Success is the progressive realization of a worthy idea.

EARL NIGHTINGALE (1921–1989)
Speaker, motivator

defined *patterns of power*, making for *certain success*, became evident.

Those patterns explain why "some must win, some must lose." More importantly, the rules evolved from those patterns eliminate *losing* for those who follow them.

YOU CAN WIN TOO!

Can you learn how to apply Dyna/Psyc to your life? Indeed you can.

In the chapters that follow, you will learn things about yourself that you never knew 'til now! You are going to learn why you have not been more successful than you have (and, incidentally, learn why you did things that you later called yourself a fool for doing). Just as importantly, you are going to learn how to have other people striving to give you what you want.

Never again will you look at a particularly successful person and sigh, "How lucky he is." Because you will know that **"luck" or "fate" has absolutely nothing to do with success or failure.** What we call "luck" is, in fact, a direct result of the correct or incorrect application of natural laws anyone can use effectively *if he/she knows how.*

Remember, the power to make things happen the way you want them to happen has always been available. You aren't going to have to create some new source of power within yourself. You are merely going to "plug-in" to the existing power.

The forces of Dyna/Psyc are very much like electricity. No one invented electricity; it existed in nature. But until man learned how to make use of the already existing natural phenomenon, he had no electric lights to turn night into day. Now anyone can perform that miracle with the flick of a switch. He knows how to "plug in" to the electricity. You are going to learn to do this same thing with yet another natural power source.

Just as electricity can serve man when handled

Luck is a matter of preparation meeting opportunity.

OPRAH WINFREY (B. 1953)
American television talk-show host, actress

Men habitually use only a small part of the powers which they possess and which they might use under appropriate circumstances.

WILLIAM JAMES (1842–1910)
American philosopher, physiologist, psychologist, teacher

properly and injure him if mishandled, the forces of Dyna/Psyc are raw power and can work for your good — or your ill — depending on how they are utilized. There is every chance that you will learn, as you study, that *you* have been causing your failures through misuse of powers you did not even know you had.

But you have taken the important first step to undoing past mistakes and *creating* a whole new life for yourself — *The Lazy Man's Way.*

HOW DO YOU SPELL SUCCESS?

What represents success to you? Your answer would probably be similar to someone else's, but surely not identical. It should cover all the things that you feel make for success in your life: money, work, health, possessions, love, and, for some, tranquility; for others, excitement. It isn't important how your view of success differs. What is important, according to scientific evaluation and research, is **for you to know what you really want out of life.**

Part of the work ahead of you will concern itself with an exact answer to that question of your desires. Why? Why do you have to have a specific inventory of what you want? Because surveys show that less than two people out of a thousand know what they want from life or have definite plans for achieving their desires.

And the same surveys show that people who do have such plans are able to make life pay off on their own terms. You will learn why this is an important factor and how to effectively create a plan.

A specific plan is only one of the factors in the success of truly successful people. Here's a list of some of the other things that come to mind when we think of a person's success. From the list, select what you feel is the other quality all *real* successes have in common.

There is only one success— to be able to spend your life in your own way.

CHRISTOPHER MORLEY (1890–1957)
American novelist, journalist, essayist

The gent who wakes up and finds himself a success hasn't been asleep.

WILSON MIZNER (1876–1933)
American author

1.   Luck . . . the "breaks"

2.   Family background

3.   Social achievement

4.   Basic intelligence

5.   Education advantage

6.   Good health

7.   Enthusiasm

8.   Winning personality

9.   Real determination

10. Plenty of financing

TAKE TIME TO EXAMINE THE CHOICES CAREFULLY BEFORE YOU LOOK AT THE NEXT PAGE!

You're wrong!

For the sake of helping you learn a *truth* that is essential to your acceptance of the natural laws that lie ahead, you've been tricked.

The correct answer, the other quality that all successful people have in common, was not listed. Think of that for a moment. Doesn't the list include every factor we're accustomed to thinking of when we think of success? Isn't the essential quality there?

No. Many people have had combinations of the qualities listed above and have failed miserably. Yet, people suffering severe handicaps of bad luck, poor beginnings, little formal education, ill health, shyness, and only a "shoestring" on which to begin have been preeminently successful.

What is that second quality common to all really successful people? The second step after knowing what you want and having a concrete plan for getting it? It is **the ability to use effectively whatever asset you have.**

Every successful person has overcome his drawbacks by making effective use of whatever time, energy, money, ideas, etc., he possessed. They knew it wasn't what you had that counted . . . but how effectively you used it.

A learned man once wrote that there were really only three kinds of failures:

FAILURE TYPE 1 WELL-DEFINED GOALS — INEFFECTIVE PURSUIT OF THEM.

This is the man who knows where he wants to go, but never quite gets there.

FAILURE TYPE 2 PUSHES HARD, USES EVERY ASSET — NO WELL-DEFINED GOALS.

. This man is like a powerful ship . . . without a rudder. He always seems to be making great headway but never arrives.

FAILURE TYPE 3 IS THE SADDEST OF THE LOT. HE HAS NEITHER WELL-DEFINED GOALS NOR IS HE EFFECTIVE.

Whatever your pattern has been in the past, whatever

Everyone has a talent. What is rare is the courage to follow the talent to the dark places where it leads.

ERICA JONG (B. 1942)
American author

A teacher can only lead you to the threshold of your own mind.

KAHLIL GIBRAN (1883–1931)
Syrian-American mystic, poet, painter

has caused your drives for success to fall short of your desires . . . your answer lies within these pages.

Think of your position at this time as though you were the owner of a palatial ocean-going yacht. I am the captain you have hired. The ship is *yours*; the choice of where you go is *yours*. My job is first to suggest the possible destinations, then, when you have made your choice, to lay out a course that will take you there. That course must steer clear of any hazard that might prevent our safe and speedy arrival.

Since you will want to sail your own ship as soon as possible, we will see to it that you learn everything you need to know on this voyage. You will be your own captain long before we finish.

In other words, Dyna/Psyc promises to assist you in finding your purpose in life and in selecting important specific goals that support that purpose. Dyna/Psyc will provide you with all the effective tools you will need on your voyage toward your purpose — to success!

What is expected of you? What must you do in order to make the transition to the successful person you could be? Very little —when you measure the reward against the effort required to attain it. That's why I call this *The Lazy Man's Way*.

However, because so little is required of you, it does not follow that you can be lazy or haphazard in doing what is required. Quite the opposite. It is important that you *perform* in order to have all the benefits that Dyna/Psyc can bring you.

But the tasks are not numerous or difficult. You have only to R.S.V.P. to this invitation to wealth, success, and satisfaction!

R.S.V.P.: READ STUDY VISUALIZE PERFORM

As you go forward in the program, think of R.S.V.P. in these terms:

READ I must read in order to learn the secrets that will make my life easier, my success in every field of endeavor certain. How else but by reading can I receive the truths that come from the natural laws expressed by Dyna/Psyc?

But if I *only* read, I cannot really *learn*. I did not learn my lessons in school by merely reading them in the same way that I read the daily paper.

Therefore, I must —

STUDY I must study the things I read. I must do more than merely apply my eyes to the printed page. I must apply myself — mind, ideas, thoughts — to the substance of the words I read. By doing this, I will begin to make the power of Dyna/Psyc grow within me. That power comes from understanding; and to understand anything more than the simplest things, one must study.

Once I am building that power, I will need to apply it to my life situations. I will need clear outlines or blueprints of when, where, and how to apply the new-found power.

For this I will have to —

VISUALIZE I must cultivate the capacity to visualize, in concrete form, everything I read and study. I must learn to take a mental or written suggestion and be able to project it like a motion picture on the hidden screen of my mind's eye. I must really see those suggestions, those plans, those goals, in solid form in my mind's eye. Then they can be mine, in fact, through Dyna/Psyc.

Visualization is far more than mere imagination. It is always more complete, more detailed. In short, it has the effect of adding the potential of *reality* to the unsatisfying dream that is imagination.

The man who creates a new and important invention often starts with mere imagination—a dream. But, as his mind ponders the idea, he begins to visualize with ever-increasing exactness of detail. He begins to "see" his invention almost as though it were physically present in

The man who does not read books has no advantage over the man who can't read them.

MARK TWAIN (1835–1910)
American writer, humorist

Vision is the art of seeing things invisible.

JONATHAN SWIFT (1667-1745)
English satirist

To accomplish great things, we must not only act but also dream, not only dream, but also believe.

ANATOLE FRANCE (1844-1924)
French novelist, poet, critic

Men are all alike in their promises. It is only in their deeds that they differ.

JEAN-BAPTISTE MOLIÈRE (1622-1673)
French comic playwright

front of him. This I must do. It is not easy at first. But the unfolding of the program contained in these pages will provide many ways to help me visualize—and turn dreams into reality.

I can reach that plateau of ability if I —

PERFORM The manner in which I perform is all outlined in great detail in the chapters and steps that lie ahead. I have only to promise myself that I will try the outlined steps. The success factor is already built into each step.

This means the scientific basis of achievement have been studied and analyzed for me in order to create Dyna/Psyc.

I have only to perform the basic, simple steps outlined by reading, studying, visualizing, and then performing.

When this R.S.V.P. is complete — success must be mine!

A SUCCESSFUL JOURNEY — A FIRST STEP

CHAPTER 5 OF PART 1

You and I have now examined together some important concepts that you must have before we commence the actual work of improvement. We are now ready for your first positive action.

It is an action that sounds easy. But don't be fooled; it is going to take you quite a lot of time to complete. And I promise you it is going to produce some truths about yourself that you never really knew until now.

Your first positive action is to answer this short question:

"WHAT DO YOU WANT?"

The work of it begins when I tell you that you must answer that question, *fully and completely* in black and white! Right now you may begin a complete list of what you want.

Why such a detailed list? Because that is the first step to getting them. This list becomes a list of your goals, your destinations.

Tell me this. Can you imagine a man going to the nearest airport to catch a plane with only the vaguest idea of where he wanted to go? If you were the ticket seller, what would you do to help him? Can you visualize what would happen?

Man: I'd like a ticket, please.

You: Certainly, sir, where to?

Man: Oh . . . uh . . . someplace nice.

You: I don't understand.

Man: Well, it's important I "get someplace." I don't want to just waste time. I want to really get someplace.

There's only one corner of the universe you can be certain of improving and that's your own self.

ALDOUS HUXLEY (1894–1963)
English novelist, essayist, satirist

41

You: Someplace like . . . where?

Man: Oh, someplace where I can be happy. Where I can have a good income. Get a new car, maybe. Perhaps become an executive with a good company or even have my own business of some sort. Be able to take care of my wife and kids. You know, I'd like to get someplace where things are really great for me and my family. Just give me a ticket; I'll pay for it.

You: But, sir, I can't sell you a ticket until you know exactly where you want to go.

Wouldn't that be your reaction? You would have no way to help that man until *he could tell you where he wanted to go.*

And isn't that what you've been saying to life? "I want to get someplace" covers everything and yet nothing! One thinks he has a goal because he wants to "be somebody." But until there is a very clear picture of that position, one cannot hope to achieve it.

Looking at your life in this way, it isn't surprising that you have not already reached the height of success you might desire — on the contrary, it is *remarkable* that you have achieved any success at all. Without clear, well-defined goals, success is impossible.

We are now going to establish those goals. We are going to first put them into the simplest practical terms. We will be exact, for simplicity requires exactness.

To make it easy for you to list your wants, I have broken the task down into three parts and included a few typical suggestions to illustrate which "want" fits each category. The three parts are:

LIST 1 — THINGS I FEEL I NEED RIGHT NOW
LIST 2 — THINGS I WANT
LIST 3 — PERSONAL QUALITIES I NEED OR WANT

Convictions are more dangerous enemies of truth than lies.

FRIEDRICH NIETZSCHE (1844–1900)
German Philosopher

Lists 1 and 2 will probably be easy for you because they deal with tangible things, but List 3 may be more difficult because it deals with intangible things, personal qualities. Don't worry about how to get the newer and better qualities any more than you worried about the "things" you need and want; just list them as they occur to you.

LIST 1 – THINGS I FEEL I <u>NEED</u> RIGHT NOW!

If I were to meet you in person at this moment and, taking out my checkbook, offered to pay to clear up everything that is currently stressing you out — things for which you have an immediate NEED — this is the list you might hand me:

Suggestions:

1. Credit card or utility bills paid.
2. Delinquent taxes (property, state, federal, payroll) paid.
3. Outstanding traffic tickets paid.
4. Medical bills (doctor, hospital, clinic, prescription) paid.
5. Deferred maintenance on yourself, your auto, home or business (needed dental work, brakes or tune-up, roof repair, carpeting, paint, computer upgrade, advertising expenses) taken care of.
6. Expenses for an operation.
7. Money for rent or mortgage payment, or anything necessary to satisfy your immediate requirements.

Don't be afraid to put everything you need on your list. Don't start off thinking in a "limited" manner. Put it all down. Even those things you may deny or that you put off because of other problems.

Turn to the next page.

Understanding human needs is half the job of meeting them.

ADLAI STEVENSON (1900–1965)
American statesman, politician

LIST 1 – THINGS I FEEL I <u>NEED</u> RIGHT NOW!

1. _____

   _____

2. _____

   _____

3. _____

   _____

4. _____

   _____

5. _____

   _____

6. _____

   _____

7. _____

   _____

8. _____

   _____

9. _____

   _____

LIST 2 – THINGS I <u>WANT</u>

Now that you have completed List 1 and have found out what you feel you need at this time, you are ready to think about the things that you want, not need particularly, but just plain want. It's important that you not limit yourself in any way as recognizing your wants is essential for your growth. Put down whatever comes to you. And remember, the sky's the limit!

The keener the want the lustier the growth.

WENDELL PHILLIPS (1811–1884)
American abolitionist, orator

Suggestions:

1. My own business
2. A $500,000 annual income
3. Happy homelife
4. A luxury car
5. A luxury house
6. A luxury boat
7. A trip around the world and time to enjoy it
8. $500,000 in the bank
9. A second home
10. Excellent health
11. To play a musical instrument (s)
12. Top-of-the-line toys (computers, cars, big-screen TV, piano)
13. To meet my idols (list several)

Turn to the next page and go for it!

Goals are not only absolutely necessary to motivate us. They are essential to really keep us alive.

REV. ROBERT SCHULLER (B. 1926)
Minister, author, social leader

LIST 2 – THINGS I <u>WANT</u>

1. _____
   _____

2. _____
   _____

3. _____
   _____

4. _____
   _____

5. _____
   _____

6. _____
   _____

7. _____
   _____

8. _____
   _____

9. _____
   _____

LIST 3 – PERSONAL QUALITIES I NEED OR WANT

Now if you consider it for a moment, it is clear that you want more out of life than just things. Mere possessions do not represent the sum total of what we need to enjoy full, successful lives.

Besides possessing things, we need certain qualities or attributes of personality and character. These intangible characteristics are needed for many reasons: To protect the possessions we might have, to guarantee our continued success, to have the respect, friendship, trust, or whatever other feelings we want from others.

Your picture of success, therefore, has another list that must be made before you can establish your goals with certainty. The personal qualities you want:

Suggestions:

1. Ability to focus (concentrate)
2. Real personal self-confidence
3. Power to stop "putting off" things
4. To be more assertive
5. Ability to finish what I start
6. More original thinking, creativity
7. Have a better disposition
8. Stop "wasting time"
9. Be friendlier to others
10. Be a leader
11. Be in good health
12. Be enthusiastic
13. Have a better memory
14. Be a more understanding parent or child

LIST 3 – PERSONAL QUALITIES I NEED OR WANT

1. _____

   _____

2. _____

   _____

3. _____

   _____

4. _____

   _____

5. _____

   _____

6. _____

   _____

7. _____

   _____

8. _____

   _____

9. _____

   _____

TOOLS YOU NEED TO GET WHAT YOU WANT

Welcome to the first day of the **Best** of your life. I said that in the first chapter, didn't I? But it's true today as well as every day if you stick to *The Lazy Man's Way*. Every page is a step in the right direction.

How many people do you know who think the best is behind them? That they have missed the boat and it's all downhill from here on out? A lot of people are washed up at 25 or 30, 35 or 40, because they think they are. But many others didn't get started on the road to success until they were in their 60s, 70s or even 80s. Colonel Sanders started his fried chicken empire at an age when most people are thinking of retiring. Dr. Forest Shaklee started his $500 million marketing and manufacturing company when he was 62. Carman K. Jones founded Kids Korner Fresh Pizza in Wausau, Wisconsin, at age 61, and Tom Duck founded Ugly Duckling Rent-A-Car in Tuscon, Arizona, at age 63. I read in the *Wall Street Journal* just the other day about a man who enjoys a six-figure income from a business he started when he was 86. I suspect you are probably younger than 86, but if you're not, don't let that stop you: the best is yet to come *if* you want it that way.

In Chapter 3 you had the opportunity to evaluate your success-ability and in the last chapter listed what you wanted for yourself. Let's look at the assets necessary to achieve those goals. Joe began addressing the subject by stating two assets absolutely necessary as:

1. Having a defined plan and

2. The ability to use effectively whatever assets you have.

Let's further identify and focus on what these qualities are that make for success.

He who has patience may accomplish anything.

FRANÇOIS RABELAIS (1494–1553)
French scholar, humorist

People who are unable to motivate themselves must be content with mediocrity, no matter how impressive their other talents.

ANDREW CARNEGIE (1835–1918)
American industrialist, philanthropist

I have a dream.

MARTIN LUTHER KING, JR. (1924–1968)
American clergyman, civil-rights leader

BELIEF AND DESIRE

Many years ago, Andrew Carnegie, an uneducated immigrant who started with nothing and built an enormous business empire, decided to find out just what made successful people successful. He knew from his own experience it wasn't family background, or education, or having money to start with; rather, it was certain universal principles or assets that *any* person could apply to become successful. He commissioned a young and talented writer, Napoleon Hill, to interview the most successful men of the times. Using the magic of the Carnegie name, Napoleon Hill was able to speak to several hundred outstanding business and political leaders and presented his results to the world in his famous book, *Think and Grow Rich.*

Mr. Hill found thirteen magic assets for finding and guiding personal success that appeared time and time again in his interviews. Of course not everyone had all thirteen assets; in fact, most people had only five or six. But there were two assets that every single person absolutely possessed, and if someone had only these assets to begin with, he or she quickly and easily acquired the others that were needed. These are the two assets I believe you are going to have to acquire before you'll ever achieve the Riches that *The Lazy Man's Way* has in store for you. Fortunately, if you don't already possess these assets, I'm going to show you how to develop them. What are these two magical qualities that absolutely guarantee success?

The first is a **burning desire**. I can hear you saying, "Oh come on — quit kidding around. I've had a burning desire for a million dollars for years and I'm not even close." Let's look a little closer at your burning desire. Is what you want really important to you? I mean really important — or is it just what I call a "wouldn't it be nice if" desire. Wouldn't it be nice if I had a million dollars, or wouldn't it be nice if we had a home on the beach?

Everybody has those kinds of desires; in fact, lots of them. But they come and go, and, more importantly, most people never allow those desires to interfere with the pleasures of the moment. In other words, "Sure I'd like to have a million dollars, but you don't expect me to give up watching Monday night football on television to get it, do you?"

I don't expect you to give up anything that is important to you, because I believe you can have everything in the world that is truly important to you. It's an essential part of *The Lazy Man's Way* that you don't have to make sacrifices. But if everything in your life now is more important than what you think you desire, maybe you really don't have a burning desire after all. There is nothing wrong if this is the case. Perhaps you're happy, just as you are, and that's great. But if you do see some important things as lacking in your life, then you'll have to find room for the things that you need to achieve — the things you desire.

What do I mean when I talk about burning desire? A true burning desire is that honest "knowing" that resides in your core being or "soul' that is undeniable and honest and when clearly defined and allowed to be brought into the light, will grow into a powerful force that will propel you forward over seemingly insurmountable obstacles. Your true burning desires are undeniable, true, absolute, and powerful. Acknowledging a burning desire is the key that can open any door to a life filled with reward, joy, and satisfaction. Recognizing a true burning desire is what gives you the confidence and therefore the power to act decisively and effectively to overcome all obstacles that stand in your way.

A true burning desire gnaws at you from the inside. It claws at your inner self trying to get out. It is something that you probably have always "known" was there because you could feel it. Well, now is the time to let it out. Stop kidding yourself that your burning desires don't exist. Stop

Hold fast to your dreams, for if dreams die, then life is like a broken winged bird that cannot fly.

LANGSTON HUGHES (1902–1967)
American poet

You're not free until you've been made captive by supreme belief.

MARIANNE MOORE (1887–1972)
American poet

hiding it because you are not sure you could ever have them or that you don't deserve them or that "they" (whomever they are) won't approve. Attainment of your burning desire has little to do with age, race, gender, background, education, experience, geographic location, the weather, the IRS, the government. . . . The only thing that matters is whether or not it's something that you truly want — what you honestly desire in your heart of hearts.

One way to determine whether your burning desires are valid and not just "wants" or "shoulds" or "ought to's" is to check where they are coming from. True burning desires come from your inner self and will elicit feelings and emotions in you that may express themselves with words like: "Yes, that's it. That's what I want!" You may find yourself smiling or on the verge of tears, or your pulse may quicken. You may simply feel yourself overwhelmed. Whatever you feel, you'll recognize the truth and honesty of the feeling as you admit your true burning desires to yourself. You'll see the significance of burning desires later when we talk about the importance of little decisions in being successful.

But for now let's discuss this second vital asset; it can be called various things, but I call it **belief**. The belief that you actually can have the object or condition you desire. If you actually have a burning desire for something and you are not making progress toward it, it's a sure thing that the lack of this second asset is where the problem lies. You really doubt you can have it. There is a simple test to see if you believe or not. Let's say you have a burning desire to be a millionaire — or maybe it's just to have all your debts paid and $10,000 in the bank. Say firmly to yourself, "Within the very near future I am a millionaire." Or, "Within the very near future I have paid all my debts and have $10,000 in the bank." Now quickly focus on the immediate thought that floods your mind. Do you have doubts about your statements? Do you make statements punctuated with "buts" followed by reasons, excuses, alibis, rationalizations,

Man is what he believes.

ANTON CHEKHOV (1860–1904)
Russian writer

and justifications for denial? Don't let your feelings be submerged by doubts. Make the statement again, and this time really get in touch with how you feel. Are you filled with a feeling of confidence that you're actually going to succeed, or are your thoughts primarily negative? The more doubts, the harder it will be for you. The fewer doubts, the easier. When you eliminate all the doubts, your goal is accomplished almost without effort. This is why we call it *The Lazy Man's Way to Riches.*

So, how do you get rid of doubts? First, you've got to identify the sources of those doubts and eliminate them. I want you to do two things: Write down one thing you really want (something that is important enough to you to be a burning desire) from each of the seven categories listed. They are: Financial, Mental, Emotional, Social, Vocational, Physical, and Spiritual. These seven categories are the areas that can help you achieve balance in your life, if you pay attention to each and every one of them. Some people seem to focus on the financial; and that's OK, as long as you don't do so to the *exclusion* of the others.

Once you are clear about your burning desires in each of these seven areas that form the foundation of a balanced life, you will find that you are driven from within to achieve fulfillment, contentment, peace, joy, and satisfaction at a level about which you only used to dream. Visualize how your life will be when you are doing only these things you truly want to be doing. You probably know of people who have already attained the things for which they truly had a burning desire. They can be your role models or mentors and can help you either by being an example for you or as active teachers. Find ways to include these people in your life.

Now it is time to write your burning desires in each of the seven areas of a balanced life; Financial, Mental, Emotional, Social, Vocational. Physical, and Spiritual. Give it some thought; and if you can't find something right away,

Man is a credulous animal, and must believe something; in the absence of good grounds for belief, he will be satisfied with bad ones.

BERTRAND RUSSELL (1872–1970)
English philosopher, mathematician, social reformer

don't worry. Later on I'll tell you three things that are probably blocking your desires. But look hard for what you really want and don't worry about locking yourself into your current desires. (You may just need permission to have a desire.) By the time you are through with reading this book I'll be very surprised if you haven't revised your goals several times. But for now, get something started and write down your desires.

Once you have done this, look at the pros, obstacles, and evaluations of your desires, in order to analyze why you are not getting the things that you really want. What has stopped you? What's holding you down? What are the obstacles or circumstances or handicaps that have held you back? The pro's — Why do you want them? What's the pay off for you? Be specific, spell it out. And the cons — What's standing in your way? Why haven't you done more? Gone on further? Made it happen? Get it *all* down on paper, every problem that stands between you and what you want. List every link in the chain that is holding you back. This may not be easy, because you'll really have to be honest; but do it. When you have all of your pro's and con's on paper, do one more thing; decide whether each obstacle you face is a problem with your attitude or your environment. If the obstacle is classified as an attitude problem, as most of them will be, that's something that can be changed because it is within your control. The dictionary defines attitude as a "way of looking at things." If your way of looking at things is the problem, then you have the option of choosing to look at them differently. Using your role models or mentors as examples, you may choose to adopt their approach to looking at things and see if it is effective for you also. It is amazing how a slight shift in your perception of things can make huge differences in the outcome of situations. In other words, making a course correction at the beginning of a journey results in an entirely different destination.

My life is one long obstacle course—with me being the chief obstacle.

JACK PAAR (B. 1918)
American author, television show host

The obstacles that you list as environmental (defined as: things, conditions, or influences) will no longer stand in your way once you learn to observe what is influencing you and realize you can make an appropriate adjustment to them. Put them in their proper perspective — go over them, around them, or through them — whatever — take action. Like your attitude, you also have the option to do something about environmental obstacles.

If you recognize and identify those obstacles for what they are — excuses — they will not be able to keep you from something that is truly a burning desire any longer. Or as Joe Karbo used to say about them, "You don't solve environmental obstacles, you just get over them."

Identifying what you believe your obstacles to be is a very important step in *The Lazy Man's Way to Riches*.

He has half the deed done who has made a beginning.

HORACE (65–8 B.C.)
Roman poet and satirist

Until you write down your dream it is just a dream. Writing it makes it a goal.

JOHN GODDARD (B. not available)
Anthropologist, explorer, adventurer, speaker, author

Now you have completed the first step in arriving at the blueprint for the future — which is the prime requisite to using Dyna/Psyc to attain Riches. You have made lists of those things you need and want, tangible and intangible, which make up your desires; and you have evaluated them carefully.

The next step is laying out those *listed* items in a manner that lends itself to the constant "use" that your success will require. In short, we must turn loose "lists" into concrete goals. This must be done by applying certain qualities or points of reference to the lists, in order to make them entirely consistent with you, your purpose and goals, your life, and with each other.

On the next page is a checklist consisting of nine questions, for goal development. Take each one of the "burning desires" you have listed; and using these questions, examine each one carefully. The desire may have to be altered slightly to meet all the tests below, but it can be done. Once the desire is in a form that will meet each test below — I want you to *write it down*. These writings are your GOALS.

Remember, this is one of the most important steps in your progress; if you do not write your goals, you cannot use them as set forth in later chapters. If they are not made to conform to the following checklist, you will find you cannot use them properly and they will be far less effective.

WHAT COMES FIRST? THE HEAD-OF-THE-LIST GOALS

In addition to the desires you have listed as needs and wants, and now are converting to positive goals, there are a few goals/declarations that are included on your list.

I ask that you include them because it has been my experience, and the experience of many others, that they do much to guarantee the fulfillment of your own unique desires.

When you read them, you will see that they are all positive in nature. I have come to call them the "head of the list" goals. This is because they are already in a form you can use — they start you on the task of *writing* goals instead of just "thinking about them"; and they are basics that underlie all that you will add after them.

So, start your list of goals with the following:

1. Each and every day I follow these procedures set out for my improvement, I become more effective, better able to function without limitation.

2. I pursue my goals free of any feelings of ill will or animosity toward others. I am a warm, friendly, well-liked person. My success is assured and does not require me to take advantage of any other person. Rather, it obliges me to help others, without telling anyone about my "good deeds."

3. I see myself with the success-eye of NOW. I have discarded the failure-eye of my infancy. I am free at last of failure or limitations.

Now, add your own goals. Add *every* goal you require to fill your needs and wants and to acquire the necessary personality factors from your early lists. Put them into your own words, being careful only that they be stated as positive, already accomplished, and set forth in great detail.

Using the checklist below, start writing your desires as stated goals. You will probably restate these goals several times, so don't worry if they're not exactly "right" at this point.

9 CHECKLIST QUESTIONS FOR YOUR GOALS

1. Do you really want this?

   (Or will it just "sound good" if someone else reads it? — Or is it so small a goal you think you have a

A strong passion for any object will ensure success, for the desire of the end will point out the means.

WILLIAM HAZLITT (1778–1830)
English essayist, critic

good chance of getting it? This must be something you *really* want — the ultimate!)

2. Does this goal *contradict* any other goal you are setting?

    (Such as, wanting a $250,000 house with a $20,000/year income?) Solution: Raise your salary or income goal.

3. Any problems with goal cooperation?

    (Would your family be against your achieving them? Talk it over and adjust your goals.)

4. Is your goal positive rather than negative?

    (As we said before — it is what you want, not what you want to get rid of.)

5. Is your goal expressed in total detail?

    (Not a big new car; not a big, new $65,000 car; not a big, fancy Mercedes; instead: a brand-new, black Mercedes, Model 600SL with . . . listing every detail as though you had to depend on this description alone after giving the company your cash!) No matter what it is, make it exact in the same degree of detail.

6.   Is it realistic?

    (And here I mean only — is it possible for some human being to achieve it? I do *not* mean is it realistic for the you of today to have it? The realism to which I have reference is shown by contrast:

    Unrealistic: I want to fly through the air without a plane or any other appliance of flight.

    Realistic: I want to pilot my own private $1,250,000 jet aircraft. (If it's a goal *someone* could attain, it's a realistic enough goal.)

7. Is this goal high enough?

(Because this factor is so important, and so often misunderstood, I want to tell you about it before we go any further.)

Number seven is the most serious checkpoint for turning your lists into goals, because it is the last chance I have to persuade you to *stop limiting yourself.*

If you have asked for an income (a paltry two or three thousand dollars more than what you are making), if you've asked for a position that is up the ladder only a rung or two from where you now stand — you are asking not to succeed!

More than that, you are guaranteeing you will not succeed! You're using what should be a FLOOR for a CEILING! Don't use the goal method as a system of limitation.

Reach out! Set the goal limit in any area of your life at the very peak of what you'd like to have — *not* at what you think doesn't sound too "greedy" or "unreal."

Be sure your goals are set high enough! I cannot emphasize this too much. There is no goal that is so high that it is not realistic if some human being can make or has made it! (Take a look at number six on our check list again.)

Nothing should enter your mind, at this point in time, as to how you are going to achieve these goals!

That's not your problem; that's *my* problem. I've made you a promise — "everything in the world you really want." All I'm asking you to do now is make up a full and complete list; your task is not to decide for yourself whether or not you could achieve a certain goal.

I'll show you the "how you get" after you've established the "what you want."

*I will go anywhere,
as long as it is forward.*

**DAVID LIVINGSTONE (1813–1873)
Scottish missionary, explorer**

*Ah, but a man's reach
should exceed his grasp,
or what's a heaven for?*

**ROBERT BROWNING (1812–1889)
English poet**

8. Am I including the personality factors necessary for goal achievement?

(If you are going to have changed circumstances, you will need the perseverance, determination, self-confidence, and other traits that you know are requisites. Don't worry about how to get the newer and better qualities any more than you worried about the "things" that are your goals. Just list them with the other goals.)

9. Is each goal stated as though already accomplished?

(That is, are the things you want worded on the goal list expressed as though you *already had* them? They must be!)

Don't write: "I want . . . I wish . . . I need . . ."

Do write: "I have . . . I am . . . I own . . ."

EXAMPLES OF HOW TO STATE YOUR GOALS

I own a brand-new, red Mercedes automobile, Model 600SL, equipped with . . . etc.
I am an effective person who always follows through on things I start . . . etc.

WARNING!

Don't tell anyone about *your* program, your new goals, your hopes for the future except someone taking the steps with you! This is of the utmost importance as you begin. Your frame of mind at this critical point can easily be infected with doubt, just as a tiny, newborn infant could fall prey to disease.

Give yourself a chance by giving no one the opportunity to keep you from the wealth and success that can be yours.

When you have started to achieve that success — they will be asking for your secret. Now, they have to deny it or admit their own lack of qualifications. Take no chances!

TURNING GOALS INTO REALITY

CHAPTER 8 OF PART 1

As set forth in Chapter 7, the form of your goals has been determined as positive, already accomplished, complete.

They have been written in the proper form and include everything in the world you really want together with every personal quality you might need to acquire. Enjoy them and keep them as a part of your life as long as you live.

Now the process of actually acquiring all these things you want begins, and it begins with a Daily Declaration — the first of three very important tools you will be introduced to in the Dyna/Psyc process.

Here is an example of a Daily Declaration:

"I _____(Space for your name)_____ accept that everything changes including myself. I am free of all past limiting attitudes."

That statement is what we call a Daily Declaration. It is a statement of belief even though when you first wrote the statement you may not have completely believed it. By constantly repeating that statement, you are planting that message in your subconscious. And there it will begin to overcome your previous training that reinforced the attitude — "That's the way I am and I can't change." Think of your subconscious as a plot of fertile ground in which all kinds of seeds have been allowed to take root. You can imagine what such a plot would look like. There might be a lot of beneficial plants there, but there will also be a lot of weeds, and the weeds tend to grow faster and be the most obvious plants. Negative limiting attitudes are like weeds. They tend to multiply rapidly. They have deep roots and, given half a chance, will take over.

PLANT PLENTY

The Daily Declaration process is just a way of planting the right kinds of seeds and planting them in such large

Life consists in what a man is thinking of all day.

RALPH WALDO EMERSON (1803–1882)
American poet, essayist, philosopher

Believe that life is worth living and your belief will help create the fact.

WILLIAM JAMES (1842–1910)
American philosopher, physiologist,
psychologist, teacher

quantities that they eventually overwhelm the weeds. Making Daily Declarations is basically very simple, but there are some important rules to follow. Your declaration must state the attitude you are trying to develop within your subconscious in positive terms as though it were already true for you. Of course when you begin working with a declaration it will not be your current attitude, otherwise you wouldn't have to work to develop it. Your whole purpose is to build your belief as the foundation for what you want to become.

THE DAILY DECLARATION PROCEDURE

Here is how they are undertaken:

EACH MORNING:

1. Immediately upon awakening, read your list of goals as you have prepared them in their positive, already accomplished form.

   Read every one of them. Read aloud if at all possible. If this cannot be done, then move your lips and form the words silently as you read. (This adds another physical dimension to the intellectual declaration.) Some people tape them so they can be played in the car.

2. After you have read each declaration . . . pause . . . *visualize* it *completely.* In your mind's eye, *see* the car, the home, the office with your name on the door. Touch the steering wheel, walk through the door. Feel the money from that first paycheck in your hands *in cash, count it,* see each bill and know its denomination.

EACH EVENING:

Just before you retire . . . no matter how late it is, no matter how tired you are, repeat the morning process.

Because it is *essential* that the Daily Declarations be carried out completely and in the most effective manner, let me give you an example of just two properly worded goals and the proper way of declaring them. As you will see, one is a declaration concerning a physical property, the other a personality quality.

We start with the need for $850 to pay an overdue debt and the desire (want) for greater confidence.

Correctly stated, those listed "burning desires" became the following goals:

1. The $850 bill from Smith & Company is paid in full.

2. I face each day supremely confident in my ability to handle every detail of my thoughts and activities. I am certain of my capacity to perform in a superior manner.

When making the Daily Declarations, the first one will be read aloud. Then the declarant will *visualize* the bill in question with "Paid in Full" stamped across it. Or, if the bill itself is in the possession of the declarant, it is taken in hand . . . examined . . . the declaration is stated again, and the bill is turned face down. Again the declaration is stated aloud.

In the personality quality declaration, it is first read aloud, giving thought to the exact meaning of each. Then the declarant *visualizes* a situation in which that quality — self-confidence perhaps — would be important. (Attempting a sale, trying to convince a superior, for example.) Now, visualize the situation as the declarant would like it to occur. The declarant shows great self-confidence; this confidence is sufficient to bring a desired result. The visualization has produced a *correct* image in the subconscious. Then, when you are faced with the *real* situation, you will have this positive material to draw on rather than the "failures" that were the only information available before.

This process is to be carried on for every single goal on your lists.

This process of Daily Declarations is *absolutely essential* to your successful practice of Dyna/Psyc. It is not necessary that you understand completely WHY it works. It is only important that you practice it long enough to learn (as thousands of others have learned) that it does work! For now, merely accept that fact as you would accept an antibiotic from your doctor without a detailed understanding of the scientific reasons for its effectiveness.

A NOTE TO SKEPTICS

Generally, at this point, in the examination of Dyna/Psyc, a handful of would-be practitioners begin to grumble things like: "mumbo-jumbo," "daydreams," "sounds ridiculous," or words to that effect.

If you are in that number, let me suggest this — *suspend your skepticism and give yourself a chance.* Notice I said "give yourself a chance." I am not concerned for Dyna/Psyc. Your doubts cannot harm it one iota. It works; the wealth that I and others have achieved using the method has proven time and time again that it *works*! But your skeptical refusal to at least TRY will once again *deprive you* of the success and the Riches that come with the success you want so badly but which continues to elude you.

Look at it this way. You have nothing to *lose* but a little time, and you have a world of wealth and happiness to *gain*. Surely, with the odds so overwhelming — nothing vs. EVERYTHING — it's worth trying.

To be unwilling to try is to cut yourself off from at least the possibility of success for the dubious pleasure of *never knowing* what might have happened.

For your convenience and in order to help you with your Daily Declarations we have included the morning and

Being a skeptic is like playing defense—you never get to score.

RICHARD GILLY NIXON (B. 1940)
American entrepreneur, publisher, speaker, author, seminar leader

You may be disappointed if you fail, but you are doomed if you do not try.

BEVERLY SILLS (B. 1929)
American opera singer, double Emmy winner, Medal of Freedom winner

evening process for you to familiarize yourself with the process and use it to guide you each time you make your Daily Declarations until the process becomes as familiar to you as your address and phone number and you no longer need this guide.

DAILY DECLARATION GUIDE

Daily Declarations are an important step on your way to Riches. They are a useful tool for obtaining your stated goals. The goals can be either tangible or intangible.

Each Morning:

1. *Immediately upon awakening, read your list of goals as prepared in their positive, accomplished form, using strong, vivid words that will capture your imagination, focusing on the results you want. If it is a personality quality, give thought to the exact meaning of each word.*

2. *Read each of them aloud if at all possible. If not, then move your lips and form the words silently as you read.*

3. *After you have read each declaration — pause — visualize it completely. If it is a personality quality, then visualize a situation in which that quality would be important. See yourself as you will be.*

Each Evening:

1. *Just before you retire — no matter how late it is — no matter how tired you are — repeat the morning process.*

The second part of the process is to restate your goal as a Daily Declaration.

HOW TO STATE GOALS AS A DAILY DECLARATION

1. *State the result or attitude you are trying to achieve as though it is already true. Say "I AM" or "I WILL" — not "I will be" or "I will have." If you want to prepare for an event in the future, say, "Whenever I am called to speak in public, I am relaxed, confident, and at ease."*

2. *Focus on the result you want to achieve — not on what you are trying to eliminate. Say "I am confident" — not "I am not nervous." Your mind tends to respond to the important words — confident, nervous — and ignores the modifiers.*

3. *Use strong, vivid words that will capture your imagination — such as beautiful, exciting, luxurious.*

4. *Be specific — state exactly the result you want to achieve. Don't be vague.*

5. *Work on yourself. Don't make declarations about others because you can't really change them, only their attitudes. The secret to changing other people's attitudes is to change your own, and that may inspire them to change themselves.*

HOW LONG WILL IT TAKE?

The answer to that question lies in assessing the following factors:

- How long did it take you to build your Inadequate Self-images?

- How bad a self-image do you have?

- Are you secretly afraid of success?

- How burdened are you with guilt from past failures?

- Will you consistently make your Daily Declarations?

- Will you really *see* when you attempt to visualize?

- Are you prepared to leave yesterday behind and live TODAY with your Daily Declarations?

- How much time and effort are you willing to give to your progress?

*Lord give me patience —
and give it to me now.*

ANONYMOUS

CAN YOU SPEED UP THE PROGRESS?

Yes! Yes, there is a method to bring about the wanted changes to your life at an even faster rate than you can achieve through your Daily Declarations alone.

While it is similar in nature to the use of Daily Declarations, it is somewhat different in use and application and totally different in the *degree of power* generated.

You might think of the comparison between the two by thinking of the Daily Declarations as the ordinary 110-volt current that is used to power electric lights and small appliances in your home. The power of Super Suggestion, which we are going to discuss, is then like the 220-volt current that is used to power heavy machinery or bigger home appliances that require far more energy.

Super Suggestion carries a far greater charge of power.

For that reason it is capable of moving your progress forward at a *more accelerated* rate than the Daily Declarations alone. Used *together,* the two kinds of motivating power, Daily Declarations and Super Suggestion, assure the most rapid results possible.

Before outlining the use of Super Suggestion and showing how it works, it is well to consider its limitations.

Super Suggestion can *only* be used on the *intangible* goals you are seeking. You can use it to build yourself, bring about in yourself the personality factors that make for success. But, you must *not use it* for acquisition of things. The realities that Super Suggestion creates in your subconscious mind must be limited to intangibles or you can do great harm to your ability to reach chosen goals.

Here's why: Super Suggestion creates full-belief even before the subject goal has been achieved. This is fine with the mental, emotional, and behavioral patterns you are seeking. Once you behave as though these intangible changes have already occurred, they dictate your behavior and you reap the benefits.

But, if the subconscious is assured (through Super Suggestion) that you already have the salary, the house, the car you are seeking, your entire subconscious mental levels cease to help you acquire them.

Remember, we said that the subconscious works without logic; it is an uncritical force. When we declare in our fully conscious state that we have things we are seeking, our conscious mind knows of their future state and "edits" the information it passes on to the lower levels of our consciousness. Then all systems will work to help us acquire them.

HOW TO DEEP CONDITION AND USE SUPER SUGGESTION

In order to understand the necessary steps you must take so that you can use Super Suggestion, it is necessary that we examine *how* and *why it works.* To help you do this

Our unconscious is like a vast subterranean factory with intricate machinery that is never idle, where work goes on day and night from the time we are born until the moment of our death.

MILTON R. SAPIRSTEIN (B. 1914)
American psychiatrist, writer

I have made the following graph. It attempts to demonstrate the levels of *consciousness* that all of us may experience at one time or another.

- **100% Consciousness** — **Wide awake** – *Alert. Some muscular tension* (participation at top level of efficiency in some sport involving quick reaction, muscular force, i.e. tennis)

- **65% Consciousness** — **Awake** – *not especially alert or tense* (preoccupied)

- **45% Consciousness** — **Half asleep** – *vaguely aware of what is going on about you*

- **20% Consciousness** — **Light sleep**

- **10% Consciousness** — **Deep sleep**

- **0% Consciousness** — **Coma** – *impossible to awaken*

As you can see, at one end of the scale is 100 percent consciousness — a wide-awake, alert condition in which there would also be some degree of muscular tension.

One of the best examples of this condition of *full* consciousness might be at the moment of participation at top level of efficiency in some sport involving careful attention, speedy reactions, muscular energy, etc.

At the very opposite end of the scale is a deep coma, an unconsciousness so complete that the person cannot even be aroused from it medically.

As you examine the various degrees of consciousness, imagine, if you will, how you would react at each stage to *suggestions* from a source outside your own body.

The top-form sports champion, intent and alert, is not swayed from what he is doing even by shouts from spectators. His own mind is in full control of his consciousness. He is not about to take *suggestions* from unskilled members of the watching crowd.

Yet, the same athlete, awakened from a sound sleep, still drowsy, might be fooled into running for an exit with the false suggestion, "GET OUT OF HERE, THE ROOM'S ON FIRE!" Every muscle of his body would then be reacting, *not to his own conscious mind*, but to the suggestion!

These two examples — suggestion rejection on the playing field and suggestion acceptance in the half-awake state — can be very helpful to our effective use of Super Suggestion.

Note that in both cases the same mind was the subject of an outside suggestion. The only differences were the *condition of consciousness* at the moment of suggestion and the power of the suggestion.

In the suggestion *rejection* case we had a fully conscious, concentrated mind. The suggestion was but one of many shouts, with little chance of penetrating the subject's consciousness.

In the *accepted* suggestion situation, the level of consciousness was far down our scale. Thus, it was more readily accessible to the suggestion. The suggestion itself was clear, urgent, and without outside interference.

Preparing to use Super Suggestion, we set up the suggestion — acceptance conditions that are best for reaching the "open" level of consciousness and presenting the suggestion in the most "powerful" manner.

When you are first learning to use Super Suggestion, it is best to:

1. Condition yourself in a quiet, darkened room.

2. Sit in a comfortable position and relax your muscles.

3. Close your eyes.

Taking these steps, you reduce many of the consciousness factors: folding your hands in your lap or resting them on the chair arms causes you to reduce muscular tension. Closing your eyes, you close off the perception of extraneous matters. The quietness of the room reduces distractions of the noise around you.

This matter of relaxing *muscular* tension is one which some people have considerable trouble achieving. If this is the case, the following procedure is suggested:

As you are sitting in your chair, visualize the various parts of your body. Start with the very tips of your toes. Think of them relaxing . . . slowly, gradually, relaxing. Proceed up your body, a section at a time, thinking of each specific part and feeling it relax. Don't make it relax, let it relax. By the time you have reached the top of your head, you will be in good muscular relaxation.

Muscular relaxation completed, you are already half-way through the mental conditioning that is the balance of the conditioning preparation required for Super Suggestion, because the very suggestion process used to relax those muscles has also been establishing mental relaxation as well.

Now, begin to count, silently, slowly, feeling yourself slip gently downward to a perfect conditioning level of consciousness. You will count from 1 up to 20. At 20, you *will* be where you need to be.

Once this physical-mental conditioning is completed, you begin to use the Super Suggestion material that you have already prepared for this session before going into your room and commencing the above conditioning.

PREPARE YOUR SUPER SUGGESTION

Unlike your Daily Declarations, in which you work on everything on your list of goals, Super Suggestion is used

◄ *Note: Do not lie down as you prepare to condition yourself to use Super Suggestion. Since you are moving to a lowered level of consciousness it would be very easy to fall asleep. In fact, I have known many people who use a Super Suggestion of sleeping in order to solve their problem of insomnia.*

on just one *intangible* quality at a time.

First, select one of the basic personality or character qualities from your list of intangible goals. Since you must work with only one at a time, making your choice should be based on the most important quality first. You will continue to use only that one quality for Super Suggestion until you have attained it. But, I promise you it will be attained in far less time than you can imagine. Super Suggestion works wonders!

Of course, you have reworded your desire for the quality into a present and positive goal. Now, select from the wording of the goal two or three key words to act as a sort of "code" for the entire goal. You do this so that you do not have to commit the entire declaration to memory. (Remember, you will use Super Suggestion with your eyes closed.)

You will read the entire declaration each time before you begin the process of "conditioning" down to the lower level of consciousness. Once there, you will repeat the "key" or "code" words and that will be all that is necessary. The speaking of those words, while in the requisite "conditioned state," will implant the entire declaration with a force and power beyond your prior imaginings.

PUTTING IT ALL TOGETHER

Let me now list for clarity the entire procedure for using Super Suggestion:

1. You have prepared a single intangible (character, behavior, or personality) goal, the one quality you feel you need most.

2. You have selected a key word or two to use as a "code" in your lower-level suggestion effort.

3. Now you go into a dimly lit or darkened room, close the door, seat yourself comfortably to relax every muscle.

4. Read the full declaration slowly and carefully. Remember the "key words" from it as you begin to condition yourself into a lower level of consciousness.

5. Go into your lower level of consciousness as outlined previously.

6. Repeat the key words silently to yourself to implant the declaration at the lower level.

7. Return to your fully conscious level, thinking as you do that you are going to feel more alert, more relaxed, more energetic than you ever have before.

That's it! That's all there is to do, and you are putting Super Suggestion to work! The desired effect will come before you know it. How soon? That depends on how well you learn to "count yourself down" into deep relaxation — and the frequency and consistency with which you perform both your Daily Declarations and utilize Super Suggestion.

The only way to know you are effectively using your Daily Declarations is to follow the instructions to *declare them every day . . . at least twice a day.* But, how can you know you are reaching the proper depth of consciousness for effective use of your once-a-day use of Super Suggestion?

This is difficult to define exactly. For it is a highly personal or subjective "feeling" that, when achieved, is evidence of the proper state. However, it is not a condition similar to the lit or unlit light bulb. It is *not* a completely "on" or "off" state.

Therefore, as you approach the essential level, you are "fading in" on it. The deeper you descend, the closer you are to the ultimate level. But Super Suggestion used anyplace along the spectrum will be effective. It will be effective in direct ratio to the degree of conditioning you have reached.

Simply put, you need not worry about your Suggestions "not working" because you have not yet developed the ability to go quickly and surely to the deeper level of consciousness. They will work better as you increase your efficiency in this conditioning, but they will be "working" for you all the time you are improving.

Practice is the secret of more efficient or more effective conditioning for Super Suggestion. Some people will find it easier than others (just as some people take to swimming or golf rapidly and with greater ease than do others). But YOU will develop an ever-increasing facility for rapid and effective descent to the lower level of consciousness as you repeat the experience.

How does it feel? There are as many answers to this question as there are people who have tried it; however, their answers all contain certain elements: relaxed, almost no body-feeling, a little drowsy perhaps, sounds fade away. You will be aware that you are you; you will not be unconscious, but you will be remote from the press of normal everyday sensation and thought.

And it is important for you to know that you will be able to reach this relaxed condition with greater and greater speed and less and less effort, as you practice it. Like the ability we develop to run rapidly along a well-known path where at first we could only inch our way.

One word of caution! Don't try too hard. This defeats the very effort itself. This is a *relaxing* effort — NOT a *concentrating* effort. *Let yourself go* — Don't try to make yourself descend!

At this point I want to remind you that this conditioning to a lower level of consciousness and using Super Suggestion is ONLY for the intangible goals, for changing qualities of basic character, personality, behavior. You don't use this method to acquire the new car, the larger salary, the new home. These goals all *require* a certain amount of time. But *personality changes* can be made as rapidly as you can Super Suggest them.

In addition to the basic and lasting personality changes

Always think of what you have to do as easy and it will be.

ÉMILE LOUÉ (1857–1926)
English naturalist

As-if principle: If you want a quality, act as if you already had it.

WILLIAM JAMES (1842–1910)
American teacher, physiologist

that we can effect through repeated Super Suggestion, you will be able to use this method of conditioning to achieve many short-term advantages.

Temporary uses to which this capacity has been put include:

- Fear of the Dentist.

  Used before the visit, fear gone!

- Late night, important work to complete, too tired.

  Super Suggestion of alertness and concentration provides both.

- Long drive, sleepy.

  Two or three minutes of a Super Suggestion of alertness at side of the road. Perfectly able to continue.

- Interview for new job, fright, and feeling of panic.

  Brief descent and Super Suggestion of calm and poise. Problem gone for interview.

- Can't sleep at night.

  In bed, a Super Suggestion of sleep, deep and restful. Success!

- Pain (dentist, childbirth, etc.).

  Used by one proficient in the preparatory conditioning — no pain.

COMING BACK

A plus factor that you can add to your conditioning when you begin to develop some degree of ease in its practice is *enhancement of later consciousness*.

This is a simple process by means of which you will return to the high consciousness level feeling *refreshed*, with new energy, vigor. Your mental outlook will be happier and more confident than it was before you conditioned for

Super Suggestion.

Adding this factor is simply a matter of counting backwards as you begin your return from the point of suggestion — 20 . . . 19 . . . 18 . . . etc. As you pass 10 and again at 5, tell yourself silently of the conditions that will be yours when you reach zero.

In other words, as you are arising from the lower level of consciousness, you make double use of the trip. Not only do you strongly implant the Super Suggestion, but on the way up, you emphasize the energetic feeling of power and well being that will be yours once you return to full consciousness.

A final point — When and how often do you use Super Suggestion in preparing to achieve a basic "personal quality" goal? As an aid to reaching the fullest efficiency of self-conditioning at the lower level, you need not limit the number of times you practice it daily, but, as a matter of effectively using a single Super Suggestion, you'll get the maximum benefit from a once-a-day use. However, you can — and should — use the Super Suggestion technique for emergencies (a trip to the dentist, a job interview, etc.).

The best time to use this powerful aid to achieving your intangible goals is when you are not tired and are reasonably alert. Thus, it becomes clear that the first thing in the morning, late at night, or just after eating are *not* the times to condition. If possible, perhaps just before your luncheon period, or just after work if you are on a tight working schedule. Otherwise, any period you can set aside while you're wide-awake.

SUMMARY

This now gives you two of the important tools that make Dyna/Psyc effective:

DAILY DECLARATIONS and **SUPER SUGGESTION**.

As you can see, they work in the *conscious* and

subconscious levels of our mind.

In the next chapter we examine the third and most powerful tool Dyna/Psyc has to offer you.

LET GO AND RELAX WITH SUPER SUGGESTION

Because of the hundreds of readers who have told us how invaluable Super Suggestion has been to them since Joe first introduced the concept 20 years ago, I would like to expand upon the procedure and the importance of learning to relax to effectively use the most powerful technique ever developed for changing habits and attitudes. This technique is based on ancient knowledge, but we have updated it with a couple of modern wrinkles. In the Bible, Jesus taught his disciples the same technique as a way to pray; and it is found in the fundamental teachings of many other religions. It has been used by mystics throughout the ages and has been given a great deal of scientific support with the work of modern psychologists beginning as far back as William James. Super Suggestion opens up *direct* communication with the amazing power of your subconscious mind. You bypass the editing function of the conscious mind and go directly to the subconscious with positive suggestions that develop in you the attitudes that you desire to obtain. The process that we will use is a combination of ancient knowledge and the modern scientific principles of bio-feedback and conditioned reflex.

Believe that life is worth living and your belief will help create the fact.

WILLIAM JAMES (1842–1910)
American teacher, physiologist,
philosopher

COMPLETELY RELAX TO RELIEVE THE TENSION

I told you the most important requirement for Super Suggestion to succeed is to quiet the conscious mind and body — to completely relax the mind and body so that you are free of all tensions. This allows you to reach the deeper levels of the mind. For most people it is difficult to completely relax. You may think you are completely relaxed when you are sleeping, but most people are in a state of considerable tension when they are sleeping. To really relax you are going to have to exercise but not the way you think. (This exercise even appealed to Lazy Joe.) The process is basically simple. You start with a mental exercise designed to open up our awareness of the tension in our bodies. Then, you use the same kind of conditioning that Dr. Pavlov used on his dogs, only you are in charge of what is going on. You take *control* of a process that has been going on in you for a long time to build a conditioned relaxation reflex. Now think for a minute about something that causes you to really get uptight — something that creates a lot of tension in your body. There are lots of examples that could be used.

RELAXING ON THE FREEWAY?

The one that used to always bug me before I understood this process was fighting traffic on the freeway. All I had to do was just *think* about getting on the freeway at rush hour, and I could feel the tension building up in my body. Now even if you haven't experienced freeway traffic, you have had the experience of being late for an appointment, being trapped behind a slow-moving car on a narrow road, and you reacted with physical tension. You get a knot between your shoulder blades, maybe a tension headache. Have you ever asked yourself why? When you think about it there is no more reason for your body to react to such a situation with tension then there was for Dr. Pavlov's dogs to respond to bells by salivating. You have simply been conditioned to react that way. Haven't you ever used the expression, "I get so uptight when" such and such happens, or, "That really bugs me." I used to say those things before I knew what I was doing to myself. I kept reinforcing "I get so uptight when I have to fight the freeway traffic," and sure enough I did. And I continued to as long as I kept *reinforcing* that suggestion. Fortunately for us, the mind can also learn how to relax our body on cue. It's just that very few of us have discovered how to do it, so we never try even though we have all experienced this process. I am sure that you can think of something right now that you find very relaxing. Maybe it is a hot shower or lying on the beach listening to the waves or stretching out in a hammock under whispering pine trees. These are things that can become relaxation keys for you. Unfortunately, you cannot always lie out in a hammock or stretch out on the beach or listen to the waves or climb into a hot shower. But what you *can* do is condition your body to respond to *symbols* in your mind just as though you were doing those things. And that is what you are learning about, with the aid of the Super Suggestion. This is an important step along your *Way to Riches*.

DEVELOP NEW HABITS

Remember, you are working with habits and habits take time to develop — about 30 or more repetitions. Developing your relaxation reflex takes time as well. So plan on using your Super Suggestion exercise daily from now on. After a while with practice you will develop relaxation abilities that you can use in any circumstance. You may worry that you will fall asleep and become completely relaxed in a situation where it would not be appropriate. Your mind will not let that occur. It is possible, with just a little practice, to completely relax your body to the extent that is appropriate for the activity in which you are involved. You will be able to use this while driving, while speaking in front of an audience, while doing just about *any* activity. You will be able to maintain the relaxation that is so helpful, so important for your body. By the way, if you practice this faithfully, I think you will notice very definite positive side effects as far as your health is concerned. Dr. Hans Selye, in his book *The Stress of Life*, estimates that 95% of all disease is either a result of, or severely aggravated by, the kind of tension we are talking about. Just think what an improvement it can be to remove that tension from your life.

SYMBOLS OF RELAXATION

Just like the bell for Pavlov's dogs or freeway traffic as a tension symbol, you will need a *relaxation* symbol. You don't want to use the word "relax," because many people have been conditioned to respond to that with tension. Have you ever been really tense and when you try to relax have the tension increase? You need a symbol that is either neutral or always has a positive relaxation association for you. One of the things that works for me is sailing. For you it might be a warm bath. For someone else, the bubbling of a mountain stream or the crackle of an open fire.

Search your experience for such an association and choose a symbol to represent that association. Make it short and one with which there is no association with tension of any kind. It could be something as simple as "Let go," which we will use as an example in our sample declaration at the end of this chapter. Initially, you will condition yourself to relax in response to this symbol. It is an affirmation of your new relaxation ability. Actually, it is an instruction to your mind, the conscious part, telling it how to behave. During the exercise you will be reinforcing this affirmation several times speaking directly to your subconscious, *teaching* it how to react.

When you do the exercise, it is important that you are physically comfortable. Make sure your neck is supported such as in a recliner or in a chair that allows you to lean back. You need to set up a situation where you can have complete quiet. You do not want the telephone ringing and interrupting the exercise. It may be that the only time you can do this is at bedtime, but if you can find some other time you can take 15 or 20 minutes to be completely alone that would be a good time to do it. It is an important little decision for your continued progress on *The Lazy Man's Way* that you actually find the time to do this exercise every single day. It is excellent for you mentally, emotionally, physically, and spiritually. I have provided you with a step-by-step guide for the relaxation declarations.

YOUR RELAXATION DECLARATION

I, ___(say your name)___ *, now realize that I have the ability to relax any and all parts for my body any time I want to. I now accept the symbol "Let Go" as my cue for complete physical relaxation. Any time I want to relax, I simply take a deep breath, hold it for a moment, then visualize or think about the symbol "Let Go," exhale, and let all the tension wash from my body with my escaping breath. I know that I have always had the power to relax my body and I now consciously choose the symbol "Let Go" as my trigger for complete physical relaxation. I accept the fact that I can automatically release all tension simply by taking a deep breath, thinking or visualizing "Let Go," and exhaling. As I exhale, all unnecessary tension flows out of my body. I also know that my relaxation never endangers me in any way. In fact, has a beneficial effect on my health and peace of mind. From now on, the words "Let Go" are my symbol for complete relaxation.*

In the creative state a man is taken out of himself. He lets down as it were a bucket into his subconscious, and draws up something which is normally beyond his reach. He mixes this thing with his normal experiences and out of the mixture he makes a work of art.

E. M. FORSTER (1879–1970)
English novelist, short-story writer, essayist

Decision-making is the most significant work you ever do. That is because it is impossible for the human animal to even exist without a steady stream of decisions.

The decision to eat or drink and the choice of what you will eat or drink is a simplified example of the decision-making process to which we give little or no importance but which is essential to our continued existence.

Other than breathing, the beating of the heart, etc., the bodily functions are generally carried on after making a decision or a series of decisions. Think of the number of decisions, each tiny and insignificant, but each essential in the process of merely scratching your nose.

First, there's the awareness of the itch. Then, the decision: Rub with the back of your hand? Rub with your sleeve? Scratch with your fingers? Which fingers of which hand? How hard, how long? Is the selected hand free to scratch or must some burden in the hand be set down or shifted to the other hand before scratching? These are merely the highlights of the number of decisions that can enter into a simple act.

And that is only part of it. In addition to making the basic decision to scratch, we must make innumerable calculations in order to effectively carry out the decisions; i.e., how far to lift the hand, the planned trajectory that will bring the fingers, flexing and unflexing properly, into just the exact position on the nose we cannot see. From a calculation standpoint, it is something like plotting a rendezvous of two spacecraft.

The hardware that the space agency has developed for such command and guidance is complex almost beyond belief. Yet, a single day's activity of an average, active human body requires that decisions and computations be made that are so numerous and must be made with so much complex input of information and in such short periods of time that no computer in existence could handle it.

Plotting and executing a space voyage is not one bit as complex as your decision and computing problems in driving downtown through busy traffic as you go to work each day. You make more decisions based on more information inputs and must make more instantaneous calculations of speed, proximity, even potential personality of other drivers (". . . that s.o.b. won't let me in here") in a half-hour drive than is required on any flight to the moon.

In short, the message is brief. NO MAN-MADE CALCULATOR OR COMPUTER EVEN BEGINS TO APPROACH THE COMPLEXITY OR EFFICIENCY OF THE HUMAN MIND.

The final step in the implementation of Dyna/Psyc — and the changing of your life — is the creation of CONSCIOUS ACCESS TO THE COMPUTER OF YOUR SUBCONSCIOUS MIND!

Make no mistake, *ordinary people* never learn to use the great Subconscious Computer. The day they learn to use it, they cease to be *ordinary.*

Searching the writings of famous men, the statements they have made as to their source of creativity (which is essentially a matter of decision-making) and reading everything I could find in this area, I can tell you this:

Edison, Einstein, Mozart, Emerson, Tchaikovsky, Steinmetz, James Watt, and innumerable other inventors, scientists, writers, composers all have given evidence of their using the great Subconscious Computer that exists in all of us. Each of them somehow happened upon this great resource. YOU are going to learn how to use it knowingly and at will.

The more extensive a man's knowledge of what has been done the greater will be his chance of knowing what to do.

BENJAMIN DISRAELI (1804–1881)
English statesman, novelist

WHAT WILL IT DO FOR YOU?

I. *Provide meaningful and productive answers to your problems.*

II. *Increase the efficiency and well-being of your mind itself.*

III. *Furnish the POWER that turns your Daily Declarations into actual possessions.*

I. In the PROBLEM area, we all know that the burden of decision-making (which is what problems are — difficult decisions) increases in direct ratio to the complexity of the problem. If the decision is yes or no, stay or go, black or white, it is usually less complex than if there are several possible solutions and you must decide which is the best course of action.

Immediately we are faced with a lot of information of varying degrees of importance, a number of answers of varying worth and, very often, emotional pressures to make one decision or another. In short, a "computer-like" problem.

Using our subconscious power we can have the answer computed and delivered to us!

II. MENTAL WELL-BEING comes into focus when we understand how the Subconscious Computer can be used to reduce stress and tension in the nervous system. Permit me to quote from a work I read some years ago:

> *Recent research on sleep has reversed some of the fashionable conceptions which were widely discussed in years past. The fact is that, although the number of hours required varies slightly between individuals and also varies with age, the idea that only four or five hours are actually required is fallacious. New findings point up that your actual requirement conforms more closely to your common practice of sleeping seven, eight, or nine hours than was previously thought. Assuming that your true requirement is eight*

hours, then the first half, or approximately four hours, is devoted to your body repairs or the rejuvenation of the tissues which have been worn down during the day. Scientists, in making observations of this period, note that during the first hour, sleep is particularly deep and there is an accompanying increase in basal metabolism. There is an extra expenditure of energy involved in the first hurried elimination of the major aspects of purely physical fatigue. The second, third, and fourth hours produce somewhat lighter sleep and require considerably less energy, while the more intricate physical repairs are accomplished — such things as reflexes and various physically derived judgments such as distance, form, and color are thus returned to normal through cell repair and reproduction.

Since this is the case, it is imperative that you have some method of reducing the tension and pressures that modern day living places upon us.

The use of the Subconscious Computer can be put to work to clear your mental system of each day's problems, as you sleep and prepare your mind for the following day's activities.

III. DECLARATION ACHIEVEMENT is accomplished through the use of this same Subconscious Computer.

Here is how that works. As your Daily Declarations are made, the subconscious computer receives that information from you. It becomes the function of this giant calculator to devise the methods that you can use to get those goals!

I will show you how to be able to receive those solutions or answers as they have been calculated.

Every time you had a "hunch" that solved a problem for you, you were using this power. When a name was "on the tip of your tongue" but you couldn't think of it, haven't you often told someone "I'll think of it on the way home." And then, just as you said you would, you "remembered" it later? That too was an example of the use of this power.

Those people who, when faced with an important decision, decide to "sleep on it" and awaken the next day with the answer are unconsciously using their computer.

But I want you to be able to use it *consciously*, not by default.

The hardest job I'll have in getting you to put this fabulous power to work is getting you to try. That's because the method of using it is so simple, it seems so easy, that many persons are totally unable to accept it. I hope you don't suffer from that limitation.

PUTTING THE SUBCONSCIOUS COMPUTER TO WORK

The three key words for putting your subconscious to work are:

WRITE — TRY — ASK

WRITE *Write out your problem.* This may sound foolish, but my experience has shown that a great number of problems exist only because they have not been clearly defined or outlined.

Once you actually write out the problem, you are going to find that you will see it in a new light. On your paper start with the words, "Shall I do this . . . ?"

Carefully, fully, yet concisely, state the problem to which you are seeking an answer.

TRY *Try to answer it yourself.* On the piece of paper which contains your stated problem, place two columns. In one column put all the reasons for taking the particular step. In the other, all the reasons against.

Put in enough time doing this so that you are relatively certain you cannot solve the problem *consciously*.

Once you are forced to reach the decision that you cannot solve the problem consciously, go to Step Three.

ASK *Ask your Subconscious Computer to solve it for you.* This is the part of the procedure which many people find hard to accept.

There is no failure except in no longer trying.

ELBERT HUBBARD (1856–1915)
American businessman, writer, printer

Ask, and it shall be given.

BIBLE
MATTHEW 7:7

They simply cannot believe that any task of such magnitude could be carried on by simply "asking" part of your mind to take care of it.

Yet, these same people drive a car to work every morning, many times becoming so involved in their own conscious thoughts that they are letting their Subconscious Computer do all the driving.

They will suddenly become aware, almost like someone awakening from sleep, that they are ready to turn off the freeway or turnpike. They will be unable to recall clearly the specifics of what occurred, in connection with their wending their way through traffic.

ACCEPT IT! Think of your subconscious as another person, an employee or assistant. Just say to that force: "I want the answer to this problem by tomorrow morning — or four o'clock this afternoon." Or, if it is particularly difficult, give the computer more time. Tell it you want the answer by next Saturday or something of the sort.

Then, FORGET IT! Forget the problem completely. Your computer will not work on a problem while you are working on it in your conscious mind. It is as though you had to release all the figures on some job to another person before he could go to work on it.

So, forget it once you have asked the Subconscious Computer to solve it for you. And you can forget it because your Subconscious Computer *will* solve it.

Simple as the use of this powerful force is, there are a number of questions that people have asked me concerning it. I have set them forth below, together with my answers, in case you too are wondering the same things.

Q. Doesn't someone have to have a really brilliant mind for this to work?

A. No. It can work for anyone if he/she will merely follow the three steps outlined.

Q. Are there any limitations on using the Subconscious Computer?

*More men fail
through lack of purpose
than lack of talent.*

**BILLY SUNDAY (WILLIAM ASHLEY)
(1862–1935)
American baseball player, evangelist**

A.   Only those I set forth already.   First, that the problem must be written out in a clear, complete form. Second, you must go through the steps of *trying consciously* to solve it.   You must put on paper the various pros and cons which you can find.

Q. How do you decide "when" the computer must give you the answer?

A.   Don't put off a decision that really needs to be made. But don't try to fool the computer. If you don't have to make the decision for some time, don't give the computer a false deadline. "Need" seems to be an important element in the speedy functioning of this power. Also, the "when" is seldom a problem *if* you have honestly gone through steps one and two.   The dimensions of the problem and the quantity of material for and against the decision will influence your timetable as well as your *need* for the answer at a particular time.

Q. How and why does it work?

A.   There are a number of theories put forth by psychologists, psychiatrists, even mystics and religious teachers. I don't really know. I simply know that it does work.

The success this method has given me is the recommendation I offer for your trying it. It does work! That's all I ever really needed to know about it.

Q. Why is it important?

A. Because really effective people cannot afford to go around carrying dozens of unsolved problems in their minds. They need the free use of their consciousness to take care of the matters of the moment. Yet, they also encounter larger problems that they are unable to readily solve for themselves *even after* defining them, laying them out fully, and going over the pros and cons.

Unsolved problems are worries!   Worries are destructive.

Q. What is its greatest value?

A. The fact that you are able to use the greatest part of your mind, a secret part, inaccessible to most people — *at will!* There is no question that the subconscious part of our mind (for reasons I still do not completely understand) has a capacity for creativity, problem-solving, etc. — *far beyond* the other portions of the mental equipment. The Subconscious Computer (S/C) is truly a *super power*. Its relationship to our conscious mind is like comparing a single man's efforts with those of a computer.

Q. Can it be used only on a basis where the answer will not be forthcoming for some time?

A. No. There is a technique for nearly "instant" application. All you have to do is "condition" yourself as though you were preparing to use Super Suggestion. At that level, ask the S/C your question. If, prior to this step you have defined the problem and tried consciously to solve it by weighing the opposing advantages and disadvantages, you will only have to wait a bit in that deeper state of consciousness and the answer will come.

Q. How will I know the answer?

A. First, let me explain you will not begin to hear mysterious "voices." It is just that the solution to the problem will come to you in a form immediately capable of application to your problem.

It will "feel" like the *right* answer. You will also "feel" you want to get right back to the problem and put that answer to work at once. If you have had some mental "block" that kept you from seeing the solution at an earlier stage, the "answer" may have to come to you in a "disguise." That is, something may keep coming to your mind, in connection with the problem, which seems to have no application — a snatch of an old song, a childhood game, etc., but then it will suddenly occur to you that "Bye Bye Blackbird" may be an unconscious suggestion to get rid of the source of the problem. And that will be one of the two courses between which you had been trying to decide.

Generally, the feeling of "rightness" and the feeling of "eagerness" to carry out the solution are all you will need to identify the correct answer from the Unconscious Computer.

Q. Can I do this right away . . . or does it take a few tries to get it working?

A. It will respond when you properly prepare and ask. However, as you continue to use it, proficiency will grow as it does with all familiar things.

But, if it *doesn't* work at all, YOU ARE PREVENTING ITS FUNCTION! It won't work if you consciously KNOW it won't. Accept that it will! And I assure you . . . it does!

A Word of Warning: Don't fail to act on the answer you are given! Or you will find it is some time before it will function again!

THE SECOND ASPECT OF THE SUBCONSCIOUS COMPUTER

As we noted earlier, there are three ways in which your subconscious can be put to work to great advantage.

We have examined one — the *problem-solving* capacity. Now, let us consider its use as an aid to mental health and to increasing your general efficiency.

During your hours of sleep, your subconscious works, primarily through the use of dreams, to lower the tensions and pressures that have accumulated during the day.

However, that function is only carried on after the process of *physical* rehabilitation is carried out, during the first four hours or so of your sleep.

If the day's problems, pressures, tensions have been particularly heavy, or if you just didn't get enough sleep during the night, your mental rehabilitation may be incomplete upon awakening. This means you will face the new day with a lowered tolerance for the day's demands on your nervous/mental capacities. Irritability makes itself felt; problems loom larger than life-size.

And, when you are at your lowest ebb the next day (for we all seem to have "cycles" of more energy, less energy, etc., in regular patterns throughout our waking hours), your reserves are shot and you're in trouble.

It is at this point that you can utilize your subconscious computer to give yourself what I call the Silent Treatment. This Silent Treatment is a method of permitting your subconscious computer to "catch up," for a brief time, on the chores it was unable to complete the night before.

It enables you to spend just a few minutes in a special manner that will increase your efficiency in every way for hours!

And what will you be doing during those few minutes? Nothing!

SILENT TREATMENTS

Here's how to give yourself this rewarding Silent Treatment:

1. Make a conscious determination that the time has come for a treatment. Don't just let yourself "happen" into it. Tell yourself you are going to turn things over to the S/C for a time.

2. Sit down or, if possible, lie down. Close your eyes and step outside of yourself. Lying there with your eyes closed, become as though you were a passive spectator of yourself. Don't try to think of anything — don't try not to think of anything. Relax — just exist for the moment with closed eyes. Think of yourself as having "stepped aside" while some workmen carry on an important task of "cleaning up" the area where you have been working. Just relax while they put everything in order for your return

after a while. Sit or lie with eyes closed and — let go!

3. When you feel an almost uncontrollable desire to open your eyes — do so. This will be somewhere from five to twenty minutes later.

Here are the results you can expect from Silent Treatments: You will find increased enthusiasm, energy, and an overall increase in your sense of well-being. Tiredness falls away.

These results will *increase* in effect after you have been giving yourself a daily treatment for a week or two.

But a warning. Sometimes, just as you open your eyes, it is such a pleasant experience you have just had, you might think of closing them again for a time. *Don't!* A second Silent Treatment, immediately upon the heels of the first, is sure to not only *undo* the benefits of the first, it will leave you feeling terrible. You will probably have a headache. One treatment only. That's the rule.

Remember, the Silent Treatment does not involve *sleep*. It is simply a means of quieting your conscious mind and permitting the unconscious to get terribly busy for a brief time. The results are well worth the trouble it may be to you to find a way to do it each day.

If you have a place at work to do it, fine; if not, perhaps you can go to your car for the few minutes required. At any rate, get comfortable, as comfortable as possible.

Another side benefit of the use of these treatments is the increasing ease with which you are able to reach your S/C. This greatly enhances the success of the problem-solving function as well.

THE THIRD ASPECT OF THE SUBCONSCIOUS COMPUTER

This utilization of the great power of the subconscious within you requires no more effort on your part than the continued use of your Daily Declarations.

Just as Super Suggestion *enhances* the speed with which you can acquire a positive trait or quality that you've set up as a goal, the S/C also makes important contributions to goal fulfillment. Both the "things" you want and the intangible goals are conditioned into your mental apparatus.

Day by day, you will perform acts that forward you in your pursuit of those goals. Your S/C enhances the speed and certainty of your goal attainment with every decision it makes, every calculation you turn over to it. It *includes* your goal needs as one more element in making each decision.

Your S/C will *suggest* moves, ideas, strategies to you that will make your declarations realities. New and creative ideas will just seem to "come from nowhere" as you progress in the application of the natural laws of power which have been summed up for you in Dyna/Psyc.

Be responsive to your own ideas! Forget the past when you had a tendency to immediately "put down" an idea that came into your mind as "impractical" or "daydreaming." Be alert and ready to be responsive to the wealth of material that your S/C can develop for you. If you turn it down, the spontaneous activity will cease. Accept it, examine it, put it into operation, and the supply will increase!

Men are made stronger on realization that the helping hand they need is at the end of their own right arm.

ANONYMOUS

Success is not the result of spontaneous combustion. You must set yourself on fire.

REGGIE (REGINALD JOSEPH) LEACH
(B. 1950)
Canadian hockey player – "Rifle"

If you have read carefully all the material presented thus far, you are 25% along the way to *The Lazy Man's Riches* I promised you. Because we have set forth the basic precepts of Dyna/Psyc.

As you recall, I mentioned at the beginning that yours must be an R.S.V.P. response to this invitation to get "everything in the world you really want." R — you must READ it all. S — more than merely reading, you must STUDY it. V — you have to VISUALIZE the steps outlined and the steps within each step. And finally, P — you have to PERFORM the works as outlined.

If all you have done so far is READ, you're 25% there. To the extent you have been STUDYING what you have read, you are even further along.

Now, let us quickly review *all* things you have to VISUALIZE and PERFORM.

I. You have DAILY DECLARATIONS. Those positive and present-tense statements made up from the lists of things (tangible and intangible) that you want and need. You are prepared to VISUALIZE them as you use them at least twice daily.

II. You have prepared SUPER SUGGESTIONS from the most important intangible goals. You have prepared code words (relaxation symbols) to summon them up for use, as you are in that conditioned state where you can offer suggestions to your subconscious levels.

III. You are prepared to use your SUBCONSCIOUS COMPUTER in three ways:

1. To overcome obstacles you perceive as problems.

2. To give yourself SILENT TREATMENTS.

3. To gain added impetus to your DAILY

DECLARATIONS.

Now, you are ready to establish:

IV. The daily programming of these elements so that you receive the maximum benefit from Dyna/Psyc. To help you do this, I have provided a chart located at the end of this chapter, page 99, on which you can check off each day the necessary actions.

By all means use it. Do not begin your program of goal attainment without a *programmed approach* that will assist you in making all these things HABITS as soon as possible.

This is the PERFORMANCE that is the last essential to success. And I assure you that *essential* means just that! There is simply no way to achieve the wealth you want without following through *consistently.*

Because the performing of these daily acts is so easy, requires so little time or effort, I think you must agree with me that it is indeed a "*Lazy Man's Way.*"

Following are a few questions many people have asked about Dyna/Psyc after they have begun its practice. I have included them in the hope that, as you progress, you may find among them the answers to your questions.

QUESTIONS & ANSWERS

Q. How many Daily Declarations do most people have?

A. The average seems to be around 20; however, the *more* you have, the better! Just be sure you use them twice daily. If the list can be handled on that basis, the number is unimportant.

Q. Why do you emphasize daily activity? Does missing a day or two hurt?

He who chooses the beginning of a road chooses the place it leads to. It is the means that determine the end.

HARRY EMERSON FOSDICK (1878–1969)
American theologian

Great works are performed not by strength, but by perseverance.

DR. SAMUEL JOHNSON (1709–1784)
English lexicographer, essayist, poet

A. YES! If you are not prepared to *regularly* practice the application of the natural laws of Dyna/Psyc, you reduce its effect dramatically. Only consistent application pays off. But it does pay off *big*!

Q. **Is one's age a handicap in practicing Dyna/Psyc?**

A. Not at all. It is equally effective for teenagers or those "four-score" and older. In fact, "keeping young" has been an important goal for many.

Q. **In discussing your approach with friends they said they thought I was too tense for such an effort. Isn't everybody tense?**

A. More or less. Some emotion is felt by everyone at all times. The pleasant emotions make you feel good; unpleasant ones make you feel bad. Repressed emotions create tension. Dyna/Psyc makes it possible to ease the tensions of unexpressed emotions. A simple way to help reduce tension is through Silent Treatments. Suggestions of relaxation and renewed energy and enthusiasm when "coming-up" from Super Suggestions are also beneficial.

Q. **What is the greatest enemy of success?**

A. Fear — the fear that caused the early negative conditioning, which, in turn, gave us an Inadequate Self-Image to begin with. And fear is the worst of all tensions. It creates *anxiety* — which creates further tensions. Declarations for *courage, confidence, relaxation and effectiveness* are all helpful in controlling this threat to success.

Q. **Are there any good ways to get rid of the tensions you feel at work so that you don't bring them home to "let loose" on the family?**

A. A minute or two of *any* strenuous physical activity can work like magic. Punch a bag you hang up in the garage for that purpose. Pound a few heavy nails into a piece of timber. Chop a piece of wood. Even "shadowboxing" vigorously will relieve the tensions.

Q. Isn't it shameful for a grown man to cry?

A. Indeed not. I was once told that many psychiatrists believe the acceptance of women's tears, but not of men's, is one of the reasons women outlive men. Human beings should be able to *relieve* grief by this perfectly natural outlet. It has been said (and I think, truly) that those who are unable to express grief in this manner are also unable to express joy.

A childish outburst is of course inappropriate. But the inability to express emotion in some physical form is also a handicap.

Q. Can one person literally give another person a "pain in the neck?"

A. Indeed! There are a number of "sayings" which we hear frequently that show how deeply our emotions affect us in physical ways. "She makes me sick — I can breathe easier, now that the bill is paid — I've got something to get off my chest — I'm boiling mad — He gets me hot under the collar — He gives me a headache — That makes my stomach turn." These are all sayings that actually describe the physical manifestations of various emotional problems. Don't let them get to you. Use Dyna/Psyc to free yourself from the destructive tensions.

Q. How can I use Dyna/Psyc to get the support of other people?

A. You will get it *automatically* when you make your Daily Declaration, "I have a warm regard for others at all times and in all situations." Your success does require the help and cooperation of other people, and a warm regard for others *communicates itself to them.* Feeling it, they must respond. Sometimes you will feel you have met someone who is immune to this treatment. But persevere; you will win! And, remember this: helping others helps you rid yourself of guilt for mistakes or wrongs in your past. Guilt is a great drawback in the search for success. Rid yourself of it by unselfishly giving of yourself without fanfare or reward. It will aid you in many ways.

Q. I had barely started on my Daily Declarations when I began to feel they were not what I had really wanted. Is this wrong?

A. No. You will find your goals *change* as you progress. Merely revise your goals to conform to your new desires. Word the new ones for Daily Declaration and continue as before.

Q. Should I tell my husband the goals I have set for myself or that I'm changing my personality and character so that things will be more peaceful and happy at home?

A. No! Keep those intangible goals to yourself. As your behavior manifests the new qualities, everyone will be aware of it. But if you talk about it, there is a too-human need to call it to your attention if, as you are beginning to establish the change, you should "slip back" to the old you for even a moment.

Remember, I have cautioned you *not* to discuss *any* of your goals or efforts with others. The main reason for this is the energy you dissipate by telling others of your projected changes or acquisitions. Sometimes it seems that, by telling, a person substitutes the "story" for true achievement. Keep your own counsel! Follow the plan!

REINFORCEMENT/PROGRESS CHART

DAY	FIRST MONTH				SECOND MONTH				THIRD MONTH			
	DAILY DECLARATION	SILENT TREATMENT	SUPER SUGGESTION	S/C PROBLEM SOLVING	DAILY DECLARATION	SILENT TREATMENT	SUPER SUGGESTION	S/C PROBLEM SOLVING	DAILY DECLARATION	SILENT TREATMENT	SUPER SUGGESTION	S/C PROBLEM SOLVING
	AM PM				AM PM				AM PM			
1												
2												
3												
4												
5												
6												
7												
8												
9												
10												
11												
12												
13												
14												
15												
16												
17												
18												
19												
20												
21												
22												
23												
24												
25												
26												
27												
28												
29												
30												
31												

BOOK ONE

THE JOURNEY

☐

PART 2: On the Road

FOCUS ON YOUR DESTINATION, NOT YOUR PROBLEM

CHAPTER 1 OF PART 2

You have been conditioned to think of situations that are inadequate for the attainment of our desires and aspirations as "problems." Then, you were conditioned to spend your life solving those problems. When you focus on solving problems, you are spending your life-energy to make something *go away* — to get rid of something. When you are focused on creating your inner vision, you are expending your life-energy toward making something you want *come into being* — your Riches. The basic intentions of these actions are opposite one another. One creates stress and frustration that can lead to anger and rage — the Los Angeles riots come to mind; the other brings us satisfaction — the Los Angeles Summer Olympics is a good example. Through *The Lazy Man's Way* you will learn to focus on creating your vision of your ideal life — finding your purpose — which brings you a life of fulfillment, satisfaction, and Riches.

I think the reason we stay with our problems is that they are comfortable and familiar. They seem to work for us. They help organize our thoughts, focus our actions, and fill up our time. Our problems relieve us of the need to think. We can just obsess instead. We can dwell on what's wrong. We can go over it in our mind repeatedly. We can worry about it. We can blame our problems for our troubles. We have something to talk about with our friends. Our colleagues will be impressed and attentive. It's us against the problem and because our victories are measured by the size of our adversaries, the bigger the problem the better. Problem solving inevitably distracts and deceives us by giving us the illusion that we are doing something important and valuable.

When we think to examine our lives in the context of having a purpose, we ask better and more useful questions. Rather than asking, "How can I get this unwanted situation

Problems are only opportunities in work clothes.

HENRY J. KAISER (1882–1967)
American industrialist

Our problems are man made, therefore, they may be solved by man. And man can be as he wants. No problem of human destiny is beyond beings.

JOHN F. KENNEDY (1917–1963)
35th President of the United States of America

Happiness is essentially a state of going somewhere wholeheartedly, one-directionally, without regret or reservations.

WILLIAM H. SHELDON (1898–1977)
American physician, psychologist

We grow by dreams. All big men are dreamers, some of us let dreams die, but others nourish and protect them, nurse them through bad days . . . to the sunshine and light which always come.

WOODROW WILSON (1856–1924)
28th President of the U.S.

to go away?" we might ask, "What results will my vision create?" "How can I get to where I want to go?" "How can I have the joy I want?" These questions direct us in a positive manner and produce better, more satisfying results than, "How can I get rid of my problems?"

WHICH WILL IT BE? THE FOREST OR THE TREES?

The difference in orientation can change your life and can change your world. Dr. Martin Luther King didn't just solve a problem. He created a vision of a new structure of equality and justice — "I have a dream."

John F. Kennedy didn't just solve a problem. He created a vision of U.S. leadership in space, education, social welfare. We began to dream of Camelot.

Mahatma Gandhi didn't just solve a problem. He created a vision that dramatically changed India, England, and the whole world.

Because a change in structure — from problem solving to creating a vision — changes the way things are accomplished (from a path of least resistance, which takes us all over the place, to a more direct, clearer path) these men, and many others like them, have been able to bring into their lives, and ours, what truly mattered to them.

This book is not just about solving problems or moving away from problems, but about how to create *your* vision of your purpose and moving your life forward under your control. As you read this book your perspective will be changed forever and lifted to new heights. You will get a "big-picture" look at the forest of your dreams, not a close-up look at the logs and stumps of your problems.

REACTIVE/RESPONSIVE VS. PROACTIVE/CREATIVE

My dissatisfaction and frustrations in any aspect of my life seem to come from a feeling that I'm not in control of whatever situation appears to be affecting me. The situation or circumstance is in control of me, if all I am doing is reacting or responding to it. Tim Timmons says that allowing myself to be in the reactive/responsive mode is living life like a Ping-Pong ball on a windy day. It is easily blown to and fro, bouncing up and down and off of everything in sight. It reacts and responds to the currents of the winds. It has no real purpose or direction, but goes with the wind (the circumstances) around it.

The real problem of the reactive/responsive way of living your life is that it assumes that you are *powerless* over the circumstances of your life. It assumes that your only options are to react or respond to a given situation or circumstance. If you find yourself repeatedly in a reactive/responsive mode, you might then want to ask yourself (are you ready for the truth?), "Who has the power here, me or the thing to which I am responding or reacting?" Clearly the power is in the circumstance and not in you, if you are reacting or responding. So you never get anything done. It's like the old saying, "When you are up to your butt in alligators, it's too late to think about draining the swamp."

I feel that power is *always* internal. If you believe, and therefore live your life, as if changing your *external* circumstances will bring you success, you are deluding yourself. *And you are the last person you ever want to delude.* Understand that nothing external, in and of itself, can bring you genuine success and happiness. If you think that people (a new boss, a different spouse, or better friend), places (a new neighborhood, world travel, or a better location) and things (inheriting money or property, a face lift, winning at gambling, a new car, better wardrobe or a new job) will make you happy, you are into a major delusion. You just can't find happiness, security, health, or peace of mind that way. (Although they may be wonderful diversions.)

There are many people who have everything you wish you had and lots more. And guess what? They are still miserable, unfulfilled, lonely, and dissatisfied. You read

Circumstances — what are circumstances?
I make circumstances.

NAPOLEON BONAPARTE (1769–1821)
Emperor of France

There are two ways of meeting difficulties; you alter the difficulties or you alter yourself to meet them.

PHYLISS BOTTOME (1884–1963)
English author

about members of the British Royal family who are in one unhappy situation after another — even to the point of trying to commit suicide. I'll bet that in your wildest dreams you never thought of having all *they* have: castles, world-class yachts, a fleet of aircraft, assets all over the world (including billions in cash) — and they don't even pay taxes. How lucky can you get?

Changing your circumstances won't change who you are. Only you can do that. CHANGE. Permanent, powerful, lasting change can only come from within. Responding and reacting to what drifts your way on the currents of life can only sweep you along with the current. If you want to visit certain Riches along the way to your destination, then look at your map, turn on your motor, and grab your rudder.

It's time to stop trying to only solve your problems — responding and reacting to the circumstances of life. It's time to *MAKE THINGS HAPPEN* — the proactive and creative way — by taking control of your circumstances when you focus on your vision. It's time to live your life on *purpose — The Lazy Man's Way*. The true way to Riches.

YOUR PERFECT JOURNEY OR JUST A JOY RIDE?

You have become used to accepting "generic" versions of almost everything. Remember when you used to order your new car direct from the factory just the way you wanted it? You could order exactly the options you wanted — your color, specified interior, your choice of engine size and transmission were all available to you. Now, with over half of our cars being built overseas, you probably take what the dealers have in stock, and your choices are most likely now limited to color selection.

You used to build your home to suit your needs and personality. Now, your choice of a new home may be a condo, or a town house, or a tract house with a couple of floor plans from which to choose. There may not be much control over room size or any of the options that make a

Destiny is not a matter of chance; it is a matter of choice. It is not a thing to be waited for; it is a thing to be achieved.

WILLIAM JENNINGS BRYAN (1860–1925)
American political leader, orator

When the fight begins within himself, a man's worth something.

ROBERT BROWNING (1812–1889)
English poet

house a home.

Weddings seem to be prepackaged and even wedding gowns mass produced. Vacations are pre-packaged for us so we buy tours that are some travel agent's idea of an ideal vacation (a five-to-seven-day cruise or a Club Med package). Health care is going the way of the H.M.O. or the P.P.O., where you can't select your own doctor. Any selection is from "their" list of doctors — not yours. It's kind of like your aptitude test in junior high school. It may be a choice, but it's limited to someone else's choices — *not yours.*

Clothes are now generally "ready to wear" or "one size fits all" or "unisex." Shoes seem to be getting harder to find in correct widths, unless you have a "medium" sized foot. Now, even much of our food is pre-packaged, frozen, or "fast." So, even if they tell you that you can "have it your way," you still have only their limited menu choices.

Well, from this moment on I want you to know you have *choices* — choices to live your life on your own terms. All you need are two documents and you can design them for yourself. They will carry you from where you are right now to anywhere and everywhere you want to go. It's your journey to Riches. It's the journey that is the rest of your life.

YOUR ITINERARY AND TICKET PACKAGE

Your journey to Riches begins with the itinerary and the ticket package. Both must be clearly identified as belonging to you with your name on the line designated as "the traveler."

Now that you have entered your name, it's time to ask yourself an interesting question. "Who is that person I just named on my ticket?" If you can step back from yourself for a moment, I would like to ask you to consider several possibilities. Is it really going to be *you* on the journey that will be the rest of your life? Or, will it be the person you have come to see yourself as over the years — either from others'

The block of granite which is an obstacle in the pathway of the weak, becomes a stepping-stone in the pathway of the strong.

THOMAS CARLYLE (1795–1881)
Scottish-born English prose writer

If you don't know where you are going, you might wind up someplace else.

YOGI BERRA (B. 1925)
American baseball player

views of you or from your own mistaken view of yourself. We tend to see ourselves through the eyes of others — through the massive amount of feedback from others — family, friends, classmates, teachers, and even strangers. We take on an identity. This is a natural process for children as they grow up. But now that you are an adult; it's time for a reality check before you plan the rest of your life. It's possible that the *dissatisfaction* you felt in your life that caused you to buy this book is a red flag. If so, pay careful attention to it.

You can only be happy living your own life. If the life you are living is the life your parents wanted for you and you're not happy living it, then it's time to start to live your life. If the life you are living is the life of any stereotype you accepted for yourself and it isn't working for you, then now is the time for you to stop living that other life and start living your life. How do you know if you are living a stereotyped life? Look at the images you have of yourself. Examine carefully the many limits and the qualifiers of these images you have embraced. These will prove to be unnecessary and unwanted baggage on the journey.

Some of the images you hold of yourself may be based on facts, yet still may be in subtle conflict with who you really are. My friend, David, who is Jewish, is a New Yorker, the grandson of a Rabbi, the son of a doctor (his mother) and a lawyer (his father). When he thought of the rest of his life, he assumed he would stay in the old neighborhood in New York City, vacation in the Catskills, marry a nice Jewish girl, go to graduate school and become a professional like his parents. He hated the whole idea yet felt compelled to live out these life-images. This he did until *dissatisfaction* caused him to awaken to the fact that he just wasn't happy being or doing any of these things. In his heart he knew what he really wanted for his life, but felt guilty even having those feelings. His parents had been so good to him. They had such hopes for him. They lived

We accept the verdict of the past until the need for change cries out loudly enough to force upon us a choice between the comfort of further inertia and the irksomeness of action.

JUDGE LEARNED HAND (1872–1961)
American jurist

We take our shape, it is true, within and against that cage of reality bequeathed us at our birth, and yet it is precisely through our dependence on this reality that we are most endlessly betrayed.

C. S. LEWIS (1898–1963)
British author

their lives for him. How could he let them down by being himself. And who was David — really?

David was a skier. David lived to ski. His whole life was skiing and when he admitted that to himself, he realized he couldn't stay on the journey he was on any longer.

David is now married to a ski school instructor and they live in Incline Village, California. And what does David do now? He is on the National Ski Patrol. In the summer David and Debbie teach skiing in New Zealand and they are making ski adventure movies. They live, love, and laugh together. They are happy doing what they love to do and being who they really are. (And they make a good living, too.) Their lives are full of the Riches they never could have had by staying on the journey that David's background prescribed. David would not have been true to who he really was.

Is your journey where a New York Jewish boy is "supposed" to go? Is this where an Iowa farm boy is "supposed" to go? Is this where a Chicano boy from Mexico City is "supposed" to go? Is this where a young black girl from Mississippi is "supposed" to go? Is this where a Smith or a Jones or a whatever your family name happens to be is "supposed" to go? Is this the ticket of the child of a famous personality, or just *whose* ticket are you holding on your Road to Riches? We seem to feel that we must fit into certain roles that we are born into dictated by family, geography, ethnicity, economics, and heritage. But is that who you really are? Maybe that's who you are only because you accepted this image as a child from the many authority figures in your life — parents, church, neighbors, teachers, grandparents, or whoever may have had an agenda concerning your life. *Well, maybe that's not who you really are at all.* Maybe there is a "butterfly" inside you after all just waiting to grow into what it wants to become. All you have to do is to allow it to happen naturally. Tim Timmons

What the caterpillar calls a tragedy, the master calls a butterfly.

RICHARD BACH (B. 1936)
American author

tells the story about the caterpillar crawling along a dusty trail. He looks up to see a butterfly flying above him and he turns to his friend and says, "You'll never get me up in one of those."

Bill Cosby, one of the highest paid entertainers of all time and one who has earned a Doctorate in Psychology, believed his role was one of a shoe-shine boy — and that's what he was — he used to shine shoes outside Temple University when he was a young man. Then he realized the name on his ticket to life didn't really fit him. Someone was to be a shoe shine boy at that stand, but he knew he wasn't the one.

It's vital that you allow yourself to know who you really are. You are the only one who can decide who you want to become and what you will be happy doing for the rest of your life. When you close your eyes, there is no one else in there with you. You are the master of your identity. You have been placed in charge of you. Only you can plan out the ideal itinerary for you.

YOUR DESTINATION

If you were to look back at your life from the end of the "Richest life," what would have made it so wonderfully "Rich?" What were the many facets that put the brilliance and sparkle on the "diamond" that was your life? Each of those facets was a part of the journey. Each of them was an important part of your life. If you want those wonderful results in your life, you have to make room for them. You have to allow them to happen by choosing and including them in your itinerary deliberately. That's how you live your life on purpose.

What's the use of running if you're not on the right road?

GERMAN PROVERB

In the next chapter, *The Power of Purpose*, we will plant a seed about seeing your life from its end — your funeral. In Charles Dickens' classic story, "A Christmas Carol," Scrooge is given a look at his life from the perspective of his funeral. The ghost of Christmas Future shows him how his life will be if he continues doing what he is doing. This scares him and makes him unhappy to see what a miserable life he has led. That was his feeling of dissatisfaction talking to him through his dream. After he listened to it, he looked at his life again from the perspective of how he wanted his life to be — how it could be if he made some changes. He looked at his life from the perspective of the *results* he wanted in his life. Now remember, Scrooge was a wealthy man and could have all the things money could buy. So where was the source of his dissatisfaction? He had only one facet to his life — money. His life stood for nothing. He was unfulfilled, miserable, lonely, unloved, unwanted, scorned, ridiculed, mocked, hated, feared, tolerated, miserly, overbearing, unhappy, friendless, and fearful. But he was rich. Yes, he was rich, but he had no Riches.

Now, look at your "perfect" life with all the facets that give it luster and brilliance. Picture your "perfect" funeral. Who is there from your family to speak for you? Who is there from your business life to speak for you, and what are they saying? Who is there speaking about your spiritual life? Who is there speaking about your contributions to society? There are many facets to a life full of Riches, and someday there will be a final celebration or memorial service to sum it all up.

We are all moving toward that final destination of our lives. So why not make some course-corrections now for the journey ahead. After all, *you will spend the rest of your life on this journey.* You want to arrive at your destination feeling fulfilled, happy, proud, with no regrets, full of love and able to take a final bow to a packed house. A standing ovation. Anything less is just cheating yourself. Make today the first day of the rest of your "new" life. Or, as I've said before, "Make today the first day of the Best of your life."

Most people are about as happy as they make up their mind to be.

ABRAHAM LINCOLN (1809–1865)
16th President of the United States

It is not the mountain we
conquer, but ourselves.

SIR EDMUND HILLARY (B. 1919)
New Zealand mountaineer

YOUR TRAVEL AGENT

As you visualize your destination, select your itinerary, and purchase your ticket for your exciting life's journey, as with any trip, you may want to seek the assistance of a travel agent. One who knows the ins and outs, ups and downs and how to avoid the pitfalls as much as possible. There are many helpful people who might act in this capacity, as your "travel agent," such as counselors, professors, and ministers, For me I have come to find that there is only one choice to make for this important role — and that is God! My life changed significantly when I discovered and accepted my creator. My purpose became more clear, I felt more fulfilled, purposeful — it just worked a whole lot better when I began using the ten commandments as my personal itinerary.

Through a relationship with a spiritual "travel agent," I believe you can gain great insight into what's most beneficial for you and others in the world. It's a win-win relationship for all concerned. Everyone knows the golden rule, "Do unto others . . .", and I believe it is true that what you give out comes back (what goes around, comes around).

For those who believe in God
no explanation is needed;
for those who do not believe in
God no explanation is possible.

FATHER JOHN LA FARGE (B. 1880–?)
American Roman Catholic priest, editor

As I grow in my relationship with my God, I grow in the realization and experience of all that I want to be and to do. Many people come to this spiritual relationship as they search out their dreams, their mission, their purpose in life. You may discover this to be true in your own experience. In a sense, you have been on a mission since the minute you were launched into this world. Realizing that your mission is actually from your heart, placed there by your God, gives you an added motivation to fulfill it with class and reflect the image of God to the world through all that you are and do. It works for me!

THE POWER OF PURPOSE

CHAPTER 2 OF PART 2

What is my purpose in life? Life's most powerful question. I am convinced that everyone has a purpose planted inside. It's like an inner label that only you are able to determine. No one can tell you what your purpose is. You are the only one who is able to look deeply enough inside yourself to discover that inner dream and desire of your heart. Finding out the answer to the question of what your purpose is should be easy but it sure wasn't for me.

Seeking your purpose is not like searching for gold. You will not "discover" it by exploration using maps, instruments, or geological studies. It is also not going to be "revealed" to you by a teacher, fortune teller, your horoscope in the paper, or even by divine revelation. It is already known to you. It's deep down inside of YOU.

If purpose — your heart's desire — is so important, then why does it seem so difficult to discover? To many it seems **hidden.** Some people never even think that they may have a purpose, are never encouraged to think about it or are so distracted by other life-issues that they don't get around to focusing upon it.

To many other people their purpose is effectively **denied.** Have you ever had a dream pop into your mind, something you really want to do? And have you shared that dream with another person only to have them throw up all kinds of obstacles to accomplishing that dream? They say things like, "How could you do anything like that without more education, more money, a miracle, etc.? You're just dreaming. Come on back to earth, pal!" You become intimidated by the thought of having a life purpose. You begin to believe that it is presumptuous on your part to have these grandiose dreams. It doesn't take much resistance to stifle your dreams and send them scurrying back to the "wish" area of your mind. After a while, you don't

A man's main task in life is to give birth to himself.

ERICH FROMM (1900–1980)
German-born American psychoanalyst and philosopher

When we can't dream any longer, we die.

EMMA GOLDMAN (1869–1940)
American anarchist

And from the discontent of man the world's best progress springs.

ELLA WHEELER WILCOX (1850–1919)
American poet and novelist

No man can produce great things who is not thoroughly sincere in dealing with himself.

JAMES RUSSELL LOWELL (1819–1891)
American poet, critic, editor, diplomat

Many people live in ugly wastelands; but in the absence of imaginative standards, most of them do not even know it.

CHARLES WRIGHT MILLS (1916–1962)
American sociologist

need any help at all in denying your dreams — you can do it all by yourself.

My purpose was hidden from me for a long while until the need to answer the puzzle of what my life was all about became overwhelmingly strong. The clue to solving it came when I began to examine why my life didn't work, what were the dissatisfactions in my life. I started looking at those things that don't work for me, things that I denied existed at all. Things that I disliked and refused to deal with. You probably have your own list of these kind of things — the things that keep you stuck. Looking at my dissatisfactions and choosing to deal with them took a great deal of courage. Once I did, I was able to open a door and walk through it into a new world where I could start looking for dreams that would take their place. And take their place they did!

The "what" in the question of "What do I want?" is already known to you. It resides within you! You were uniquely created to be who you are and to do what you can do. You can access it either rationally by observation (detection or discernment) or through your intuition, by what we call "hunches."

Hunches are creative thought. In this society we were taught that logic is the better thought process, but most creative thoughts don't come from logic at all. Logic takes us from step to step, from idea to idea, from concept to concept, and from detail to detail. Hunches skip all that and just jump to a conclusion.

So what am I saying here? Simply this! In order to create the answer to the question of "What do I want?" the "what" is just something you *"make up!"* Whoa! Did you get that? You just make it up! It's really that simple! It's *The Lazy Man's Way* — and it works!

At one time or another all of us experience momentary flashes of what we really want. But most of the time, we are too timid, unaware, not sure or embarrassed to accept them so we don't share these flashes with anyone. These "silent sentences" in your heart are valuable gold mines where you will discover the key to all the riches you are looking for! Let's get started!

THE "WHY" OF YOUR LIFE — THE PORTRAIT OF PURPOSE

Focus on your purpose — the *"why" of your life!* What does your life stand for? Develop a personal mission statement that focuses on what you want to be (your character and values) and to do (your performance and achievements).

Dr. Viktor Frankl, a prominent German psychiatrist who survived the Holocaust in Auschwitz said, "Everyone has his own specific vocation or mission in life — he cannot be replaced, nor can his life be repeated. Thus everyone's task is as unique as is his specific opportunity to implement it." He goes on to say:

> Ultimately, man should not ask what the meaning of his life is, but rather must recognize that it is he who is asked. In a word, each man is questioned by life; and he can only answer to life by answering for his own life; to life he can only respond by being responsible.

In other words, your life communicates a message whether good or bad, effective or ineffective. You have a life message — a purpose for being and doing. Find out what it is!

You can look at your purpose as a personal constitution much as the Constitution of the United States. The U.S. Constitution formulated a road map for our living together. This road map has given us our primary direction for the life of this great country. It serves as a guide for knowing who we are and what we are all about, what our values are, what we stand for, what we want as a nation. Doesn't it make sense to do the same thing for you and your life?

By allowing yourself to *access* (detect and discern)

He who has a "why" to live for can bear almost any "how."

FRIEDRICH NIETZSCHE (1844–1900)
German philosopher

If a man does not keep pace with his companions, perhaps it is because he hears a different drummer. Let him step to the music which he hears, however measured or far away.

HENRY DAVID THOREAU (1817–1862)
American essayist, naturalist, poet

your purpose you will become involved in taking control of the direction of your life. Personal involvement is crucial in obtaining your Riches. You can't allow anyone else to suggest, define, set, or in any way become involved in your purpose. This is a job *only* you can do. It demands your total commitment! No involvement means no commitment, and no commitment means no results!

MY LIFE MATTERS!

Because your purpose is such a personal issue and there is no one answer as to what your purpose might be, I will talk on this subject from my personal experience of finding my purpose. I believe that my life matters and this thought leads me to strive to be useful and feel useful. My life is really empty without feeling useful and fulfilled and I feel I deny a primary purpose of my existence if I am not useful! By not being useful I am wasting my gifts and talents. By not being useful I allow my creative forces within to wither and even be destroyed. By not being useful I would feel that I had sacrificed my purpose and with it my sense of fulfillment, peacefulness, contentment, happiness and joy. I would have sacrificed my Riches!

I also believe that I was born to be thoroughly used up when I die — not to go to my grave with my music still in me. Getting your music out, whatever it is, is the beginning to acquiring the great Riches you desire. It will empower you! It will inspire you! It will propel and compel you! Your "music" is your message, your meaning, your *purpose* in life! I like the statement, "It's not how long you live your life, but how well you spend it that counts"! **A well-spent life is a life lived on purpose!**

For some, purpose means achieving extraordinary things! For me the examples are everywhere. Buckminster Fuller, thinker, teacher, inventor, and scientist. A man who could have gone in many directions and been outstanding in all of them. Frank Lloyd Wright, one of the finest architects of all time, who strove for new horizons with a burning

I cannot believe that the purpose of life is to be "happy." I think the purpose of life is to be useful, to be responsible, to be honorable, to be compassionate. It is, after all, to matter: to count, to stand for something, to have made some difference that you lived at all.

LEONARD Q. ROSS
(Pen name of LEO ROSTEN) (B. 1908)
Polish-born American writer and political scientist

Life is ours to be spent, not to be saved.

D. H. LAWRENCE (1885–1930)
English novelist, poet, essayist

vision. Abraham Lincoln who went through repeated failures but persevered to become one of the most effective and memorable men of all times. All with apparent extraordinary purpose.

Do all of us have to achieve these kinds of monuments to history with finding and fulfilling our purpose? As Robert Kennedy pointed out: "Few will have the greatness to bend history itself, but each of us can work to change a small portion of events. It is from numberless acts of courage and belief that human history is shaped." Regardless of the scope of our purpose, finding out what our purpose is and pursuing it is what is really important.

When you don't have a purpose or mission (or worse yet, don't follow the one you have), you may experience an empty life without a sense of meaning and joy. This is where the daily objective is simply a struggle to solve one problem after another to survive. This lack of purpose shows up as apathy, fear, low self-esteem, and often leads to disease, alcohol and drug abuse, crime, and becoming a burden to family and society!

I believe the purpose of life is to be a growing, contributing, involved human being and that life is at its best when you are willingly and happily contributing to other people and society. The idea of service and contribution is not new, but to many people the idea of serving suggests an inferior status. To the great leaders of our world the notion of service is evident in the contribution that they make to the world and to themselves. Social philosopher Marshall McLuhan suggested that, *On Spaceship Earth there are no passengers — only crew.* As a crew member each of us is free to choose our assignment.

I feel the power of a purpose is what makes living more worthwhile, more meaningful, regardless of the challenges that come your way. It's a Richer life that will give you access to the inner confidence you need to move forward through any and all obstacles in your path.

My mother said to me, "If you become a soldier you'll be a general; if you become a monk, you'll end up as the Pope." Instead, I became a painter and wound up as Picasso.

PABLO PICASSO (1881–1973)
Spanish painter and sculptor

Do not wait for extraordinary circumstances to do good; try to use ordinary situations.

JEAN PAUL RICHTER (1763–1825)
German novelist, aesthetician

Purpose gives you the power to handle life's "piles and pits" more easily!

PURPOSE IS A CONTINUUM

A first grader told his preschool sister, "Don't ever learn to spell cat; once you do that, they keep on giving you harder words!" Good advice, but life still goes on! Life is a process that progressively builds. You are the sum total today of all of your prior experiences, whether you interpreted them to be good or bad. And no matter what your experiences have been, your purpose is best discovered through those lenses. For many, their purpose is developed out of a past trauma, an indelible mark upon them that now drives them to be more sensitive, more impassioned, more focused, more driven. People who have had an illness as a child may develop a purpose in life to work with children suffering from disease or a physical disadvantage. A person who was embarrassed may incorporate a great sensitivity or compassion for anyone who might find themselves in the same situation. People who have experienced loss in their past have a greater sense of appreciation for those who are experiencing similar loss, therefore they have a "message" for people in the same situation. Not only does purpose build upon your past experiences, it also continues to be in process throughout your entire life. It's a continuum!

THE "WHERE" OF YOUR LIFE — YOUR SENSE OF DESTINY

In order to answer the question "What do you want?" most fully you must walk through the process of the "Why" of your life (purpose) and the "Where" of your life (results). Your purpose will become even clearer by *picturing* the results you want for your life!

An ancient Chinese proverb states: "If you don't know where you are going, you won't know when you get there." Deciding what *results* you want — not just the things you want — is the vital step toward achieving the Riches you are looking for. This all helps to define your purpose or mission in life.

As the architect begins with a clean sheet of paper or the artist with an empty canvas, so I suggest you begin in the same way. Start with nothing. Start fresh with a blank sheet or an empty canvas. Fill in the blank sheet and canvas by "making up" what you want out of your life.

The best place to begin is to look at what the end might look like. The results you want! If you were an observer at your own funeral, what would you expect you would say about the results of your life? There are two possibilities to you. One is — you liked your life. It worked for you because you experienced joy, happiness, excellent health, and felt satisfaction. Or, like Scrooge, you didn't like your life. It definitely didn't work for you. You were dissatisfied. You spent a great deal of energy and time doing those things you disliked and you missed out on a lot of joy and happiness. You missed out on experiencing loving relationships. Are you hearing the result of your life that you want to hear? Were you treating your life as if it mattered? Did you take your life into your own hands to create the life you wanted? You can. If not you, who?

The amazing thing I've discovered over the years is that virtually everyone already possesses a picture of the desired results he/she wants to achieve. Those pictures are down deep *inside* you. They were placed there when you were originally created. The images of those dreams, those intended results for your life, were implanted within your very soul. They are waiting for you to develop them into pictures of reality. It's your **personal sense of destiny!**

IT'S AN APTITUDE PROBLEM

When you were in school, you probably learned *how* to do things. Therefore, it's natural for you to approach your life like all of the assignments you were given in school. It's what you were taught to do. You were taught how to do

You can only have two things in life, reasons or results. Reasons don't count.

ROBERT ANTHONY, Ph.D.
(B. Withheld by request)
American psychologist and writer

Great minds have purpose, others have wishes.

WASHINGTON IRVING (1783–1859)
American essayist, biographer, historian

things: *how* to read, *how* to spell, *how* to solve math problems, *how* to play football, *how* to use a computer, etc. What you learned in school was *process* — the *how* to do things! You probably never learned about finding your dreams— the *what you want*. There were no classes in vision — creating a purpose.

Even if you think that what you want isn't possible for you or you can't possibly have what you want, that you aren't worthy, or don't have the education, or whatever limits you put on your true wants — *you still want them!* So, be honest with yourself; allow yourself to have them — at least, in your thoughts and dreams. Thoughts and dreams are seeds. At least plant them!

Even though Riches primarily come from within, other people make a major contribution to your Riches as they help you build and develop them. So if you want Riches, it's wise to fully understand that other people are going to play an important part in your getting what you want. It has been said, "You can get everything in life you want, if you will just help other people get what they want."

Before we do a simple exercise, let's sum up the basic truths about purpose:

1. Your goals are not your purpose. Your purpose drives and threads your goals together, By your purpose you know what you are to do and what you are not to do.

2. Your purpose must have a people connection.

3. Your purpose may or may not have anything to do with your job. It enables you to abandon the job you hate and find the vocation you love. It creates the excitement that keeps you awake at night and gets you up in the morning with anticipation and eagerness.

4. Your purpose may emerge out of your life-struggles and pain.

No horse gets anywhere until he is harnessed. No steam or gas ever drives anything until it is confined. No Niagara is ever turned into light and power until it is tunneled. No life ever grows great until it is focused, dedicated, disciplined.

HARRY EMERSON FOSDICK (1878–1969)
American theologian

5. You never retire from your life purpose. You may
   have more than one purpose throughout the course
   of your life.

6. Your purpose will continually be revised as you go. It
   is made out of patchwork experiences — the latest
   added on to the list.

YOUR RICHES AND YOUR SUCCESS ARE TO BE AND TO DO
ALL THAT YOU WERE CREATED TO BE AND TO DO.

*The great and glorious
masterpiece of man is to know
how to live life on purpose.*

MICHEL DE MONTAIGNE (1533–1592)
French moralist, essayist

Now let's look at a simple exercise that will show you
what you are all about — your values — your purpose or
mission in life! All you do is write it down. You fill in the
blanks of the assignment we offer. Sounds easy, doesn't it?
But there is just one hitch. There is an *outer* you and an
inner you. I don't want you to do the assignment in a
surface way using the outer you. Use the inner you, your
heart of hearts, your conscience — the private you. This
will ensure a more honest expression of your feelings. The
outer you has been colored and conditioned to behave in
certain ways, but these very ways are the "identities" that
got you where you are today. Listen to the inner pangs of
dissatisfaction down deep inside that are trying to express
themselves. It needs to be heard, if you are to resolve the
cause of the dissatisfaction in your life and move forward to
the Riches you know you want.

So how do you do this? Start with identifying the
things in life that make you feel good, that make you come
alive, that make you say "Yes!"

They may be small things, large things, everyday
things or extraordinary things. It doesn't matter as long as
they "speak" to you. They are the "hunches" I spoke of at the
beginning of this chapter. You continue by putting those
feelings together with activities that when you think about
doing them, bring about these same feelings. Once you get
a sense of that then take practice runs in filling in the

blanks to this question:

"My purpose in life is to _____
_____ to _____."

The first blank needs just one simple verb; i.e. help, organize, strengthen, educate, support, guide, etc. The second blank requires a description of who — individuals, groups, subsets, classes, types — with whom you want to serve or work. The last blank to fill in is to describe the goal or result you wish to co-create with these people. As an example, an elementary school teacher might answer the question in this way:

"My purpose in life is to___inspire___ _____children_____ to_____learn_____."

Remember, anything you dream can be yours. Listen to the possibilities that "pop" into your head for these are those messages coming from the *inner* you. Sit quietly for a while and let the blanks be filled in by that *inner* you. You will know when the words are truly yours.

A lofty vision stated clearly contains the power to move mountains! It helps you to focus on your goals and bring them into existence! The goals that make up that clear path that will take you to your purpose like a rocket to the moon! Operating from a clear sense of purpose assures that all your efforts are directed toward doing the right thing in the right way for you.

Remember, you have the right to live your life to its fullest, so be involved in your own life. If you want to live, not just exist, a *vision* of what you want your life to be will make it a rewarding, rich experience. Actively create that life rather than be created by the circumstances around you. Instead of being manipulated by various life-molds, manage your own life by making your life happen. It's called living your life on purpose!

All right, let's get on with filling in the blanks.

When I look into the future, it's so bright, it burns my eyes.

OPRAH WINFREY (B. 1953)
American television talk-show host, actress

SETTING UNBELIEVABLE GOALS

Setting goals is one of the most popular topics in the business world and in the psychological arena as well. And yet the selecting, setting, and securing of goals is still one of the most frustrating of life's experiences. The goals path is filled with frequent disappointments and is littered with all sorts of wreckage due to misplaced, unattained, and abandoned goals.

Here are some ways you might be using to solve the problems of goal setting in the absence of tying goals to a purpose.

FIRST *Aim at nothing!* The problem with this method is that when you aim at nothing you'll hit it every time and get *nothing* accomplished. Using this method of goal-setting is for those who have come to adopt the "couch potato" approach to life, that is best lived by sitting around as a spectator — going nowhere! This approach will prevent you from making any kind of mark on your world or ever having what you want!

SECOND *Aim at everything!* This was my best method for years. I shot at everything I could. And then, when I happened to hit a somewhat significant target, I'd be quick to point out that I had been aiming at that goal all along! Using this method of goal setting is for those who have chosen to live by the roll of the dice — by accident going everywhere. This approach will enable you to make an indistinguishable mark on your world by scattering and splattering bits and pieces of you everywhere!

THIRD *Aim at things!* This is a most common target as people set goals. Accumulating things is neither right nor wrong, but if it is all you are out

The person who makes a success of living is the one who sees his goal steadily and aims for it unswervingly. That is dedication.

CECIL B. DEMILLE (1881–1959)
American filmmaker

Make no little plans; they have no magic to stir men's blood . . . make big plans, aim high in hope and work.

DANIEL H. BURNHAM (1846–1912)
American architect

to do, you will eventually feel most empty. Just remember Mr. Scrooge. There is more to a quality life than just money and the things money can buy. AIM HIGH!

The most common problem with goal-setting is best stated in the following way: "The problem with most people is not that they aim too high and miss it, but that they aim too low and hit it!" Most people long for an arrival point. But when they do "finally arrive," the process of death and dying begins! So, in too many cases these people "die" at 35 or 40 and we bury them at 75 or 85! This is the world of the uninvolved — the "walking dead." It's a world of boredom and monotony, dissatisfaction and depression. But this doesn't have to be your reality. To be fully involved in life, set, select, and secure your goals by aligning them to your purpose."

In 1972, *Life* magazine published a story depicting the adventures of John Goddard. His story was one of undying determination filled with personal purpose. When he was fifteen, he overheard a visiting friend of his parents lament, "If only I had done this when I was young." Determined not to spend his life playing the "if only" game, John Goddard sat down and decided what he wanted to do with his life. When he finished writing, 127 goals existed. John Goddard decided there were eight rivers he wanted to explore, along with sixteen mountains he wanted to climb. He decided to become an Eagle Scout, visit every country in the world, learn to fly an airplane, and dive in a submarine. He wanted to retrace the travels of Marco Polo and ride a horse in the Rose Bowl parade. This was just the beginning. John Goddard committed himself to reading the Bible from cover to cover, reading the entire works of Shakespeare, Plato, Dickens, Aristotle, Socrates, and several other classic authors. He planned to read the entire *Encyclopaedia Britannica* and yet have time to learn to play the flute and violin. Marriage, children (he had five) and a stint with church missions were also in his plans, along with a desire for a career in medicine.

As of 1993, John Goddard has accomplished 108 of his original 127 goals. Goddard exemplifies the excitement of determining a purpose in life, setting goals and pursuing them with determination. The goals that John Goddard wrote out at age fifteen were unbelievable — but he still wanted them. How do you go about attaining your goals?

Napoleon Hill in his classic work, *Think and Grow Rich*, presented a bold theme: "Whatever the mind can conceive and believe, it can achieve!" *Belief is the key!* And all truly lofty goals start out as unbelievable. It is the dynamic of "picturing" that transforms your unbelievable dreams into the realities of the Riches you will find along *The Lazy Man's Way!*

To dare is to do; to fear is to fail.

JOHN GODDARD (B. not available)
Anthropologist, explorer, author,
adventurer, speaker

If you think you can win, you can win. Faith is necessary to victory.

WILLIAM HAZLITT (1778–1830)
English essayist, critic

PICTURING

Picturing is the first part of the process of bringing desired results into physical reality. You do it naturally, almost automatically, literally thousands of times each day. Take, for example, the turning on of a light switch. That's a very modest and simple function, but it's picturing at its most basic level.

You think, "Turn on the light" and the mind commands the body to perform this act. The goal is realized. It's one thing to set a modest goal for oneself and reach it, but it's quite another to set a lofty goal to be reached. Yet by analyzing the first (the modest goal) process you can gain insight into the second (the more lofty goal). The modest goal of switching on a light switch is a most certain process, because there is no credibility gap. It requires no faith — no stretch of the imagination — to believe this goal can be achieved. The possibility is unquestioned, so the results are certain. This is in agreement with Napoleon Hill's theme of *"Whatever the mind can conceive and believe, it can achieve!"* In cases where the possibility is

The Possible's slow fuse is lit by the Imagination.

EMILY DICKINSON (1830–1886)
American poet

It's not the attainment of the goal that matters, it is the things that are met with along the way.

HAVELOCK ELLIS (1859–1939)
English psychologist, essayist, art critic

beyond question, then to conceive is to achieve! Where your belief is not an issue, where there is no credibility gap, then to will it is for you to own it.

When asked how he accounted for his amazing inventive genius, Thomas Alva Edison replied, "It is because I never think in words; I think in *pictures*." Edison was a master at picturing in his mind the objects he desired to invent.

Phenomenal achievements have been accomplished by people who were able to visualize what they wanted. Edison was told no light could exist in a vacuum, but he *visualized* it and *believed* it could be done. The experts scoffed at Louis Pasteur's theories of germ life. William Harvey's far-out notion that blood flowed through the body was rejected, and Samuel Langley's vision for a flying machine was ridiculed; however, each of these men were able to visualize their dream into reality. Conrad Hilton said, "Man, with God's help and personal dedication, is capable of anything he can dream." Visualize your dreams!

Remember, a goal is not the end. In the games of hockey or American football, a single goal generally won't win the game. In the game of life the more goals you score toward your purpose, the Richer your life will be. A goal by itself is not the victory. It takes several goals to be a winner. A goal is a score, not the victory. As you attain one goal have another ready to tackle.

Too often one thinks of the goal as the finish line or the arrival point. The purpose is the entire journey, departure to arrival. This is especially true of very lofty goals. Picturing is a journey. There is normally a credibility gap, but somewhere along the line that gap is defeated and in its place come feelings of total confidence, assurance, and personal knowledge that the destination will be achieved. And by paying the price along the way you will arrive at your goal. The credibility gap is conquered in gradual increments — a process. The process goes from "if only" to "maybe" to "I think so" to "I know so." These are the natural stages of development for achieving your goals — the process of picturing.

NATURAL FACT

Emerson said, "Every natural fact is a symbol of some spiritual fact." Natural facts are representative of spiritual facts in the growth of people.

One of the earliest processes we all studied in grade school was the life cycle of the butterfly. Butterflies don't just happen out of an egg. Changes take place gradually and they are not the least bit perceptible to the casual observer — larval stage, chrysalis stage, pupa stage. Finally, after weeks of gradual growth and passing through stages of development, there emerges into the world one of nature's most marvelous creations, the mature, adult butterfly. This process is one of the miracles in our world. But this incredible transformation is nothing compared to the miracle of a human life finding his/her purpose and being fulfilled. Purpose attainment is like that. It is a process made up of many stages — your goals.

Here is how Paul Meyer of Success Motivation Institute sums up the goal process. "What you ardently desire, sincerely believe in, vividly imagine, enthusiastically act on, must inevitably come to pass."

TERRY FOX — AN UNBELIEVABLE GOAL

I'd like to introduce you to Terry Fox. Terry has been an inspiration and a "friend" for many years. I was introduced to him through a picture of him in a magazine. I never met Terry in person, because he died before I had a chance to meet him, but I felt his death as one can only feel the loss of a friend. Terry died at the age of 23. He lived only 23 short years, but he will be remembered by millions for years to come.

Terry was a great athlete (basketball, cross country,

Only in men's imagination does every truth find an effective and undeniable existence.
Imagination, not invention, is the supreme master of art as of life.

JOSEPH CONRAD (1857–1924)
Polish-born English novelist

and track) with enough talent to "letter" in several sports in college and the desire and drive to turn professional. A leg problem that bothered him caused him enough concern to have a doctor look at it. The doctor diagnosed it as cancer. It was ravaging his leg. The doctor told Terry, "I'm sorry, but we've got to amputate the leg. And since you are an adult you must sign for us to do the surgery." Terry signed off his own leg and with it his hopes and dreams of an athletic career.

The surgery was successful in that the leg was gone and Terry wasn't. Convalescing from a leg amputation is a long process that includes physical therapy and learning to walk again with an artificial leg. Convalescence was also a great time to rethink his purpose, since his original purpose of being a professional athlete was now a physical impossibility.

Terry's new purpose was to raise awareness and money for cancer research, so others might be spared the suffering and the torment he had experienced. Terry's new purpose was not only to raise money for others with similar conditions, but to raise people's consciousness for the need for cancer research as well. He wrote down his purpose and announced it to family and friends. Then, he planned the way to attain his purpose by writing down his goals. He organized what was called "Terry Fox's Marathon of Hope." He truly set out an unbelievable goal — to traverse Canada on an artificial leg!

How far is far. How high is high? We'll never know until we try.

FROM THE CALIFORNIA SPECIAL OLYMPICS THEME SONG

His parents suggested he first go to college, graduate, and then make his contribution. But that was their dream, not Terry's. He knew his purpose and would not be swayed from it. He went to the Canadian Cancer Society and proudly told them of his plan to raise awareness and money for cancer research through his "Marathon of Hope." The Cancer Society told him they were already involved in many other activities, but thanked him for thinking of it and suggested he forget the whole idea.

Well, you don't just forget a purpose and go on doing the same old thing. Terry and his college roommate dropped out of school and flew to Canada's eastern coast of Newfoundland. Terry touched the waters of the Atlantic Ocean and turned around to start his "Marathon of Hope" journey to walk across the entire length of Canada to the Pacific!

Day after day he walked, trying to generate interest and enthusiasm in his mission to raise awareness and money. It was difficult to get cooperation in the French-speaking part of Canada for an "Anglo" from British Columbia. It was discouraging, but Terry was not discouraged. Terry had a purpose! He was walking over 30 miles a day and it wasn't getting any easier. The artificial leg was awkward and painful. The constant walking caused sores that brought a grimace to Terry's face. There were times the sores opened and bled. People slowly began to notice this man with a mission. Media attention began to build. Radio stations talked about Terry as he came through their towns. Local papers talked about him and ran his picture and his story. Local TV stations picked it up too.

He knows not his own strength that hath not met adversity.

BEN JONSON (1573–1637)
English playwright, poet

His notoriety caught the attention of politicians including the Prime Minister of Canada, Elliott Trudeau. The Prime Minister and Terry shook hands for the press. Terry suggested that he had revised his original goal from raising $100,000 to $1 million!

The attention Terry was getting spread from Canada to other countries as the story of this young man with an *unbelievable* goal was told. The wire services carried his story to local papers all over the world and quickly Terry's story was featured in the national press and media throughout the United States.

By the time he got to Thunder Bay (about halfway across Canada) he developed breathing problems that required him to see a doctor. A thorough examination

The only measure of what you believe is what you do. If you want to know what people believe don't read what they write, don't ask them what they believe, just observe what they do.

ASHLEY MONTAGU, Ph.D. (B. 1905)
American anthropologist, educator

The courage we desire and prize is not the courage to die decently, but to live manfully.

THOMAS CARLYLE (1795–1881)
Scottish-born English prose writer

showed Terry's cancer had spread to his chest. The doctor told Terry he had to stop his run. Terry told the doctor he obviously didn't know him or the purpose of this run. Both Terry and his purpose would go on.

He explained to the doctor: "My folks said I couldn't do it, but I chose to go on anyway. The Canadian Cancer Society told me no, but I chose to go on anyway. The provincial government told me to stop because I was disrupting the roadways, but I chose to go on anyway. The Prime Minister offered me no help, but I chose to go on anyway. Well, the provincial governments are now behind me, the Prime Minister is behind me, the people are behind me and we have exceeded our goal of $1 million! So, when I leave your office today, I plan to continue and I'm going to raise a dollar for every single, living Canadian. That's $24.1 million!" The doctor protested that Terry had already accomplished his goals of raising awareness and money for his cause. Terry had already exceeded all expectations and had become a worldwide hero and an inspiration to all. He pleaded with Terry to go home and rest. The doctor's sound advice and concern along with Terry's weakened condition persuaded Terry to go home. Terry never finished his "Marathon of Hope," because he died of the cancer.

Did he meet all of his goals? No. He met the goals of raising awareness and of raising over $24 million for the cancer research fund, but he didn't reach his goal of walking across Canada. Did he fulfill his purpose? You bet he did! He raised our awareness.

I "met" Terry through an article in *Time* magazine that showed a picture of him in his running shorts with his artificial leg. The story was an inspiration to me that has marked my life. I taped that picture to my bathroom mirror, where it reminds me to this day of the power of purpose. Terry achieved his *purpose* without being able to fulfill all of his goals. His purpose was so strong that most of his goals were "assumed" and attained almost automatically, like learning to walk on an artificial leg. But for Terry, that was an assumed goal if he were to achieve his purpose!

Terry never viewed his circumstances as terminal. He saw them as a new supply of raw material with which to build a new purpose. Terry looked inside himself for a new purpose for his "ruined" life and found that his "problems" were not going to keep him from accomplishing it. He chose to "accept" his purpose which, in turn, revealed to him the goals that to us seem so extraordinary.

You don't have to lose a leg to know that you need a "purpose" in life or a new purpose. Your dissatisfaction tells you that! It's been called Divine Dissatisfaction. I've often felt that I was "on the wrong bus" in life, because it just didn't feel right, nothing was working, nothing was going my way. I couldn't get a break and my life felt out of my control. I wasn't driving my own life. I wanted off, but didn't know how. I continued on "hoping" and "wishing" that "it" would get better. If only someone or something would rescue me. Let me repeat, maturity starts when you accept that there is no one out there to rescue you, so you plan to rescue yourself.

I was stuck. There is a profound piece of Texas wisdom that says, "When your horse is dead, get off!" I should have gotten off, but didn't know *where else to go* or *how to get there*! Now I know. "Purpose" is where to go and "goals" are how to get there! Don't confuse purpose and goals — a purpose is not a goal. Your purpose can never be reached and then checked off like a goal. Your purpose is fulfilled, continuously, in every moment. Goals can be defined, obtained, reached, satisfied but, they are just milestones along the way to your life's purpose. But your goals must be big enough to fulfill your purpose — your mission in life. This is the answer to the questions: "Why am I here?" "What is my job as a crew member on

The buck stops here.

HARRY S. TRUMAN (1884–1972)
33rd President of the United States
(handwritten sign on his White House desk)

*The American economy cannot
be revived without someone
getting rich: why not me?*

RUSH LIMBAUGH (B. 1951)
American radio & TV talk-show host

Spaceship Earth?" "What is my contribution to humanity?"

Big enough goals will give you thrust and momentum all by themselves! Big enough goals will give you the opportunity to get your Riches! Big enough goals will motivate you to make changes. Big enough goals will be **unbelievable goals**! Ask yourself four progressive questions:

WHY?!
WHY NOT?!!
WHY NOT ME?!!!
WHY NOT NOW?!!!!

ATTITUDES — YOUR BIGGEST ROADBLOCKS

CHAPTER 4 OF PART 2

Greetings. Ready for the next step on *The Lazy Man's Way To Riches*? Don't tell me you haven't got enough time. I can't tell you how many failures I've met who were too busy to be successful. Most of the steps will take you less than 15 to 20 minutes to complete. Over a month's time that's only 10 hours. Suppose that all you want to get out of this book is to discover a way to pay off all your debts and have $10,000 in the bank. Is your time worth $1000 an hour? It can be if you'll stay with us every step on *The Lazy Man's Way*. Can 15 minutes per day really make that kind of difference? Suppose I said I'd give you all the $20 bills you could count in the next fifteen minutes, could you find the time? You bet you would! Well, the fifteen minutes you will spend on each step will be worth much more than those $20 bills over the rest of your life. Right? Right.

You now have at least one thing written down that you really want out of life in each of the seven areas, and you have listed the things that are standing in your way. If you haven't done the same for all seven areas, do so now; if you have, congratulations. Now we are going to discuss how you free yourself from the obstacles and limitations that are holding you back. I am going to tell you the problem that underlies every roadblock you have experienced. I'll start you on the first step toward wiping out that obstacle, and all of the roadblocks that stand between you and the Riches you want. But first I'd like to tell you a story, a true story. In fact it's just about the truest story I know. A story I learned about through watching a movie of a very important experiment conducted by a research psychologist several years ago. The movie had a tremendous impact upon me, and I'd like to share it with you.

. . . Everything can be taken from a man but one thing: the last of human freedoms — to choose one's attitude in any given set of circumstances — to choose one's own way.

DR. VIKTOR E. FRANKL (B. 1905)
German psychiatrist, author

Even if you're on the right track, you'll get run over if you just sit there.

WILL ROGERS (1875–1935)
American actor, humorist

LEARN FROM A PIKE

The experimental study begins with the psychologist putting a Northern Pike in a large aquarium. A Northern Pike is a large strong fish that feeds on smaller fish, and a pike's favorite dish is minnows. When the psychologist put minnows in the aquarium, the pike would just snap up a minnow anytime the mood struck. It's amazing how fast a pike can move when it wants a minnow. In a split second, the minnow disappeared. After showing how the pike feeds, the psychologist then placed clear glass cylinders in the aquarium and this time put the minnows inside the cylinders.

Now when the pike tries to feed, something very painful happens. He can't see the glass cylinders, doesn't know they are there, but every time he tries to take a minnow — bam. He gets a very painful bump on the nose. You can see the pike shake it off — like a fighter who takes a good one on the chin. Then he tries again — Bam. Another bump on the nose. He tries again. Bam. Bam. Bam. Bam. You've been hit on the nose, you know how painful it can be. Well, evidently it's painful to the pike as well, because after a while he stops trying. He has learned his lesson. He can't have the minnows. No matter how tempting, no matter how hungry he gets, he just can't have them. And furthermore, not only can't he have them, it hurts to try.

When the psychologist is satisfied that the pike has stopped trying, he removes the glass cylinders, thus releasing the minnows. Now minnows apparently aren't very bright because they will swim up to the pike, look him right in the eye, practically swim into his mouth, and the pike will not make a move to take one. His favorite food easily within his reach and he won't move a muscle to get it, because he's learned it hurts to try and thinks (or whatever fish do) "What's the use, I can't have it anyway." That fish will literally starve to death in the midst of an abundance of his favorite food before he will move his tail and open his mouth to eat it.

What a shame; it shouldn't happen to a poor fish. What a tragedy — it shouldn't happen to a human being either and yet it does — constantly to more than 95% of the people in this world. They sit and "starve" in the midst of the greatest Riches the world has ever known. They hunger for wealth, for friends, for love, for respect, and it's all within easy reach. All they have to do is move their tails and open their mouths. They are surrounded by glass walls; glass walls that exist only in their memories, in their past, in their *imaginations*, but not in the here and now. Everything they could ever desire could be theirs if they could simply believe in it, but they have learned that it hurts to try, and — "What's the use? They can't have it anyway."

GLASS WALLS MADE OUT OF ATTITUDES

Let's look at the obstacles in your way. I asked you to decide if they were in your attitude or your environment. What did you come up with? Look at your list of obstacles and think about that pike. Without even looking at your list, I can tell you that any obstacles that you have that refer to your past experience or lack of experience or to your current situation are entirely in your attitudes. Are you thinking, "Now wait a minute, the fact that I'm heavily in debt is my attitude? You're crazy. My debts are real!" I know your debts are real. But your debts are not the thing standing in your way, it's your *attitude* about your debts. Your *belief is* that they are holding you back. That's the imaginary glass wall that's keeping you from the Riches you need the most.

The same logic applies to every single obstacle you have written down. It's not what you have or haven't. It's not the interest rates or the economy. It's not who you know or don't know. It's what you believe about these

Men can starve from a lack of self realization as much as they can from a lack of bread.

RICHARD WRIGHT (1908–1960)
American novelist, short-story writer

The meaning of things lies not in the things themselves but in our attitudes towards them.

ANTOINE DE SAINT-EXUPÉRY (1900–1944)
French novelist, essayist, aviator

things that's standing in your way. Change your attitude and your external circumstances change.

Now there's good news and bad news in this. The good news is that you don't have to change a whole lot of circumstances in your present or past in order to become successful. All you have to do is learn to change your attitudes about those circumstances and they will no longer block you, even though they still exist. Now here is the bad news; it seems to be pretty hard to do. As Master Motivator Zig Ziglar often says, "Hardening of the attitudes is more common in this country than hardening of the arteries." Have you ever said, "Sure I know I would be more effective if I would do such and such, but I'm just not good at that sort of thing." Or, "That's the way I am." Those are words of power — tremendous *negative* power that freezes you in a self-defeating attitude. Just eavesdrop on our friend the pike's mental process: "Oh boy am I hungry — I'd sure love to have a minnow, but I know I can't. I've tried and tried and all I got was a sore nose. That's the way it is with me; I just can't have any minnows."

Look at the list of the things standing in your way. You can't change the events of your past, and you can't really alter the circumstances you are in right now. You can change your attitudes about those things and when you do, you can do anything you want with your future. Unless, of course, you think that changing your attitudes is impossible, in which case, move over brother pike, you've got company.

CHANGE YOUR ATTITUDE — CHANGE YOUR LIFE

Unless you are willing to accept the reality that everything —including you — is constantly changing, and that you can take charge of that change, and cause it to go in any direction you want, you will never be able to walk *The Lazy Man's Way* to your own Riches. You'll just

The greatest discovery of my generation is that a human being can alter his life by altering his attitudes of mind.

WILLIAM JAMES (1842–1910)
American philosopher, physiologist, psychologist, teacher

Success or failure is caused more by mental attitude than by mental capacity.

SIR WALTER SCOTT (1771–1832)
Scottish novelist, poet

flounder and starve like that fish — everything you want and need within easy reach, but forever kept from you, no matter how hard you work, by glass walls that exist only in your imagination. On the other hand, if you'll accept one of the fundamental principles of all existence, you can take another easy step on *The Lazy Man's Way to Riches*. You see, the major difference between the struggling Joe Karbo who was deeply in debt, and with no job and no hope, and the Joe Karbo who started getting everything he wanted, certainly wasn't hard work. It wasn't an invention or any idea no one else had ever had. It was a change in attitude, coupled with the simple steps I am going to teach you in the next few chapters, that made the difference. Suddenly he was working less and making more progress. Formerly impossible things became easy. The new T-Bird he wanted but thought was impossible to obtain was his within a few days. The sailboat and the home on the water had seemed 10 years away, if then. He had the sailboat within a couple of months and the home on the water within three years. How? By following the simple steps I am going to layout for you in these chapters. Are you ready for the next step?

Good. Go back over the obstacles you've written when reading Chapter 6 of Part 1. Focus on the ones you thought were environmental — outside you. Try to identify the attitude that's really creating the obstacle. For example, suppose one of your obstacles is, "Not having enough money to develop my ideas." Actually the real obstacle is your *belief* that you don't have and can't get enough money to develop your ideas. See what I mean? Take each of your roadblocks and rephrase it. *Accept the responsibility for your thoughts*. This is a tremendously important step. Because if you'll accept that the roadblock is in your mind, and not in the outside world, then all you have to do is change your mind to get you on the straight track.

Nurture your mind with great thoughts.

BENJAMIN DISRAELI (1804–1881)
English statesman, novelist

I don't ask you to buy all this at once. It was a struggle for me at first, but do it even if you don't believe me. Look at each of your obstacles and tell yourself — "This is holding me back only because I believe it is holding me back. If I change my attitude, this will no longer stand in my way." Now write down each obstacle you identified and this time after each of them, write, "This is holding me back only because I believe it is holding me back. If I change my attitude, this will no longer stand in my way." This exercise may seem foolish to you, but writing it down helps your focus and produces results. Each time you do it, it will get easier. Do this at least twice today, once right away and once before you go to bed tonight. Believe that it works; *do it.*

EVERYTHING CHANGES — WHY NOT YOU?

Remember that fish I told you about — the pike who starved to death? He starved with plenty of food all around because he did not understand the most important and fundamental principle of all existence; and most people I know are struggling for the same reason. They are beating their brains out against glass walls that exist only in their imagination and in their yesterdays — not in their todays.

The most exciting step on *The Lazy Man's Way* is when you understand the full implications of this simple principle — EVERYTHING CHANGES. You are saying, "I know that all I have to do is look at myself now and ten years ago and realize how much I've changed physically." And you have, just as everything else has changed and is changing constantly.

I'm not saying that there are no absolute, no eternal truths. There are, but in the physical world, in relationships between people and in your own mind, change is the natural order. Physical objects age. Relationships between people deepen and mature as we grow in wisdom and experience. Everything is constantly changing and yet most people refuse to accept that premise in one crucial area of their lives — their attitudes about themselves and their abilities. Have you ever said something like, "I know I could be more successful if I were just more organized but I've always been disorganized, that's the way I am." Or maybe in your case you're organized but you are not outgoing, or you think you don't have enough drive or you have never done really well at anything in the past, so why should you expect success now? After all, if you are a failure you are a failure! Right?

Wrong! "That's the way I am" is one of the most negatively powerful sentences in the English language.

Change is the law of life. And those who look only to the past or the present are sure to miss the future.

JOHN F. KENNEDY (1917–1963)
35th President of the United States

We change when the pain to change is less than the pain to remain as we are.

ED FOREMAN (B. 1933)
American entrepreneur, engineer, author, speaker, member of U.S. Congress

*The absurd man is he
who never changes.*

AUGUSTE BARTHELEMY (1796–1867)
French poet, satirist

Every time you say it or think it you are reinforcing the attitude that everything changes BUT YOU! That everything changes but those glass walls, the walls that are keeping you from the things you want and need the most, the Riches you are looking for.

You are not entirely responsible for the walls being put there in the first place any more than the fish I told you about was responsible for putting the glass wall between himself and the minnow. Your walls were erected by well-meaning friends or relatives, by teachers and classmates, and by situations in your past in which you tried something new that didn't quite work out. There are thousands of events in everyone's life that can result in a glass wall. People who laugh at you when you express your dreams; people who, out of love, warn you not to get your hopes too high so you won't be disappointed; classmates who make fun of you, when you make a mistake reading aloud; or loved ones who tell you hurtful things in anger — things that are not true and are not really meant but that you take as gospel. As a result a wall is formed. A wall that can last forever if *you let it.*

IT'S YOUR CHOICE

Now you have a choice. You can sit around and blame your parents and teachers and the other people who helped to build your glass walls and stay right where you are. Or you can let the past go and get on to the more important business of tearing those walls down so that you can get at the Riches life has to offer you.

*For they can conquer who believe
they can.*

JOHN DRYDEN (1631–1700)
English poet, dramatist, critic

You see, while you may not be the one who put those walls there in the first place, you definitely are the only one who keeps them there, and you keep them there by denying the fundamental principle that everything changes, including you, and your attitudes. Not only is everything changing, but it's possible to take control of and guide that change in any direction you want. You can let go of these walls and keep new ones from appearing if you'll just accept, understand, and believe *The Lazy Man*. There is no amount of physical work you can do to knock down those walls, but with a few simple mental exercises you can make them disappear. That's the key to doing things *The Lazy Man's Way*. Don't work harder, work *smarter!*

BETTER LATE . . . ?

Let me tell you about someone who learned this concept in her late sixties. Dorothy was the kind of person who always got stuck with the menial jobs — you know, the ones with lots of work and no glory. She was always the secretary in the clubs she joined. She always had to make the coffee and clean up the mess. In the civil service job she held, and hated for over twenty years, she frequently did work for which others got credit. She accepted all this because deep down inside she really didn't think too much of herself. Besides, that's the way it had always been. When Dorothy finally retired she was worn out, depressed, bitter, and physically ill. She was "dead" but just hadn't discovered it yet. Well, not totally dead, because there was some spark left and there was a dream. That spark led her to *The Lazy Man's Way* at the age of 67. She grasped the principle that everything changes and applied it to herself. She learned to use the three simple tools that I'm going to give you, tools that will give you immediate results.

You should see Dorothy now after using these tools to achieve her dream. She went back to college when she was 69, and earned her master's degree — her lifelong dream — at the age of 72 with straight A's. Not only that, but this woman who had been part of the background all her life suddenly found herself center stage. She was elected president of the senior citizens student body and became a university spokeswoman for other senior citizens thinking of returning to college. She also served as a consultant to the president of the university on problems of returning students.

A living thing is distinguished from a dead thing by the multiplicity of the changes at any moment taking place within.

HERBERT SPENCER (1820–1903)
English philosopher, social scientist

It is better to live rich than to die rich.

DR. SAMUEL JOHNSON (1709–1784)
English lexicographer, essayist, poet

Change is not made without inconvenience, even from worse to better.

RICHARD HOOKER (1554–1600)
English theologian

The Riches Dorothy went after weren't financial. They involved self-respect and self-appreciation. She achieved every one of her goals and at the age of 72 is now looking for new worlds to conquer. Dorothy's first step and yours too, if you want to attain your Riches *The Lazy Man's Way*, is to accept the full implications of the statement — EVERYTHING CHANGES. And everything is possible for you now! When she grasped the meaning, as it applied to herself, she was able to shake off over forty years of frustration. Forty years of putting herself down in comparison with others. Forty years of wishing but not having. After forty years of bumping her nose on the glass walls, she easily began to achieve her lifelong dreams that had seemed impossible. And you can too once you've dissolved the barriers. Remove the roadblocks and you've got a clear road to your Riches. How? Very simply. So simple you may not believe it can work until you try it.

You can start this process by writing the following declaration *"I,* _your name_ *, accept the reality that everything changes — including myself. I am free of all past limiting attitudes."* Carry this declaration with you and look at it at least 25 times each and every day. Even though it may seem excessive, do it. It works! Make numerous copies of this declaration and put them where you'll see them; on your mirror, on the dash of your car, someplace where you'll see them frequently. And each time you see them, read them aloud and think about what it means to you. You've got a lot of brainwashing to undo and the only way to do that is to do your own brainwashing. Only this time you are in charge. So go to it; and when you are through, you'll be a giant step further on *The Lazy Man's Way to Riches.*

THE TURNING POINTS

CHAPTER 6 OF PART 2

In this chapter I'm going to talk about your greatest gift and your greatest power, the power that can change your life and take you anywhere you want to go once you know how to use it. But first I'd like to ask you a question. Are you finding it a bit difficult to do all the exercises that I am suggesting? Do you think that some of them may not be necessary or are silly? Well, don't feel alone; most of us have the same response in the beginning. What's happening is that you are beginning to run up against the biggest roadblock of all, namely YOU! You see, there is a constant flow of thought moving through your mind at any given time. I call it self-talk! These are the *silent sentences* within you. Some self-talk is positive — your inner dreams, your unrealized purpose, your wants, your secret desires for your life, loved ones, and your livelihood. I have been encouraging you to listen to this self-talk throughout our experience together. I warn you that some self-talk is negative — the brainwashing of the past that has gotten you nowhere. It brings you down, limits you, discourages your dreaming process, and posts "STOP" signs in your path at almost every turn. How do you tell the one from the other? It's simple! Negative, destructive self-talk is just that — negative and self-destructive! Avoid this kind of self-talk and listen carefully for the positive dimension, where the seeds of your personal success have been planted. In a couple of chapters I'll tell you how you can take charge of your "inner voice" — your self-talk — and start it working for you, instead of against you!

Now let's talk about your greatest gift and how most people throw it away without realizing what they have. I'll start with the second fundamental principle of life.

WE ARE ALL CREATED EQUAL!

Respect yourself if you would have others respect you.

BALTASAR GRACIAN (1601–1658)
Spanish prosewriter, Jesuit priest

People are always blaming their cicumstances for what they are. I don't believe in circumstances. The people who get on in this world are the people who get up and look for the cicumstances they want, and, if they can't find them, make them.

GEORGE BERNARD SHAW (1856–1950)
Irish playwright, critic, social reformer

Like the first fundamental principle — EVERYTHING CHANGES — the full meaning and importance of the principle is easy to overlook. Maybe you're like Joe Karbo used to be and can't even accept the truth of the statement at first. Joe really worked to understand and accept this, because all around him he saw evidence of inequality — some people were born rich, some poor, some healthy, some challenged with physical infirmities. Some who seemed to come into the world loaded with talent and some who seemingly had no talent *whatsoever*. Some were born into freedom and some into slavery. "Where is the equality?" he kept asking. How can you possibly accept the truth of this statement when all the evidence of your experience seems to contradict it?

Initially Joe discarded the principle that all people are created equal and with it any chance he had at finding *The Lazy Man's Way*. Around him he saw people who were successful and happy, who had truly found the Riches that life offers to all of us and had overcome what seemed to be enormous challenges. He also saw people who had what seemed to be every advantage and were frustrated in their efforts to be successful. And he saw others who seemingly had little natural ability and few advantages of birth or position who became enormously successful.

As time went on and the more he studied, the more convinced he became that the apparent inequalities of birth were only some of the many factors and not the most important one. Then he realized the obvious — the people who attain the Riches they desire are the ones who use their greatest gift, well, even though they don't always understand the power they are using. The ones who become bogged down are the ones who throw their gift away, not realizing the power they possess.

What is this gift? Very simply it's FREE WILL, or if you prefer, FREEDOM OF CHOICE. The freedom to make a decision, to choose the road you wish to follow. It is the freedom to sit still and wallow in your own failure or the freedom to change and move ahead. To accept your so-called limitations or to find a way around them. The freedom to deny the realities of change or to accept change and make it work for you. Every day of your life you are faced with thousands of decisions and in every case you have a choice of which way to go. **Your life is the sum total of the consequences of all your decisions**. When Joe accepted this principle — when he understood and began to apply the power of the gift of the freedom of choice — his whole life began to change faster than he ever could have dreamed possible!

INCH BY INCH — IT'S A CINCH

The major problem for most people in taking charge of their decision-making gift is that they fail to realize that a lot of small decisions, which are usually made without thinking, are more important than the few major ones that they really think of as life-changing decisions.

Everyday we make thousands of decisions, 95%, no, 99% of these decisions are made with little or no conscious thought. In one way that's good; it would be terrible to think about which shoe you were going to put on first or how much sugar you were going to put on your cereal or what route to take to work. We make these decisions out of habit, and rightfully so, to free our mind from the trivial details of life. It's a marvelous capacity of the human mind that we can reduce even complex procedures to habit. It is unfortunate, however, that we do this with many decisions that are not trivial in terms of their impact on our lives.

How often have you made a New Year's resolution to make a radical change in your life — perhaps to stop smoking or to lose weight or to become more organized? And how often have you failed to follow through and had to make the same resolution the next year, and the next, and so on? Your major decision did not affect your life the way

One change leaves the way open for the introduction of others.

NICCOLÒ MACHIAVELLI (1469–1527)
Florentine statesman, political
philosopher

you wanted it to because you didn't realize that the major life-changing decision is really the end result of a lot of little decisions, most of which you make out of habit.

BURIED IN A PAPER TRAIL

For example, one of the best and fastest ways to become more organized in your business or profession is to minimize the number of times you handle any particular piece of paper and to always know where to find it. This, in turn, requires that you have a good filing system.

Suppose you decide to use these principles in your life. That's a major decision. So you buy the file cabinets and folders and spend a week setting up your system and getting it in order. But none of this does you any good if you don't make the right decision every time a piece of paper crosses your desk. If you don't develop a new set of habits for making decisions each time you handle a document, all your expense and effort will go for nothing.

The same thing is true of *The Lazy Man's Way to Riches*. You made a decision to buy this book and then make a much more important decision every day when you reach out and open the book. You make another important decision when you follow through by actually performing the steps and exercises in this book. If you don't decide to reach out and open the book and don't complete the steps it outlines, you cancel out all these decisions you made in starting this journey; and you have to live with the consequences of your decision. Remember, "if you just keep doing what you're doing, you'll just keep getting what your getting."

WHAT TRIGGERS THE TURNING POINTS?

One of the easiest ways to understand the importance of the little decisions is to examine the so-called turning points in your life. Were they really the result of clear-cut decisions where you knew exactly what the outcome would lead to? Or were your turning points the end result of a lot of *little* decisions that were made with hardly any or no thought of the consequences? For example, two of the most significant events in most of our lives are marriage and the choice of a career. But are these cases of major decisions made after a great deal of analysis? Usually not. Most people arrive at these turning points in their lives as a result of a lot of earlier decisions that were made without any idea of the consequences.

Joe said his decision to marry Betty, and hers to marry him, came as a result of a lot of little decisions about going out together and working out the conflicts in their personalities; so by the time they decided to get married, it was the only logical thing to do. Zero in on the little decisions that affect your life.

Your next step on your road to Riches is to examine the turning points in your life. Try to examine the *little* decisions that added up to a major change. Pick out the major events in your life and write down all the reasons you made the choices you made. Then, look closely at your reasons and try to figure out what little decisions really created the situation that influenced your choice.

He who is outside his door already has a hard part of his journey behind him.

DUTCH PROVERB

C ongratulations! You just made a very important little decision that's going to mean a lot to you. You decided to complete the steps necessary to continue your journey on *The Lazy Man's Way to Riches*.

Was examining the Turning Points in your life a revelation to you? Are you getting an idea of how crucial the little decisions are in your life? It's kind of scary, isn't it, to think how a bunch of little decisions can really add up to a big change in your life. Scary — but also very exciting because that means you have a lot of chances every day to influence your life in a positive way.

Have you ever made a mistake, recognized it as a mistake, and turned right around and made the same mistake again? If you are human you have. We all have this experience — making the same mistakes over and over again and basically for the same reason. Habit. We get into the habit of making certain decisions without thinking. That can be great if the decisions are success decisions, but it can be disastrous if they are (and they usually are) failure-oriented decisions. Now why does this happen? Why do we make the same blunders over and over again?

THE POWER OF SUGGESTION

Joe was convinced that we act as though we have been hypnotized. Have you ever seen a hypnotist work, especially on stage? Pat Collins, the famous hypnotist, once owned a night club in Los Angeles. In her act she asked for volunteers from the audience whom she determined were good hypnotic subjects. She hypnotized them and suggested certain situations to them. The hypnotized volunteers behaved as if her suggestions were true. During the show Pat demonstrated a technique called "post-

God will not look you over for medals, degrees or diplomas, but for scars.

ELBERT HUBBARD (1856–1915)
American businessman, writer, printer

hypnotic suggestion." She told her volunteers that after they came out from under hypnosis, each time she mentioned the name of her club they would jump up and start shouting "The British are coming! The British are coming!" She then brought them out of their relaxed state and thanked them for helping her at the "Pat Collins Celebrity Club." Immediately they jumped up and started hollering "The British are coming! The British are coming!" Of course the audience thought it was hilarious. Each time she mentioned her club she got the same result. One of the volunteers said, "I was aware of what I was doing and each time I did it, I really decided I wouldn't do it again, and yet each time Pat mentioned the name of the club, I found myself reacting the same way."

SUGGESTION GAINS IN INTENSITY!

Doesn't that sound familiar, haven't you felt that way, repeating the same mistakes over and over again? This simple nightclub gag really explains a lot of human behavior. All of you have been hypnotized at various times in your life. All that means is that you have accepted certain suggestions about yourself and your behavior as a result of your experiences. You get a certain cue or trigger and off you go shouting "The British are coming! The British are coming." Of course, it is more subtle than that. Often the trigger is a certain kind of situation rather than a word or words.

For example, let's say you have a great idea for doing a certain part of your job more effectively. If you can sell your employer on the idea, it will probably mean a promotion and a raise; but each time you try to approach the boss with the idea you become nervous and tongue-tied. You begin to doubt the real value of your idea and as a result you really don't get it across. Your whole presentation is a shambles and you lose out. A couple weeks later, one of your co-workers gets the same idea. Worse yet, "borrows" your idea,

He who does anything because it is the custom, makes no choice.

JOHN STUART MILL (1806–1837)
English economist, social critic, writer

takes it to the boss, and sells it. He gets the credit and the raise and you wonder why you can't seem to communicate effectively with someone who is above you.

Well, now you know. Sometime in your past you accepted the suggestion that you don't do well talking to "The Boss" or "authority figures." Maybe it was a bad school experience with a teacher or principal or other authority figures or maybe it was a problem speaking to your parents. It doesn't really matter, because the damage has been done. The important thing is learning how to break the pattern. We start that process in the next chapter.

THE WINNING EDGE — PREPARE TO WIN

Why do you have these problem areas in your life, such as not winning with authority figures? According to the very successful basketball coach, Bobby Knight of Indiana University, it is because you are not *prepared* to win. He was asked how he instilled the will to win in his players. He replied, "Everybody has the will to win. What I work to instill in my players is the will to prepare to win!" That's a key step in *The Lazy Man's Way to Riches*. If you have the will to prepare to win and engage in the right preparation, you will make the right little decisions automatically. Those little decisions really add up into a winning way of living your life.

One of the roadblocks that stops a lot of people from getting the things they want out of life is the belief that to be really successful in life you have to: work much harder, be much smarter, or be luckier than the average guy. And it just isn't so! For one thing, if you had to work much harder than average, Joe would have been out of it — because he was the original Lazy Man.

THE WINNING EDGE — BY A NOSE!

Actually, the winning edge is much smaller than you think. Some years ago Nashua became one of the first

We are all, it seems, saving ourselves for the senior prom. But many of us forget that somewhere along the way we must learn to dance.

ALAN HARRINGTON (B. 1919)
American social critic, writer

Showing up is eighty percent of life.

WOODY ALLEN (B. 1935)
American filmmaker

million dollar racehorses. Now you don't have to know very much about horse racing to know that a million-dollar racehorse is not a hundred times faster than a ten-thousand-dollar racehorse. In fact, he is not even twice as fast. If you have ever seen a horse race you know there usually isn't very much space between the winner and the rest of the pack. In Nashua's case 60% of the races he won were by photo finishes. In racing that means the horses were only *inches* apart as they crossed the finish line after more than a mile of racing. In other words, Nashua became a million-dollar racehorse even though 60% of the time he was one or two inches ahead of his competition after over 70,000 thousand inches of running. That's a difference of less than 1/100 of 1%. It's just as true in life. The winning edge is not a matter of miles. It's often just a fraction of an inch.

THE WINNING EDGE — A FEW EXTRA HANDS!

There's not a salesperson in the world who doesn't want to make or exceed his quota. They want to win. But whether they make it or not will often depend on as small an effort as one extra call a week. Dick Johnson relates the story of his own business experience.

In several small wholesale distribution companies this truth is clearly illustrated. The figures show that people who put at least fifteen hours per week into the development of their business succeed spectacularly. They often develop $50,000 to $100,000 incomes annually within three or four years. The figures also show that people who put less than eight hours per week into the development of their business usually struggle to make anything and often fail completely. In this case the winning edge is an extra seven hours per week — just one hour per day — and that little extra makes an enormous difference in income. How big a decision is it to make an extra call or to spend an

Action may not always bring happiness, but there is no happiness without action.

BENJAMIN DISRAELI (1804–1881)
English statesman, novelist

extra hour each day developing your future? Not too big and yet it's this kind of decision that really makes the difference. There's one big problem with little decisions — they are usually made out of habit.

Go back over your experiences and identify the post-hypnotic patterns that are blocking your progress. In other words, where are the areas in your life where you are creating the same mistakes over and over and over again.

Mistakes like:

- Somehow I always spend more than I make

- I'm still in the same dead-end job that I vowed to get out of last year

- I have great ideas but somehow I never carry them through to completion

- I'm the same 30 pounds overweight than I was last year

- People never take me seiously because I always seem to turn everything into a joke.

CHANGE YOUR HABITS — CHANGE YOUR LIFE

CHAPTER 8 OF PART 2

It really opens your eyes, doesn't it, to see how post-hypnotic suggestions or habits are dominating your life? Day after day, most of us make virtually all our decisions, important or unimportant, out of habit. If the decision is not made automatically, as some are, the thought processes that go into our decision making are dominated by our attitudes, which are just habits of thought about ourselves, our abilities, and our environment.

Most, if not all of our attitudes are not valid most of the time. I will explain that in more detail later, but you have probably already realized that you are not always 100% right about everything.

CHANGE YOUR HABITS AND CHANGE YOUR LIFE

Since habits dominate your life, to change your life you have *to change your habits.* It has been observed many times that successful people are those who make a habit out of doing the things unsuccessful people won't do. But what are those things? W. Clement Stone, who certainly has one of the twentieth century's most exciting success stories, has pretty well narrowed it down. W. Clement Stone started in the insurance business at the age of sixteen with a one hundred dollar investment. When I last heard, his net worth was over seven hundred million dollars and is still strong. Mr. Stone is also the founder of *Success* magazine and the P.M.A. (Positive Mental Attitude) seminars and rallies. Mr. Stone says that in his experience, successful people all exhibit the following characteristics.

DO IT

First, when faced with an opportunity where they have a great deal to gain if successful and little or nothing to lose if they fail, *they try.* How often have you seen people with a clear opportunity in front of them paralyzed by indecision

It seems, in fact, as though the second half of a man's life is made up of nothing but the habits he has accumulated during the first half.

FYODOR DOSTOEVSKY (1821–1881)
Russian novelist

We are all of us failures—at least, the best of us are.

J. M. BARRIE (1860–1937)
British playwright, novelist

and fear? And what are they afraid of? The fear of failure itself, not the consequences of it. The sad thing is that often there is no real risk. No risk of losing their savings, or self-respect, or good name, or anything of value.

DO IT NOW!

The second of W. Clement Stone's attributes of successful people is they have a *"do it now"* attitude. Procrastination — putting things off — is the greatest destroyer of success that I know. And I should know, because in the past I was one of the greatest procrastinators ever known, and it has cost me dearly. Opportunity is almost always lost when people put things off, and problems usually become much worse when they are not solved immediately. There is another negative aspect of procrastination — it saps your energy. Usually when you put something off you don't forget about it — it nags at you constantly. You run over the situation several times a day in your imagination. The amazing thing is that you burn up just as much or more energy *thinking* about the problem as you would *solving* it. So the longer you procrastinate, the more tired and frustrated you get as you go over and over and over it in your mind. You will be astonished at how much more energy you have when you start developing a "do it now" habit!

DO IT PERSISTENTLY

W. Clement Stone's third attribute of successful people is that they have *persistence*. In his words, *"Success is achieved and maintained by those who try and continue to try with a positive mental attitude."*

Life has a way of testing your desires by setting some obstacle in your way. Too many people give up at the first setback. The history of failure is full of stories of people who quit just inches away from success. And the history of success is full of stories of people who failed more than once

Procrastination is the thief of time.

EDWARD YOUNG (1683–1765)
English poet

Habit is habit, and not to be flung out of the window by any man, but coaxed downstairs a step at a time.

MARK TWAIN (1835–1910)
American novelist, humorist

before they finally clicked.

Developing these three habits — *willingness to try, do it now,* and *persistence* — with a positive mental attitude is certainly fundamental to your progress in *The Lazy Man's Way.* But let's be realistic. Just recognizing the desirability of a new habit is not enough. Developing habits takes attention, time and continued effort, especially if you are trying to replace an old habit that conflicts with a new one. Habits such as these can take a long time to establish. That is why you need some tools to help you keep on track and moving. You will have a lot of powerful tools before you are through.

DRAW UP A CONTRACT

And here is the first one. The Habit Contract. The idea of The Habit Contract is simple. We are usually motivated by *rewards* and our nature is such that we are usually motivated more by near-term, easily achievable, tangible rewards than by more distant, less tangible rewards. It is important, therefore, that you set up some near-term rewards, so you may become aware of the progress you are making, and to teach you to be good to yourself.

The process is simple. First, *identify* the habits you want to develop. And second (because you always develop new habits — you don't break or give up old ones) you must *develop a new response* as a substitute reaction for the old one. Changing a habit is like changing the course of a river — you must divert the flow into a new channel. The old channel is there, and in the beginning it is fairly easy to revert to it, but as time goes on the new channel becomes deeper and deeper. The old one fills in and there is less and less likelihood of going back to it — your old ways. It would be easier to change a habit if your mind automatically made you stop and make a conscious choice about changing. You need something — a symbol — to trigger you to remember you are no longer responding in the same way to situations

The only people who never fail are those who never try.

ILKA CHASE (1905–1978)
American actress

Nothing is more powerful than habit.

OVID (PUBLIUS OVIDIUS NASO)
(43 B.C-A.D. 17)
Roman poet

— to your old habits. I call this a Habit Trigger. For example, when you pour yourself a cup of coffee in the morning, it could trigger you to remember the new habit you are trying to establish.

To adopt a new habit, you must first identify the long-term payoff that will result from adopting it. It may be more success, higher income, better health, more self-esteem, more freedom, peace of mind, or whatever long-term benefits appeal to you. You are probably feeling it would be nice if you could have all those things, but you are also not really excited about the prospects. They are too far away, not sufficiently specific to get you excited enough to generate the energy it takes to develop the new habit. That is why you need the specific award aspect of The Habit Contract to inspire you to put out the effort to change now!

REWARD YOURSELF

This is the way The Habit Contract works. You select something as a reward for yourself. Something you will give yourself as a special treat for accomplishing a milestone toward your goal of developing a new habit. To be effective, this reward must be something you really want, but would not ordinarily get for yourself. It could be something that would cost a little more than you would normally spend on yourself. Perhaps a custom-made suit or dinner at a very fine restaurant. It could be something that cost very little, but seems a little selfish.

One woman's choice of the height of luxury was to have her husband and kids take off on a camping trip for three days, so she could be totally alone in her home for that time. That was a great reward for her. It was something she had always wanted but had never felt right asking for so it made a perfect reward for establishing a new habit. The habit she was working on developing was a "do it now" attitude. When she successfully performed thirty consecutive acts of completing tasks rather than putting

The nature of man is always the same; it is their habits that separate them.

CONFUCIUS (551–479 B.C.)
Chinese philosopher

them off, she rewarded herself with three days of peace and quiet.

So what kind of habits should you be adopting? The number-one habit I want you to adopt is faithfully performing the steps I have introduced, and particularly, Daily Declarations and Super Suggestions. If you will do that, I am confident you will start developing the other habits you need. To help you develop the habit of continuing on your *Lazy Man's Way to Riches*, I have put a sample of a Habit Contract on the follwing page. The next page contains a blank Habit Contract for your use. You might want to make a copy of it for your individual contracts with yourself. So select your reward, and then earn it by carrying out your journey in *The Lazy Man's Way*. Keep in mind while deciding on your reward to make it something that really motivates you; and make it something you would not ordinarily do for yourself, unless you felt you had *earned* it. Pick a Habit Trigger (something you see or do frequently) that will remind you of this contract. Sign the contract and have it witnessed by someone who won't nag you about it.

By the way, do not feel limited to just one Habit Contract. You can probably handle up to three habits simultaneously, but do not try to change everything at once. You have plenty of time; trying to do too much at once will diffuse your concentration and defeat your purpose.

How long does it take to develop a new habit pattern? Psychologists tell me that a rat can learn a new behavior in about 30 repetitions. So draw your own conclusions. To help you measure your progress, I have included the numbers one through thirty so you can check off each time you are successful in reinforcing the new habit.

EXAMPLE
HABIT CONTRACT

MY DESIRED HABIT: Spend some time each day developing myself and enriching my future by reading "The Lazy Man's Way to Riches."

MY LONG-RANGE PAYOFF: Everything in the world I really want.

MY HABIT TRIGGER: Every time I brush my teeth, I am reminded of this contract and the reward I'm working for.

MY REWARD: When I have successfully adopted this habit, I will reward myself by taking my wife to dinner at that fancy French restaurant we both enjoy so much.

SIGNED, WITNESSED, AND DATED:

I will fulfill this commitment to myself for I realize it is the first step in enabling me to
create the kind of life I have always wanted!

REINFORCEMENTS

1	2	3	4	5	6	7	8	9	10
11	12	13	14	15	16	17	18	19	20
21	22	23	24	25	26	27	28	29	30

(Check off as you do your reinforcements)

Now look at the next page and complete your first habit contract. Write in the desired habit, the long range payoff, the trigger you will use, and your reward for establishing your habit. Sign the contract and have it witnessed. Each day you complete a step cross off the next number. By the time you reach 30, reward yourself!

HABIT CONTRACT

MY DESIRED HABIT: _____

_____

MY LONG-RANGE PAYOFF: _____

_____

MY HABIT TRIGGER: _____

_____

MY REWARD: _____

_____

SIGNED, WITNESSED, AND DATED: _____

_____

I will fulfill this commitment to myself for I realize it is the first step in enabling me to
create the kind of life I have always wanted!

REINFORCEMENTS

1	2	3	4	5	6	7	8	9	10
11	12	13	14	15	16	17	18	19	20
21	22	23	24	25	26	27	28	29	30

(Check off as you do your reinforcements)

Habit is like a cable; we weave a thread of it each day and at last we cannot break it.

HORACE MANN (1875–1955)
German novelist, essayist

Wherever we go, whatever we do, self is the sole subject we study and learn.

RALPH WALDO EMERSON (1803–1882)
American poet, essayist, philosopher

I believe that it is harder still to be just toward oneself than toward others.

ANDRÉ GIDE (1869–1951)
French novelist, critic, essayist, editor, translator

A very wise man once said that there is a gift that all our true friends would love to give us, that gift that we probably need desperately, but a gift capable of utterly destroying even the deepest friendship. That gift is criticism. And, the more personal the criticism, the greater the sting it carries.

At the risk of endangering for the moment your sense of self-satisfaction, let me tell you something about your inadequacies. How do I know they are your inadequacies? Simply because you bought this book, the odds are overwhelming that you suffer from some feelings of inadequacy. (But if it makes you feel any better, almost everybody does.) However, by buying this book, you also proved that you were willing to make some important changes in your life. You've already taken the most important step!

Now when I speak of inadequacies, I am not concerned with your size, weight, physical appearance, strength, manliness or femininity. The concern here is with the most important inadequacy from which any person can suffer — an *Inadequate Self-Image*. For brevity I will refer to it as ISI.

This *ISI* is one of the first things formed in your life. It has an influential and *lasting* effect on your failure or success. It plays a more prominent role than *any other single factor*. This is true because it is the giant *controller* of your personal destiny.

If that seems hard to believe, let me ask you this: Would you like to try to face the daily task of your present world (job, friends, love-life, etc.) knowing and believing only what you knew and believed when you were *five or six years old?*

Think of the mess you could make of even the

simplest tasks assigned to you, functioning as a grown person with the knowledge and beliefs of a young child! Think of the impossibility of a mature relationship with others if your capacity to "get along" was that of a kindergartner!

Well, your ISI, in all those areas that are important to us as adults, was largely set in concrete by the time you were six years old! Challenging though that statement may seem to some, there is overwhelming scientific evidence to support it.

Once we have ascertained the point of woeful inadequacy at which ISI was established, surely you must wonder if it doesn't change as you get older. The answer (and we'll see why later) is, "No, hardly ever," unless you deliberately set about to change it!

Your next question might be, what does this ISI control or affect? The answer: To a greater or lesser extent, *every single activity of the human being!* And it does this by placing a clamped-down, nailed-down, ceiling on success! It prevents the adult from ever reaching a potential beyond the concept of the *child.*

The direct result of this ISI is that the average person uses less than *10% of his/her potential*! And it's no wonder. At the age of five or six few of us were convinced of our own great strength, power, abilities. We didn't feel very *effective.*

HUMAN CONDITIONING

That feeling of ineffectuality was the result of the many pressures that were applied to us in those first few years. These pressures were the "do's and don'ts" of our early years as expressed in the *habits* we established. Scientifically these things are referred to as "conditioning."

Those pressures can be divided into two categories: Those which *help* us in later years and those which *hinder* our progress. The *helps* of those years were the

We are so constituted that we believe the most incredible things; and, once they are engraved upon the memory, woe to him who would endeavor to erase them.

JOHANN WOLFGANG VON GOETHE
(1749-1832)
German poet, playwright, novelist

conditioning we acquired that today lets us perform many of our daily tasks almost without thinking. In this group are included such diverse things as tying our shoes; using a knife, fork, and spoon; walking; talking, etc.

But what of the conditioning that hinders our effectiveness? Consider this example:

As a very little boy, Johnny goes out to the garage where his father is working in his woodshop. Fascinated, he watches his father as he is "making something." Soon, watching is not enough. He wants to "help." At this point two things may occur. One will result in a conditioning that will *help*; the other will *hinder* the self-image structure and the later-life development as well.

If his father gives him some safe but satisfying task of the utmost simplicity to perform, lets him do it, guides him to some small success, and then praises his efforts, the lad's self-image has received a tremendous boost. If this pattern of events is repeated again and again, confidence is built through the *habit of success* in this area of activity. It will *help* him build a better self-image.

If, on the other hand, "Daddy's" time and/or patience is short, if the lad's interest and desire to participate result in only an irritating interference with the work at hand, no such helpful image-building results. The repeated efforts to participate (for little ones are not easily discouraged) may result in a final rejection by the father as he is banished from this fascinating scene or punishment for what the father sees as deliberate disobedience.

Either way, the child has been taught a lesson. He has been "taught" or conditioned into a belief that he is "no good" at a certain kind of manly activity, or that he is "no good" merely because he has wanted to participate — *"bad"* because he was *ambitious*. His self-image has taken a blow, his fear-factor (of which we will talk later) has received a great boost.

To the same degree that this was an occurrence

Creative minds have always been known to survive any kind of bad training.

ANNA FREUD (1895–1982)
English psychoanalyst, daughter of
Sigmund Freud

charged with *heavy emotionality* (loud voice, a physical punishment, lasted a long time), it will have a proportionately large and lasting effect on the self-image.

Few of us have been so fortunate as to have had only *helpful* ego forming, or self-image, experiences in our early years. That is why today it is a scientific evaluation that the *average person is working at only 10% of his/her potential!*

Where does that put you? Well, since you care enough about the future to buy a program like this, to read it, to TRY to improve your chances of success, you are already considerably *above average*! But the fact that you are not already a smashing success means you are still not functioning near the maximum of your potential power.

I CAN BE MY OWN WORST ENEMY
OR MY OWN BEST FRIEND

Hello. I'm Richard Gilly Nixon and the reason I am introducing myself to you again is that I am not the same Richard who talked to you earlier, anymore than you are the same person you were when you started this book. You and I are constantly *changing* and can be constantly *improving*. It is usually hard to see the changes from day to day, yet just look at how you have changed since we started our page by page get together.

How have you changed? Well, for one thing, you know a lot more about yourself than when we began. You know that you have *all* the qualities you need to be an outstanding success. You know that the roadblocks that used to block your way are really products of your attitude. And you know that you and everything else in the world around you is constantly changing, so those attitudes that block you from the Riches you want can be changed too. You've been thinking about where you want to go in life and you have begun to identify some patterns in your life that lead you to make the same mistakes over and over again. The knowledge you have gained in these pages makes you a new person. As you start learning to apply that knowledge, you will begin to see changes take place. And this raises a very important question. Are you willing to change? I know I asked you this question at the beginning, but I find that in the beginning most people don't realize how significant these changes will be. Are you willing to release some old attitudes? Admit some of your most cherished beliefs aren't working for you? If you are not, it is going to be very difficult to release the barriers between you and the Riches you want.

> *Progress is impossible without change; and those who cannot change their minds cannot change anything.*
>
> **GEORGE BERNARD SHAW (1856–1950)**
> **Irish playwright, critic, social reformer**

YOU CAN PREDICT YOUR FUTURE

Look at it this way. You can absolutely predict your progress in the future by looking at the progress you have made in the past, *if you choose not to change your thinking.* But, when you change your thinking you can make your future anything you want. Resist change in your attitudes and your future will be just like your past. Post-hypnotic suggestion explains our habitual behavior.

How many mistake patterns can you find in your life? Let me check for a few you might have overlooked. How is your temper? Do you find that you often lose it when a little diplomacy would really help the situation go more smoothly? How is your procrastination level? How often do you put things off and compound a problem that could be solved by a simple action? How is your self-confidence? How often do you let someone else talk you out of your good ideas? How about your impatience? Do you find yourself doing things impulsively when a little patience would make things work smoother? How forgetful are you? How often do you forget an important appointment or a person's name or a priority task that must be done? Quick temper — habit. Procrastination — habit. Low self-confidence — habit. Impatience — habit. Forgetfulness — habit. All habits. All post-hypnotic suggestions that have you behaving in ways that contradict your reason and intelligence. Fortunately, all post-hypnotic suggestions can be removed once you understand and use the process I am going to teach you.

Earlier when I was telling you about the Pat Collins Show, I left out an important part. Before Pat finished her show she was very careful to remove all post-hypnotic suggestions. After all, it could be embarrassing to suddenly jump up and shout "The British are coming" at a dinner party just because someone happened to mention the Pat Collins Celebrity Club. Pat Collins is a conscientious professional and would never fail to remove post-hypnotic

Laws are never as effective as habits.

ADLAI STEVENSON (1900–1965)
American statesman, politician

suggestions.

But suppose that one night she forgot? No need to worry. The results would not be too serious because a very important feature of hypnotic suggestions is that eventually they wear off, if they are not renewed or reinforced frequently. In other words, if you go to a hypnotist and ask him/her to help you stop smoking, the hypnotist might suggest to you that cigarettes taste terrible. They will for a while. But unless the hypnotist teaches you how to reinforce that suggestion it will soon wear off. Because smoking is such an ingrained habit for most people, they will continue to smoke even if the taste is bad; and after a very few cigarettes their minds will begin to forget or throw off the bad-taste suggestion and soon everything will be back to normal. Just as one of Pat Collins's volunteers would have been able to resist or forget that "The British are coming" within a day or so, any post-hypnotic suggestion will lose its effect within a very short time unless it is reinforced frequently. Right about now you may be thinking, "Wait a minute, you just told me that my repetitive mistakes were examples of post-hypnotic suggestions planted in my mind years ago and now you tell me post-hypnotic suggestions wear off quickly unless they are reinforced? That's a contradiction. How come my habit patterns have not worn off?" Very simple. They have been and are continually being reinforced by you.

YOU ARE YOUR OWN HYPNOTIST

Who is the most influential person in your life? Who do you listen to more than anyone? Who do you always agree with even when they put you down? Your spouse, your parents, your kids, your boss? No. None of the above. The most influential person in your life is YOU. When someone else is talking, you may or may not be listening. If you are listening, it is probably not to them but to your inner voice translating and restating what they are saying.

I know you believe you understand what you think I said, but I'm not sure you realized that what you heard is not what I meant.

ANONYMOUS

And as your inner voice tells you its translated version of what it is hearing you will attach more importance to that information than what is actually being said. You may or may not believe what others tell you, but you will always believe what your inner voice tells you, even if it puts you down — especially if it puts you down.

The fact of the matter is, there is no such thing as being hypnotized by another person. You can only be hypnotized by yourself. All the other person does is make certain suggestions and you either accept them or reject them. For example, if the hypnotist says, "Your eyelids are getting heavy," you have two choices. You can either accept the suggestion by saying, "Yes, my eyelids are getting heavy," in which case your body will respond to you and your eyelids will feel heavy, or you can say, "No, my eyelids are not getting heavy," in which case, nothing will happen. So, in fact, you hypnotize yourself. All the hypnotist does is tell you how to do it. If that is true, then how do we develop all of our bad habits? Simple. This process is going on all the time, and much of it happened when you were just a child. A lot of your limiting programming came from your lack of understanding of the world around you and the natural inclination of children to look up to and accept what bigger children and adults tell them. You *accepted* all kinds of suggestions about yourself and the world around you. Some were valid and helpful, many were false and worked against you and continue to work against you.

You can't really go back and change the kind of programming you received as a child. Nor is there any point in blaming your parents, teachers, brothers, sisters, other children, or anyone else. They were all going through a similar process and they did not know what was going on anymore than you did. So, if you cannot go back and change your past, does that mean you are stuck with you the way you are? When I was going to school, that was pretty much what psychologists believed. Supposedly our whole lives were influenced by things that happened to us when we were infants. There was not much we could do about it without a lot of very expensive psychoanalysis.

Events in our childhood do influence us later in life; but the idea that we are stuck with our behavior and attitudes just because we were not toilet-trained correctly is nonsense. We can change any aspect of our personalities or behavior if we want to; but we must want to and then learn the process for doing it.

SELF-TALK

You begin this process by becoming aware of how you talk to yourself. How often do you use the expression "I AM" as in statements like, "That's the way I AM" or "I AM temperamental," or "I AM lazy," or some such expression that means the same thing as, "I can't do it." To utter such statements is the same thing as saying, "I AM the kind of person who can't do it," or "I don't know," which is just another variation of the same thought. Almost anytime you use the word "I," you are making a statement about your talents and abilities — a statement that reinforces a false and limiting attitude about yourself. Statements like: I always do the same dumb thing. I was just born that way. I just can't remember names. I'm just not lucky. I'm always so disorganized. I never seem to have enough time. I always pick the wrong people. Recognize any of these? They are the kind of statements that reinforce your attitudes and tend to lock you into being just a product of your past training — good and bad.

For the next few days, I want you to become very self-aware of the kinds of statements that reinforce your attitudes and tend to lock you into being just a product of your past training — good and bad. Pay attention to what you say to and about yourself. As you go through your day, keep track of how many times you reinforce your past training with one of these phrases or a similar statement.

What is this self inside us, this silent observer, / severe and speechless critic, who can terrorize us. / And urge us on to futile activity, / and in the end, judge us still more severely. / For the errors into which his own reproaches drove us?

T. S. ELIOT (1888–1965)
American-born English poet, critic, editor, playwright

True Riches are yours when you really believe you are entitled to them — when you just *allow* yourself to have them and can freely *choose* to have them in your life. True belief in your ability to attain your purpose and the fundamental goals that support your purpose will grow in direct proportion to your level of positive self-esteem and even to your self-images. It's been said that belief is the foundation upon which our lives are built. If that's true, then a healthy, positive self-esteem and the many self-images we have of ourselves are the bedrock upon which the foundation is built!

A man can stand a lot as long as he can stand himself. He can live without hope, without friends, without books, even without music, as long as he can listen to his own thoughts.

AXEL MUNTHE (1857–1949)
Swedish physician, author

SELF-ESTEEM DEFINED

Self-esteem is a confidence and satisfaction in oneself. It's that deep down, inside-the-self feeling of your own worth. Our self-esteem is a total picture of how we see ourselves — a unique concept of who we are. It's the value you place on yourself — a favorable appreciation or opinion of yourself.

You've got to take the initiative and play your game. In a decisive set, confidence is the difference.

CHRIS EVERT
(B. 1954)
American tennis player

- Self-respect!

- Self-possession!

- Self-confidence!

  - Self-dignity!

  - Self-sufficiency!

  - Self-assurance!

    - Self-responsibility!

    - Self-pride!

    - Self-reliance!

- **BELIEF IN ONESELF!**

SELF-IMAGE DEFINED

Self-image is a *conception* of oneself or of one's role in a particular and singular area. It's the way you see yourself — viewing yourself as an exact likeness of another. It's a tangible or visible representation of oneself. *It's a view of self, based on an ideal.*

We have many self-images and they are based on our beliefs or ideals of how things should be. We have an image of ourselves in every aspect of our make-up!

- As a student..........I'm good in math, but I'm lousy in history.

- As a swimmer..........I tell myself I'm a poor swimmer, so I am.

- As a cook.............My belief is that boys don't cook, so I don't.

- As an employee..........I'm a good employee.

- As a spouse..........I'm so-so as a spouse.

- As a speaker..........I'm terrified as a speaker.

- As a seamstress..........Boys don't sew.

- As a football player.........I'm a good center but a lousy tackle.

- As a parent..........I do my best to be a responsible parent.

- As a child..........I'm learning how to handle my parents.

IT'S YOUR BELIEF

We view ourselves from the perspective of the ideals or beliefs we have come to accept about each role in our lives.

We tell ourselves I am a good cook, but a lousy mechanic; a good tennis player, a good golfer, but a bad swimmer. We see ourselves either competent or incompetent in every role and then we perform to the standard we set up for ourselves. We live out our self-fulfilling prophesies that are based upon the *image* we have of our competence in any given area. That's a wonderful concept! It's only your belief, that you buy into, that affects your performance in your role as a dancer, swimmer, mechanic, etc. Therefore, you can freely, willingly, and easily change your belief! You can replace failure-belief (I can't dance, I can't swim, I'll never understand mechanics) with a factual-belief that you can do or have or be something that you had previously denied yourself. That's *The Lazy Man's Way*. Because the human experience is universal — *that which any human being can do we all can do* — I call it a "factual belief." You can't go wrong if you remember these two things. First, all of the potential of the universe is inside you. Second, it's inside every other human being, too. As Joe always said, "All men are created equal."

A word of caution here: Whenever there is a conflict between your burning desire and your self-images, self-images will win every single time. That's why it is important to look carefully at the results of your life, objectively and truthfully. Is your life as good as it could be in each of the seven goal areas you listed after reading Chapter 7 of Part 1?

CHANGE YOUR PRESENT SELF-IMAGES!

A self-image that will work for you can easily be created in any area of your life to replace the present self-image that isn't working for you. You simply determine which areas just aren't working by simply asking yourself, "Are these the results I really want?" If they aren't, it's not the desire that's at fault or too weak; it's the idealized self-

Take charge of your thoughts. You can do what you will with them.

PLATO (428–327 BC)
Greek philosopher, prose writer

It may be all right to be content with what you have;
never with what you are.

B. C. FORBES (1880–1954)
American publisher

image of false belief that's getting in your way. Replace the image and the false belief it's based upon with a new image based on the new belief that "I can dance" (or whatever). Why not? Four billion other human beings can and do dance. Why? Simply because they think they can. You can, too; and you probably did as a two-year-old. You then work in an easy progression toward your new image, until you are able to develop the experience and self-confidence necessary to change your new ideal image into a real self-image. You won't start out as well as Fred Astaire or Paula Abdul, but neither did they! They started out just like you. You have to go out and do the things you're not very good at doing — yet!

They can do all because they think they can.

VIRGIL (70–19 BC)
Roman poet

JESSE JACKSON SAYS:

Reverend Jesse Jackson teaches people to say to themselves, "I am somebody!" What a wonderful start! It's true! But suppose for a moment you were switched at birth with the child of the rulers of your ancestral homeland. Your parents got the rulers' kid and the rulers got you. How would your life be different? You would have had the best of everything life had to offer — food, clothing, education, private tutors, arts and sports. You would have power, prestige, wealth, fame, and confidence galore! Could you dance (or whatever)? Of course! And so you can! You are still you regardless of how you grew up. *You are somebody!*

MUHAMMED ALI SAYS:

Muhammed Ali used to proclaim "I'm the greatest!" and he was. He proved it over and over. But he knew it deep in his soul even before he became the boxing champion of the world. His claim of "I am the greatest!" was not an idle boast or self-delusion. He worked for it! His claim was based upon the experience of success after success starting out as a beginner and moving up in weight class to better opponents. You can start out doing what you want to do also (dancer, swimmer, whatever), and you won't get "punched out" in the process!

SO WHAT'S THE DIFFERENCE?

There is a difference between "I am somebody!" and "I am the greatest!" The difference is between mere existence and existence with a purpose backed by *action* toward that purpose. It is your Performance. It is Accomplishment. It is Achievement toward your purpose.

To establish real self-esteem, concentrate on your *growth* toward your idea of success. Look at the stumbles and tumbles (and sometimes even outright failures) as corrective and necessary feedback — course corrections that get you back on target again! Instead of comparing yourself with others, see yourself in terms of your abilities, your ideals, your new beliefs, your growth and your goals. You can start now by making a conscious effort to change your life, raise your sights, and become more aware of your behavior, your personal habits, your posture, and appearance — in whatever you do try to do it just a little better each time — always try for your personal best performance. Doing your best will boost your self-esteem. Successful people believe in their own worth, even when they only have a dream to hold on to. That dream is based on a purpose and a plan! More than any other quality, a healthy, positive self-esteem is the key to your Riches!

High self-esteem must always include self-trust because when we trust ourselves we have no need to control anything or anybody. High self-esteem also includes self-respect because when we respect ourselves we find within ourselves all that we need and have no reason to fix things outside of ourselves (other people, possessions, etc.). Of course, high self-esteem can only exist in a state of genuine self-love. For in a state of genuine self-love there is no fear.

Many persons have a wrong idea of what constitutes true happiness.
It is not attained through self-gratitude but through fidelity to a worthy purpose.

HELEN KELLER (1880–1968)
American memoirist, essayist

Self trust is the essence of heroism.

RALPH WALDO EMERSON (1803–1882)
American poet, essayist, philosopher

BE CAREFUL NOT TO KID YOURSELF!

What happens when you have a conflict between the ideal you hold for yourself and the opposing belief you also hold about yourself? Suppose you believe you are just a bad person. You might then try to balance out that belief with the ideal of being a "good" person in your mind. You will then attempt to fulfill the ideal image of a "good" person by doing what a "good" person does. Your behaviors and actions would thus be motivated by *avoiding* or moving away from the problem of being a bad person. No matter how many "good" deeds you were to do to contradict the belief of being "bad," you would only be kidding yourself! Why do that? You'll just be hurting the self-esteem you are building up.

Look at your motivation. *Being good is not just the absence of bad any more than being healthy is just the absence of illness.* You don't become healthy just by moving away from bad habits, although that helps. If you want to be healthy, you must believe that you are a healthy person (it's a state of mind). That motivation will cause you to then do the things that a healthy person does, moving you toward good health automatically. You will no longer have to think about not doing things that are bad, because as a healthy person you will only do those things that are good for you. Self-esteem is self-love! It is a vital step along your journey to Riches.

IS FEAR HOLDING YOU BACK?

CHAPTER 12 OF PART 2

Now we are going to talk about one of the biggest roadblocks most people face on *The Lazy Man's Way to Riches*. We have already discussed the fact that all it really takes to get what we want out of life is a *burning desire* and the *belief* that we can have it. So why don't we have everything now? It is not that we don't have motivation, and it is not that we don't have the right kind of experience. It is not that we don't have the right basic equipment with which to start. The problem is not what we don't have at all. It is something that we do have that gets in our way. And that something is FEAR.

I am not talking about the kind of fear that keeps us from placing ourselves in danger or risking our lives unnecessarily. There is nothing wrong with being afraid of stepping in front of a speeding car. There is nothing wrong with being afraid if someone is holding a gun on you and robbing you. Fear, in this case, plays a very important role — it is protective. Also it is generally short-lasting. Once the real danger is gone, the fear usually disappears. There is another kind of fear that is not valuable to us. In fact, it is always destructive to our success and happiness. It does not involve any real danger or life threat. It usually arises in anticipation of something that almost never happens, and this kind of fear can hang around for a long time and be a continuing blight on our lives and happiness.

Suppose you have a great idea. It is an idea for making a lot of money and it has tremendous potential. Suppose that you tell me your idea and I am impressed by it. A week or so later I call you up and say, "I would like you to come over and go through your idea again in front of some friends of mine." Your feeling would probably be "Great, I would like to do that," and you would look forward to it with some anticipation. But suppose I go on and say, "The group of

People are afraid of the future, of the unknown. If a man faces up to it, and takes the dare of the future, he can have some control over his destiny. That's an exciting idea to me. Better than waiting with everybody else to see what's going to happen..

JOHN H. GLENN, JR. (B. 1921)
American astronaut, U.S. Senator

No passion so effectively robs the mind of all its powers of acting and reasoning as fear.

EDMUND BURKE (1729–1797)
English statesman, orator, writer

So let me assert my firm belief that the only thing we have to fear is fear itself—nameless, unreasoning, unjustified terror which paralyzes needed efforts to convert retreat into advance.

FRANKLIN D. ROOSEVELT (1882–1945)
32nd President of the United States

people to whom I want you to explain this is a group of the most successful people in the country. There will be about 200 of them there, and you will be on a stage in front of this group." Now what happens? How do you feel? What changes? All of a sudden it becomes something frightening. "How will I ever impress the most successful people in the country? What have I got to say that they will be interested in? Suppose I goof up?" All kinds of things go through your mind that have nothing to do with the actual situation. But they have everything to do with the kind of fear I am talking about.

WHAT DO YOU FEAR MOST?

I read a national survey some time ago in which people were asked to identify their greatest fears. Believe it or not, the number-one answer was fear of speaking in public. Ahead even of the fear of death. More people were afraid of speaking in public than dying. Now I have spoken many times in public and it is neither dangerous nor life-threatening so why are people afraid to do it? Why are they so much more afraid of public speaking than of real dangers? They are in the grip of nonessential fears. What are these fears? There are a lot of variations in the area of nonessential fears, but there are three that seem to be the most crippling. Starting with the Fear of Criticism, which leads to the Fear of Rejection, which, in turn, leads to the Fear of Failure. And these three — Fear of Criticism, Fear of Rejection, and Fear of Failure — are the biggest roadblocks that stand in most people's way to success.

ORIGIN OF FEARS?

So where do you get these fears? And if they are so limiting and so destructive to us, why don't you just get rid of them? It all starts when you are young and defenseless. As a baby you do not want much. You are not afraid of anything when you are born, except loud noises and falling.

All you really need is to be held fairly often, to be fed and changed, and basically left on your own to sleep and just "be" the rest of the time. But as you begin to grow up, life begins to make demands on us and in the process of meeting those demands you sometimes make mistakes. You encounter the anger or disapproval of your parents, who are extremely important to us, which results in a feeling of rejection — and it hurts. You begin to experience pain. You believe that when things go wrong, it is your fault — that there is something wrong with you. Now that is a very painful feeling to a child.

Because you are criticized for making mistakes and feel the pain of rejection, you grow up with the false idea that making mistakes is failing. And because failing is the biggest mistake of all, what do you do if you feel there is any risk of failure? You don't try. And what happens when you don't try? Then you fail absolutely. That really puts us into a trap, doesn't it? You're dammed if you do, and dammed if you don't. To escape the criticism of others for trying and failing, you procrastinate and don't try at all, which opens you up to self-criticism. That is the worst kind, because there is no way you can escape that.

FEAR CONDITIONING

Although few people ever realize it, fear plays an overwhelmingly important role in the early-child conditioning. Since you have that early conditioning to thank for our later Inadequate Self-Image (ISI), it is important that you understand two unique qualities of fear as a conditioning factor.

1. Fear is always a "hindering" force.

2. Fear is generally a "buried" force.

Let me illustrate those two qualities by two specific examples of fear-conditioning.

Praise for a job well done, as in the case of the wise

It is hard to fail, but it is worse to have not tried to succeed. In this life we get nothing save by effort.

THEODORE ROOSEVELT (1858–1919)
26th President of the United States

Feelings of inferiority and superiority are the same. They both come from fear.

ROBERT ANTHONY, Ph.D. (B. Withheld by request)
American psychologist, writer

father with the child who wants to participate in the workshop project, is a "helping" force. It is positive in nature; it is a happily remembered experience. Praise is something to be sought after. You want to repeat the pleasure of the feeling of being praised so you try again and again to do something that earns more praise.

What of the other side of the coin — the rejection or punishment unwisely meted out? It is designed to be and operates as a "hindering force." It is negative in nature. It creates fear. It creates fear of the painful experience being repeated; and, since it is unpleasant to remember, it is shut out of the conscious mind as soon as possible. Notice I said the "conscious" mind; for with the strong impact of fear, *it is not lost entirely.* It plays its conditioning role long after the conscious remembrance is gone. It is suppressed and slips down into the subconscious mind.

So, we have fear, which hinders us in years to come, but which is *hidden* from our conscious thoughts.

To observe this in action, let us assume that some years after the child had been rewarded or reprimanded (perhaps on several occasions) in the manner outlined, a new situation arises.

The father calls his son and announces the time has come to "learn how to handle tools." Father anticipates great joy on the part of his son at this announcement. He is looking forward to the fun he and his son will have working together in the wood shop. But such will not be the case.

The son does not *remember* the things that happened so long ago when he was so young, but he *feels* very uneasy. He has been conditioned to fear the woodworking, or anything in connection with it. Is it surprising that the son probably won't be very excited about the idea, will have trouble trying to do what his father asks, will be prone to fail when he tries (thus releasing him from having to continue)?

Some prime examples of the kind of *deliberate* remarks that become conditioning for the very young carry in their own terms the fear-factor they will create.

"You're stupid."
"You never do anything right."
"'You're always so clumsy."
"You'll never learn anything."
"You'll never be as (smart, nice, good, etc.) as your (brother, sister)."
"I know you're always lying . . . I'll never believe you."

When we add to this the number of unintentional conditionings that come about accidentally (through spilling things, breaking objects, saying the wrong thing, various other childhood mistakes) it is not surprising that many, many fears of failure have found a permanent home deep in our subconscious minds. All these fears help shape our view of ourselves. And so fear is largely responsible for our ISI.

Why is the conditioning of the early years so effective in shaping today's image and even activities of an adult? Because the subconscious levels of the mind, while powerful, are *noncritical.* What is fed into them is all accepted as fact without any regard to logic or later learning.

NEW CONDITIONING

To alter conditioning of this sort, you must bring new conditioning to bear. It does not matter that we know *today* that a failure at the age of four does not decree similar failures as an adult. The conscious mind uses logic, the unconscious does not.

The best way to understand this is to think of dreams you have had in the past in which impossibilities seemed quite reasonable while you were asleep. "I was flying through space," "I was in this house . . . but it became a boat," "I fell off the cliff but I just floated to the ground."

Where fear is, happiness is not.

SENECA (4 B.C.–A.D. 65)
Roman philosopher, playwright

None of these things seem unreasonable while we are sleeping, but awake we would recognize them immediately as impossibilities.

They are accepted while asleep because the lower level of consciousness has *no critical* judgment or logic. This means that all those fears you have suppressed to the below-consciousness level stay there unchallenged by reality as you have grown and matured in your conscious mind.

The fears and repressed impressions of your childhood years, based on the most childish lack of understanding, often rule your activities today!

You can give yourself *new conditioning* thru Dyna/Psyc to replace that faulty old conditioning that is blocking your way to success.

That conditioning permits you to both be a more adequate person and also to see yourself as more adequate. These two things accomplished, you are a success!

For realizing to the maximum *your* true potential, instead of limiting yourself to the ISI view of your potential, will make all the difference in the world.

THE CHAIN OF FEAR — A DEAD END

How do you get rid of the fears that are so destructive to your life? How do you avoid hanging on to the dead-end of the chain of fear? The answer is really quite simple: You have to take control of the chain by becoming aware of it and how it is formed. This is not to say that you can wave a magic wand and banish fear forever; but understanding where the chain starts — with criticism — and how the next links are formed, you can take steps to stop forging those links.

REDEFINE REJECTION

The first linkage in the chain of self-limiting fears you can break is the idea that criticism necessarily means

Nothing in life is to be feared; it is only to be understood.

MARIE CURIE (1867–1934)
French chemist

rejection and there is something wrong with you. Again, nothing could be further from the truth. Most of the time criticism from others really comes from one of two things. They may be feeling self-critical and vulnerable and criticize you before you have a chance to criticize them. Or maybe they are angry about something and criticism is simply their way of venting that anger. In either case, the problem is theirs, not yours, and that is important to realize. When someone criticizes you, remember, their criticism is probably an expression of their own insecurity and doubt or of their own anger, which is not necessarily directed at you. You just happen to be there at the time, and if it weren't you it would be someone else experiencing their anger and frustration.

REDEFINE FAILURE

Second, you can break the chain by taking a good look at what it means to try and fail — to understand it intellectually. What is failure? Most of us have the idea that failure is a sin. Our schools tend to reinforce that idea. We study the final results of peoples' lives and don't look at their early mistakes. We look at Leonardo Da Vinci or Michelangelo's masterpieces and not at their initial attempts. We don't look at the poems that did not work for Keats and Shelley, only the masterpieces that survive. Their first efforts wound up in their wastebaskets. We get the impression that these people were somehow born with a mature talent, fully developed skills, never made mistakes and that everything they did was perfect. Nothing could be further from the truth!

I'll bet their wastebaskets were as overflowing as yours and mine are. Every great artist, every great scientist, and every businessman made thousands of mistakes before they made the masterpieces that we study and admire.

Thomas Edison is a great example. He tried thousands of different ways to make the light bulb work. And once

Everything we say about other people is really about ourselves.

MERRIT MALLOY
American poet

Never confuse a single defeat with a final defeat.

F. SCOTT FITZGERALD (1896–1940)
American novelist, short-story writer

Experience is the name so many people give to their mistakes.

OSCAR WILDE (1854-1900)
Irish-born English poet, playwright, novelist

Failure is only an event in your life—not a life.

ANONYMOUS

We fear the thing we want the most.

ROBERT ANTHONY, Ph.D. (B. Withheld by request)
American psychologist, writer

when an interviewer asked him how he could continue to go on after thousands of failures, Edison replied, "I haven't failed thousands of times. I succeeded in finding thousands of ways that the process won't work." That's how you have to learn to regard failure, as attempts that just didn't work — *or as another way to define experience!*

Failure is nothing more than a successful way of finding out how a process won't work. If you try, make a mistake and then analyze why you made the mistake, and through that analysis find out how the process really works, you will have learned a great deal! There is no shame in failing. Failing is a necessary part of growth and development. If you have never made a mistake it means you have not really tried anything new. And if you have never tried anything new, that is the biggest failure of all. You see, the only real failure occurs when you stop trying.

BUT YET ANOTHER FEAR

Now that we have looked at the fear of failure, let's take a look at the opposite side of the coin — the fear of success. How can success be something you are afraid of? Easy, you have been programmed that way and you may be reinforcing that bad programming every day. Most often it is the fear of success that is the cause of our failures rather than tangible reasons. You can see abundance all around you. It's there for you to enjoy. You can even understand the ideas necessary to claim your share of that abundance and still not make a move to get it, if you don't understand how to root out this fear.

One of the keys to overcoming the Fear of Success is what I call "Just Consequences." In this world there are no rewards or punishments. There are Just Consequences. And *Just* means both only and fair. If you believe in a Creator who is responsible for all life as you believe that our Creator gave us free will, which is a fundamental belief in every major religion, if you believe that our Creator is just and fair, then it's essential to accept the principle of "Just Consequences." Does it seem reasonable that our Creator would give us free will and then slap us down if we did not make the right choices? I am not talking about the after life. I am talking about the here and now. I believe God does not reward or punish us for our choices. With God's blessing we can make any choice we want and then live with the consequences of our decisions. That is what our lives are — the total of all the consequences of all the decisions we have made.

LEARN TO ENJOY

I also believe that our Creator intended us to enjoy the fruits of his creation — not to suffer in this life in hopes of reward in heaven later on. I realize I may step on some toes with this concept, but this is important to your progress down *The Lazy Man's Way.* Some religions teach that the requirement for heaven is suffering and pain in this life. You may likely have picked up some of that kind of teaching at least down in your subconscious. How many times have you heard expressions like "Poor, but happy," or "Poor little rich kid?" How many times have you seen news stories about some rich person or family that suffered some kind of loss or catastrophe and thought to yourself, "I wouldn't want to be in their shoes for any amount of money?" Sure, there are rich people who suffer, and you read about them because it makes a good story. But there are a lot more wealthy people who are very happy. They raise families of wholesome kids, who contribute significantly to our society, and about whom you don't read because there is no news value in their lives. Every one of the tales you have heard about the sufferings of the rich or successful people is a roadblock, a speed bump, on your way to Riches.

Whatever the source of your beliefs, most of us have been taught to fear success or to distrust it. Haven't you

In nature there are neither rewards nor punishments— there are consequences.

ROBERT GREEN INGERSOLL (1833–1899)
American lawyer, public official, agnostic

The man who fears suffering is already suffering from what he fears.

MICHEL DE MONTAIGNE (1533–1593)
French moralist, essayist

heard expressions like, "You have to pay your dues," or "Sure you can be rich if you want to do nothing but work all the time," or "I would rather have health than wealth." As if you can't have both!

These statements create an attitude of fearing success, and if you have that sort of attitude you have a mighty big roadblock to get past. It is difficult to sustain the effort required to change your course in life if you are afraid you will lose something of value along the way. There's no doubt that you have to pay a price for your success, but the essential truth of *The Lazy Man's Way* is that you actually learn to enjoy that price while you are paying it. You don't make sacrifices. Besides, it is also a fact of life that you pay a price for failure as well. The difference is you never learn to enjoy the price of failure and you never stop paying it.

THE PROCRASTINATION HABIT

We have discussed how the three big fears lead to the habit of procrastination — a big problem in anyone's life. There is no question that putting off until tomorrow things that could be done today is one of the most serious obstacles you encounter on your journey through life. Living courageously is taking action in the presence of fear, making a conscious growth choice rather than a fear choice. Part of the fears that produce this habit lie buried in your subconscious. To get at them on that level, you will need the power of Super Suggestion, which is available to review in Chapter 10 of Part 1, as well as other simple tools you can start using right now that will begin to break the procrastination habit. As in all changes of habit, you need to be reminded that you are changing that habit. First, make a positive statement about that change and a positive statement about the attitude you are trying to develop. Write a note to yourself on a Post-It and put it up in a prominent place, someplace where you will see it often

To live with fear and not be afraid is the final test of maturity.

EDWARD WEEKS (1898–1989)
American editor, lecturer, essayist

Men never plan to be failures; they simply fail to plan to be successful.

WILLIAM A. WARD (1812–1882)
English theologian, writer, editor

One of these days is none of these days.

ENGLISH PROVERB

during the day to remind you that you are becoming a different person and that you are doing things differently. Each time you see this sign take the time to read it. Plant it deeply in your mind and think about what it means.

The note is very simple. It contains the three words "Do It Now" and it applies to any situation or problem that you meet that needs resolution. Remember, each time you read the words "Do It Now," that good judgement is the result of experience — of learning from your mistakes. So accept mistakes as a necessary part of your development.

Knowledge of what is possible
is the beginning of happiness.

GEORGE SANTAYANA (1863–1952)
Spanish-born American philosopher,
poet, novelist, critic

Y ou can use the material in this book to get everything you really want out of life. The only thing
that's in your way is you: The old you; the old
habits; the old attitudes.

The reason it's so hard to be free of these negative
forces is that they're *comfortable.* You've had them a long
time. You've grown used to them. You've accepted them.

You've brainwashed yourself, or more likely, someone
— your parents, your friends, your teachers, your boss —
has done it for you. They meant well. They wanted you to
be "happy," and their notion of happiness is that you should
be satisfied with things as they are.

You accepted their definition of "happiness" because
you wanted to please them. Well, I want you to be *unhappy.* Or more to the point, I want you to be *creatively unhappy.* I don't want you to accept things as they "are." I want
you to make life what it *can* and *should* be for you.

How will you do that? By letting Dyna/Psyc take over
your life! Right now. This minute. If you say you "will" do
it, you've postponed making a decision until some future
date. Now is the time to act, because today is the first day
of the rest of your life.

Don't waste time looking back, savoring old regrets,
cherishing old mistakes, crying over lost opportunities.

When Eleanor Roosevelt was asked how she had so
much energy for so many different projects, she replied,
"Because I never waste time looking back."

Let's say that you had your choice of two routes to take
you to work. Both were the same distance and took you the
same time; but one route was along a tree-lined freeway
with little traffic, and the other route was ugly, choked with
traffic, bristling with stop signs —and ran right alongside a
garbage dump. Which one would you take?

The first one, of course! Then why, as we go through life, do most of us take the second route — inhaling deeply as we pass yesterday's garbage, bringing the stink of yesterday's waste into today?

The answer? We don't know that there's another, more pleasant route to get where we're going. It *doesn't* take the same amount of time — It's faster! And the destination can be the one you *choose* — not the one you thought you had to accept.

Don't tell me you "can't." What you really mean is you "won't." And that's not you talking — It's that Inadequate Self-Image — your ISI.

Let me show you, once again, how ISI works:

A number of years ago I handled the advertising for a Ford agency. One day, when the manager was making out the salesmen's paychecks, he commented on something that, at first, seemed unbelievable. He noted that each and every salesman earned just about the same amount each month as he had made the month before. If there was a monthly variance, the salesman would almost always earn, within a few percentage points, during the current year what he had earned the year before.

I checked into it further and found that there was an even stranger "coincidence." The Ford agency divided its sales-month into three 10-day periods. About 50 percent of the salesmen plugged along each day and ended up with the commission check they expected to make. Another 25 percent made enough sales during the *first* 10 days to provide what they anticipated as their monthly income and — never made another sale. Oh, they showed up for work, all right, and went through the motions; but nothing ever clicked. If you asked them what had happened, they would have told you it was "bad luck" or someone else was getting all the "buyers." The last 25 percent made little or no sales until the *last* 10 days of the month. Then suddenly, during those final 10 days, these salesmen got "hot."

Give me where to stand,
and I will move the Earth.

ARCHIMEDES (287–212 BC)
Syracusan mathematician, astronomer, inventor

The fact is, regardless of the pattern of sales, each salesperson made what they expected to make. Not what they wished they could make or would *like* to make (and really didn't think was possible) — but what they expected to make. Without exception, each person got what they *really* wanted!

LET ME GIVE YOU ANOTHER EXAMPLE Another advertising account of mine was a real estate firm. They were expanding and wanted to attract some new, top-flight salesmen. So they placed an ad that stated, truthfully, that people who were willing to come to work for them could earn $100,000 a year. The ad laid an egg. So they changed one word and had so many responses that they could pick the cream of the crop.

The word, or rather the figure, they changed was "$100,000." They made it "$40,000."

And now that you know a little bit about ISI, you can see why the first ad failed and the second ad was successful. Very few people can imagine what it would be like to earn $100,000 a year, or more important, truly believe that they're worth that much, so they didn't even bother answering or investigating the "impossible" (for them) ad.

That's why the *prettiest* girls spend a lot of lonely nights. Most of the boys think they're "unattainable."

And here's the payoff on my true story about the real estate firm. Many of the people who couldn't imagine themselves making $100,000 a year wound up making that much and more because the real estate firm had a training program to raise their ISI!

I mentioned that the real estate firm "picked the cream of the crop." They did — but the standards were not age, education, or experience. They picked those people who were willing to *change,* to accept the "possibility" that life could be a lot better.

Once you've picked your destination, Dyna/Psyc is the vehicle capable of taking you there swiftly and pleasurably.

It requires only routine maintenance and that you do not cripple its performance with an ISI governor.

You don't have to understand the principle of internal combustion to drive a car, but you do have to turn on the key. I've given you the key. It's called Dyna/Psyc. Use it.

ACCENTUATE THE POSITIVE

I talk a lot about money. That's because it's an easy way to measure "success." As Pearl Bailey said, "I've been rich and I've been poor, but rich is better."

Not that money solves all problems. Some of the most miserable people I've known have been millionaires. They were miserable because they thought that money would make them happy. But they weren't miserable *because* they were rich. If they lost their money, they'd just be poor and miserable.

That's why it's important that you let Dyna/Psyc change *all* of your life, let it make you the kind of *person* you want to be and can be.

You can be a loving, forgiving, and generous person. (In fact, you can be one heck of a nice person to be around.) You can be an understanding but firm parent. You can be a true friend. You can be a trustworthy, hard-working, and loyal employee. (And if you can't, fire yourself and get another job. You'll be doing the boss and you — especially you — a big favor.) You can be a good neighbor.

You can be anything you really want to be.

And as you change, so will the people around you. Remember that if you want to teach someone to love, give them affection. If you want them to have confidence, give them encouragement. If you want them to be truthful, tell the truth. If you want them to be generous, share. If you want them to be patient, be tolerant. If you want them to be happy, give them understanding.

You can't affirm for other people. You can — and must — affirm how you *respond* to them. If you allow someone to

I don't like money, actually, but it quiets my nerves!

JOE LOUIS (1914–1981)
American boxer

Learn what you are and be such.

PINDAR (522–438 BC)
Greek poet

"bug" you, it's *your* problem. You may not be able to change how they act, but you can change how you react.

Remember Dr. Eric Berne's *The Games People Play?* You'll be surprised at how often people stop throwing the ball to you, if you never make an effort to catch it.

Finally, accept yourself as an imperfect, fallible human being — not that you ever stop trying to improve; but you recognize that you'll probably never quite attain 100 percent in all of your zones.

When you realize — and truly accept — that you're imperfect, isn't it easier to accept and understand other people's imperfections?

To illustrate, I'd like to tell you about a friend of mine in Los Angeles.

Late one night, he received a phone call that his son was confined in a mental health clinic in San Francisco. The boy, about 19 years old, had made an unsuccessful attempt at suicide. The psychiatrist on the phone reassured the father that his son was in no physical danger but suggested that a personal interview with the father might be helpful. Could he fly to San Francisco?

When the father arrived the next day, in the late afternoon, the son was angry because the father had "taken so long." He demonstrated his anger by refusing to speak to his father.

When the psychiatrist had them both in his office, he asked the boy why he was giving his father "the silent treatment." The boy told him.

"I see," said the psychiatrist. "So you've made up your mind as to what your father should have done. And you won't settle for any less. You think that a good father — a 100 percent father — would have taken an earlier plane. So you're discounting him for every hour he was late, by your standards.

"Well, the fact *is* that he is here. So he must care at least a *little*. Maybe 10 percent? Are you saying that, if you can't have a 100 percent father, you won't take any less?"

My friend told me later: "I flew up to San Francisco filled with guilt and anger. 'How had I failed my son? How could he do this to me?' But the psychiatrist's question started me thinking. 'Maybe I have been a 10 percent father. And he's been a 10 percent son. O.K. I'll try to do better. But starting right now, I'd better accept his 10 percent instead of rejecting *all* of him because he hasn't entirely lived up to the standards I've set for *him*.'" It was the start of an understanding between father and son.

People like people who like them. After all, anyone who has such good taste must have other redeeming qualities. And people reward the people they like with favors, love, promotions, business — everything. But they can't like you unless you like you — and them. I'm talking about your *genuinely* admiring that percentage of the whole person — in yourself and others — that you find likeable.

The amazing thing is that, as you reprogram your life through Dyna/Psyc, you'll find that everything else literally falls into place. One day, very soon, something you are affirming — something you thought was "impossible" — will happen. You will have *made* it happen.

You are indeed the cause of all your effects.

All things are possible until they are proved impossible—and even the impossible may only be so, as of now.

PEARL S. BUCK (1892–1973)
American novelist, humanitarian

BOOK ONE
THE JOURNEY

□

PART 3: The Destination – Your Way!

BALANCING YOUR LIFE — WHAT A CONCEPT!

CHAPTER 1 OF PART 3

At the beginning of our journey together I was telling you what this program was all about. I mentioned that there were three basic questions we were going to ask that are fundamental to all existence:

1. Who are you? (Repeat "Who am I?")

2. Where are you going? (Repeat "Where am I going?")

3. How do you plan to get there? (Repeat "How do I plan to get there?")

Most of what you have done up to now has been working on the question "Who are you?" (Repeat — "Who am I?") and you still haven't quite finished answering that question. I will cover some important parts of the answer to that question in later chapters, but right now I want to talk about exactly where you want to go. Before you answer that question, let's examine the limits of your potential. Of what are you really capable? If you really don't see yourself as successful at this point, you may have a limited view of your capabilities. Let me tell you about some people who started out with several strikes against them and still became exceptional human beings and achieved tremendous things in life.

EINSTEIN — GREAT SCIENTIST

We have all heard of Albert Einstein, discoverer of the Theory of Relativity. The advances in physics that Einstein has made will affect human lives for generations to come; yet Einstein was a notoriously poor student. Teachers could not communicate with him. He had difficulty in getting his ideas across, and he nearly flunked the eighth grade.

LINCOLN — GREAT PRESIDENT

Another name you will recognize is Abraham Lincoln.

Never look down to test the ground before taking your next step; only he who keeps his eye fixed on the far horizon will find his right road.

DAG HAMMARSKJOLD (1905–1961)
Swedish statesman, U.N. Secretary General

Some men succeed because they are destined to, but most men because they are determined to.

ANONYMOUS

*Few great men
could pass personnel.*

PAUL GOODMAN (1911-1972)
American writer, educator,
psychoanalyst

*Nothing great will ever be
achieved without great men,
and men are great only if they
are determined to be so.*

CHARLES DE GAULLE (1890-1970)
French general and statesman
President of the 5th Republic of France

*God gives the nuts, but he does
not crack them.*

GERMAN PROVERB

Lincoln is almost universally recognized as one of the greatest American presidents. Still he lost more elections than he won and at one point in his life suffered a complete nervous breakdown. And we all know where he started — in a humble cabin reading by candlelight and going barefoot. If Lincoln could rise from that to the presidency of the United States of America and become one of its greatest leaders of all time, what are you capable of accomplishing in your life?

ROCKEFELLER — RESPECTED NATIONAL LEADER

Let's look at another person, one of whom you may have a more recent memory, Nelson Rockefeller. When Rockefeller was a child he was classified as "learning disabled." Now I suspect that if the Rockefeller family had less money he probably would have been called "dumb." But Nelson Rockefeller overcame that learning problem to become a respected national leader. So if you have had people call you "dumb" in your life, you are in good company. Perhaps learning did not come easily to you. Your grades in school may have reflected indifference or a mental block which kept you from being a super achiever. That does not need to hold you back now!

EMERSON — GREAT THINKER

One hundred and sixty years ago the great thinker, Ralph Waldo Emerson, wrote that there is nothing capricious in nature. Nature will not plant a burning desire in your mind if you do not have the innate capability to achieve that desire. Whatever you truly and sincerely want out of life you can have because it is within your reach. *You do, however, have to reach out for it!*

If I asked you to name the happiest person you know, who would you name? If you did not respond with, "Me," why not? Why are you not the happiest person you know? If you are not, a lot of reasons come to mind. Stop and think for a minute. How can you measure someone else's happiness? Don't we usually measure someone's happiness relative to ours by the things they seem to have that we don't — good or bad. How can you possibly know what their life is really like? How can you appreciate someone else's problems? If you put someone else's name down, it is an indication that you think you could be happier. Even if you put your own name down as the happiest person you know, certainly you will accept the idea that life can be better for you. You would not be reading this book if you didn't.

It is not easy to find happiness in ourselves and it is not possible to find it elsewhere.

AGNES REPPLIER (1858–1950)
American essayist

AND YOU — ????

Well, how can you be happier? The key to happiness lies in understanding two concepts. *One is the need for balance in all areas of your life. And the other is the need for continuing expansion in those areas.* What do I mean by the areas of life? What are they? All of us have certain basic needs in many areas. You probably responded to this book because you felt a need in the financial area of your life. But that is only one of many areas as we discovered when we did Chapter 6 of Part 1 and dealt with the seven basic areas of life: Financial, Mental, Emotional, Social, Vocational, Physical, and Spiritual. Let's look at these areas more fully at this time.

The Financial Area is obvious. We all have needs here. Strangely some people will deny those needs and live in poverty and for some this is possible. For some people it is possible to become a hermit and live away from society. But most of us have basic financial needs. We need to feed and clothe and to shelter ourselves and our families. That takes money.

What is the Mental Area of our life? Our needs in this area are our needs for stimulation and growth, for challenge to make our mind work and keep it active. All of us benefit from the stimulation and challenge of developing our character and our skills as we continue to grow.

The Emotional Area is of prime concern for most of us. It is the area in our life that determines how we feel inside about ourselves. And because this feeling dictates how we

Our duty as men is to proceed as if limits to our ability did not exist.

PIERRE TEILHARD DE CHARDIN
(1881–1955)
French clergyman, philosopher, paleontologist

make most of our decisions, it is extremely important to be "whole" in this area.

The Social Area. This is about your relationship to your fellow man, your communications with him and his communication with you, your mutual support and cooperative progress toward understanding one another and achieving harmony.

Most of us feel that our family is the most important part of the social area of our lives, so growth here is paramount. Too often I've heard people say, "If only . . . " as regards to a departed loved one. Have the relationship you want now.

The Vocational Area. As I said earlier, we are ultimately our own boss so if your career isn't all you want it to be, do what any good boss would do for an employee who needs help — get it for them! Coaches, mentors, tutors, additional education, retraining — whatever it takes for your vocational growth and prosperity.

The Physical Area of our life is obvious. It is our physical health and fitness, our bodies, our sense of well-being, our energy level, how we feel. With a healthy body everything else seems more easily obtainable.

Finally, there is the Spiritual Area of our lives. Our need to understand our spiritual mission in life, our relationship with our God, and our place in the universe.

I feel it is vital to realize the importance of *balance* in all of these areas. It makes no more sense to deny your spiritual needs than it does to deny your financial needs. They exist. And if you do not put some effort into this area, your life will be out of balance no matter how financially successful you are and you will miss out on a lot of the Riches that life has to offer. In fact our experiences have shown, when the spiritual area of your life expands, the other areas seem to develop and balance out much more easily.

It is indeed from the experience of beauty and happiness from the occasional harmony between our nature and our environment, that we draw our conception of the divine life.

GEORGE SANTAYANA (1932–1952)
Spanish-born American philosopher, poet, novelist, critic

WHO'S DRAWING YOUR REALITY MAP?

Let's go on to an examination as to why fears have such a hold on us. The reason is the way you actually think and act. When we observe something we go through a process that virtually involves our entire mind and experience, but we do it so fast that it is usually completed before we are aware of the process. It works in four steps: We see something, we compare it with all the information we have stored in our brain, we make a decision based on this stored information and then we act on that decision. SEE, COMPARE, DECIDE, ACT.

In a sense it is kind of like using a road map. Suppose you wanted to visit our office. You have a map of the area with some intersections marked and the directions you should turn. When you see an intersection coming up, you compare it with your map and decide which way to go and then act on your decision. All of our stored information is kind of like that road map. It is our whole concept of reality: The whole ball of wax; what we think of everything in the universe including ourselves. It is our map of the world, our reality map, and like any map that you have ever seen, it is inaccurate and incomplete. "What's that?" you may say. "Everything I do in life is based on this reality map that I have, and you tell me it is inaccurate and incomplete? How can I ever expect to get anywhere?" Relax. Joe Karbo's map was just as inaccurate and incomplete as yours and it didn't keep him from getting where he wanted to go.

The key is to know when your map is accurate and when it isn't and how to clean it up in the critical areas. For example, when that pike I told you about bumped his nose against the glass wall enough times his reality map contained a road block that permanently prevented him from getting to the minnows. Now as long as those glass walls were there, the pike's reality map was accurate. He

The great thing in this world is not so much where we stand, as in what direction we are moving.

OLIVER WENDELL HOLMES, SR.
(1809–1894)
American physician, professor, man of letters

saw the minnows and he associated it with the pain of his bumped nose. He knew he could not get to them. But the instant the glass walls were removed, the pike's reality map became tragically inaccurate. Like that pike, you have locked into your reality maps certain obstacles and roadblocks — detours that are no longer there. When you think about how your reality map was drawn, it's amazing that it works at all.

As we talked about earlier, as far as we can determine a baby comes into this world basically neutral. He or she has certain physical needs and some emotional needs, but there are no real fixed attitudes about the world that the child has entered — good or bad. If you liken the baby's mind to a balance scale, it starts off perfectly balanced. As you develop from infancy and encounter a concept or a new idea you do not know quite where to put it on the scale. How do you form your attitudes? Well, when you first encounter a new concept or experience you tend to rely on the reactions of other people.

SPINACH — YUK!

Let's go back to your childhood, say around age three or four. Suppose you have never had spinach or have never been aware that what you were eating was spinach. You're out playing with some friends and one friend says, "Gee, would you like to eat over at my house tonight?" Then the friend adds, "Uh oh, maybe you had better wait until tomorrow night. Tonight we are having, ugh, spinach." Now what has happened? Your friend has given you his value judgment with respect to spinach. You had no previous experience with this thing, so you make a decision based on your friend's judgment and your assessment of your friend's credibility as to whether spinach is a good or bad thing. You put some sort of weight on either the positive or the negative side of the balance. Let's say your friend previously told you that ice cream was good and you tested that out and found that the friend was right — it was good. You probably respect that person's judgment in the area of food and so you slightly tip your scale in the direction of thinking the spinach is not such a hot idea.

Now let's suppose that your next experience with spinach is some days later when your mother serves it. You see this green stuff on your plate and you say "Gee, what's that?" And your mother says, "That's spinach." So you say, "I don't think I want it." And your father, who has had a trying day, says, "What do you mean you don't want any. You eat your spinach or I will crack you one." Now something very important has happened. Spinach has been associated with something very negative. A heavy weight comes down on the negative side. Even though you have never tasted it, you already know it is something that has caused you stress and problems. That is the way most of our attitudes are formed. You encounter something and make a decision as to which side of the scale the rock goes on. It's a turning point.

Once you have made a decision, positive or negative, the next piece of information relating to the same subject is going to be evaluated and influenced greatly *in respect to the first decision.* And if the experience has been a strong emotional one, it will further reinforce biases that influence the forming of this belief, as in the case of the desirability of spinach. Your friend's assessment of spinach was probably not that important; but when your father threatened you with a spanking if you didn't eat your spinach, it had a lot of emotional impact behind it which caused the weight that you put on the negative side to be much heavier.

The impact that emotion plays on forming your reality structure is really critical. The stronger the emotion, the heavier the judgment you will develop as a result of the incidence. And the stronger the emotion, the more likely it is that it came from irrational behavior. Here is an example of how this can happen.

I grew up to have my father's looks, my father's speech patterns, my father's posture, my father's walk, my father's opinions and my mother's contempt for my father.

JULES FEIFFER (B. 1929)
American cartoonist

REMEMBER YOUR REPORT CARD?

Suppose as a child you bring home a report card and your parents are sitting there assessing it. They say, "Hmm, you got a 'B' in arithmetic, that's OK; 'A' minus in English, that's fine. You got a "D" in science. What's the matter with you?" And suddenly there is a big issue. Here is an area where strong emotional impact can be made. Now whatever your reasons for getting a 'D' in science, it is probably not the result of any incompetency in that area. Perhaps you felt bad on the day of the test. Maybe you misunderstood a concept that later you would have been able to grasp. Or perhaps you simply have difficulty with that particular teacher. But once your parent comes down on you for your inability in science, the result is a very negative feeling toward the concept of science. You may even accept the irrational conclusion that, "I'm just not good in science." Another turning point. When you feel negative about something it is hard to like it and pay attention to it. So, you find it much more difficult to study, which in turn makes your grade worse, and so on down the line. So the initial impact of an incident augmented by emotion can add up to a very strong negative bias and a very false impression of your true capability.

The other area where you have to be careful is that part of your reality structure that is formed by things that you vividly imagine. One of the worst villains in this area are so-called movie or television comedies. Have you ever noticed how much comedy is derived from putting someone down or making someone look ridiculous? Now laughter is one of our greatest blessings, and you should not take yourselves too seriously; however you need to guard yourself against a lot of garbage that is thrown at you That is really the role of your conscious mind, to filter out your experiences. When you relax while watching TV or a movie or reading a book, you tend to let your guard down. Your imagination becomes involved in what you are seeing, and you start adding these impressions to your reality map without really thinking about what you are doing.

EVALUATING YOUR ROAD MAP

Evaluating the road map you have created may be one of the most challenging things to do as you walk *The Lazy Man's Way.* Seeing if it is as true and accurate as you think it is will take some examination. Is it a true representation of who you are and can be? Comparing how one imagines himself, with one's actual personality and capabilities will reveal the areas of distortion in one's reality road map.

HOW DO YOU PICTURE YOURSELF

I call the pictures of ourselves that are stored in your reality map your self-images. Actually your reality map has three pictures of you: You as you see yourself, You as you want other people to see you, and the real You. And the real You most likely is someone you hardly know is there. The real You probably has capacities far beyond even the picture of yourself you try to present to others. Unfortunately, the real You is the picture you usually believe in the least. Like everything else in your reality structure your pictures of yourself create feelings in you. These feelings about your self-images create your self-esteem.

This is the time to really examine your self-esteem and self-images and start locating some of the biggest inaccuracies in your pictures of yourself. Ask yourself questions that will reveal where you are really short-changing yourself, questions like the following. Do I make decisions based on my own beliefs or those of others? Am I envious of others? Do I approach new challenges confidently? How do I take criticism? Do I accept responsibility for my actions? Do I change the facts a little to preserve my image? How do I accept credit and recognition? Can I respect the feelings of others even if I don't agree with them? Am I embarrassed by the actions of people I'm with? Bottom line — how do I accept myself without regard to what others think?

What you think of me is none of my business.

TERRY COLE-WHITTAKER (B. 1939)
American evangelist, author

You've no idea what a poor opinion I have of myself — and how little I deserve it.

W. S. GILBERT (1836–1911)
English dramatist, librettist, writer

I f your experience with your self-esteem questions was the same as mine when I went through it, you might be feeling pretty low about yourself about now. One of the toughest things in the world is to look at yourself and see what is really there. The questions that you just went through doesn't do that. What it does is show you what you *think* is there. What you have to do is get to what is really there. If you were not happy with the answers to your questions, don't let that worry you, as it doesn't mean you are doomed to failure. All it really means is that you need to do some extra work. You can make best use of this questionnaire in a very important way.

Go back and look at the questions that you believe show low self-esteem and ask yourself *why* the question and your answer is important. Why does this indicate that you don't think as highly of yourself as you might? Make a decision as to whether or not you want to change yourself in that area. For example, if you found that you are constantly sensitive to other peoples' opinions about you, you may feel that this is a virtue. This can be a desirable characteristic, but the degree to which you are sensitive to other people is also very important. Some people are so sensitive to other people's feelings that they give no thought to their own. They worry constantly about what others will think and are never able to take care of their own needs. As a result they live inhibited and bitter lives. You have to make a decision. You can be considerate of other people's feelings, but at the same time you must recognize that you have a right to your own feelings.

As we continue through the book and particularly as you begin to practice utilizing Super Suggestion you are going to develop some specific tools that help you raise your self-esteem and self-images in a hurry. The tools that will

It is easy to live for others; everybody does. I call on you to live for yourselves.

RALPH WALDO EMERSON (1803–1882)
American poet, essayist, philosopher

help you release those false and limiting pictures of what you are really capable. Tools that build in you feelings of confidence and self-appreciation of what you really can do. The reason your self-images and self-esteem are so critical to your development and growth along *The Lazy Man's Way* is because of a basic self-defeating cycle that all of us get trapped in at one time or another.   It looks like this.

When you encounter a new situation, one which challenges you to take some action, to grow and develop as a human being, you create in your own mind an expectation as to how well you will handle this challenge. This is all looked upon as previous experience by your self-image and self-esteem. On a conscious level, you may anticipate success; but your self-images and self-esteem will subconsciously determine an expectation that is lower than what you state you would like to achieve.

EXPECTATIONS DETERMINE PERFORMANCE

Now the interesting thing about your expectations is they absolutely determine your performance. If you wish to accomplish something and your expectation is below what you would like to achieve, your performance will also be below that which is necessary to achieve the results you wish. And what happens then? You evaluate your performance. You sit in judgment of yourself not based on your expectations but rather on what you wanted to achieve. The net result is that you did not live up to what you really wanted to do, so you put yourself down. You become critical of yourself. This self-criticism lowers your self-esteem and self-images and the cycle begins again.

YOUR TOUGHEST CRITIC — YOU

How often do you *praise* yourself for something you have done and accomplished as opposed to the number of times you put yourself down for not really measuring up to what you wanted to achieve? That is the real key as to how the self-defeating self-image cycle works. When you evaluate your performance you rarely praise yourself. Usually you cut yourself down and are harder on yourself than you would be on any other human being. How many times, for example, have you patted yourself on the back for sticking with the exercises in this book? When you pick up this book and start listening to me talking to you, do you give yourself a little congratulatory pat on the back for doing it? I hope so. When you complete each of the steps asked of you do you acknowledge that you have just done an important step for your own improvement? I hope you do. From this point on, I would like you to do that for yourself.

When you successfully accomplish any task, do you give yourself a congratulatory pat for doing it well? Probably not. Suppose you do *not* do something that you feel you should have done. Do you take the opportunity to jump all over yourself for it? If you are human, the answer

If you think you're a second-class citizen, you are.

**TED (ROBERT EDWARD) TURNER III
(B. 1938)
American sportsman, businessman**

is probably "YES." Most of us have been conditioned to put ourselves down more often than put ourselves up. You have been taught somewhere along the line that patting yourself on the back is a bad character trait. You have also been taught somewhere along the line that to be self-critical is a valuable trait. That is a bunch of nonsense! As you can see from your understanding of the cycle I just described, it is extremely important that you put yourself up more than you put yourself down. And when you are in a situation where you are evaluating performance that does not measure up to what you felt you wanted to accomplish, don't be too hard on yourself. I am not saying that you shouldn't evaluate yourself at all. It is essential that you evaluate yourself and learn from your mistakes so that you can grow. *But it is not essential that you put yourself down in the process.*

After all, when you try something new, the chances that you are going to make a mistake are much greater than the chances that you are going to do things perfectly. This is especially true if what you are trying is really new to you. If you are reaching out and trying to change your life, you are going to make mistakes. You have two choices. When you make a mistake or fall short of what you are trying to achieve, you can stamp all over yourself with hobnail boots and use words like "You dummy, you always make mistakes." Or you can say, "I made a mistake." "I was trying something new and I can learn something from that mistake and next time I will do a better job." Which do you think will have a more positive effect on your self-image and self-esteem? If you jump all over yourself it is not going to help because you believe the things you say to yourself. That's true even when you say such things in fun. Your subconscious has no sense of humor and it accepts them as deadly serious. But if when you make a mistake, look at it, evaluate it, figure out why you made the mistake and then tell yourself: "OK, I made a mistake. But I was trying something new. It was a stretch for me and I have learned something from it, so next time I will do a better job"; then

Do not find fault; find a remedy.

HENRY FORD (1863–1947)
American industrialist

what happens to your self-esteem? You have grown. You have learned. You have improved yourself. That improves your self-image and self-esteem. You know a little more than you used to and this in turn will increase your expectations and pulls you in a positive direction toward better performance the next time. Put yourself down, you diminish your performance. *Put yourself up, you increase your performance. It is that simple.*

CHILL OUT! EASE UP!

What is not so simple is to break the habits of a lifetime that have you jumping all over yourself when you make a mistake. You can learn to do it. Learn to look at what you have done wrong, recognize the mistake, and approve of yourself for learning from that mistake. Learn that when you do something right, even if it is an everyday sort of thing, you should give yourself a pat on the back; and never, never, never, under any circumstances, miss an opportunity to praise yourself for doing something significant and new correctly. Too often when we do something right we think, "Oh, anybody can do that." *But you actually did it!* You have to pay conscious attention to the process of building your self-images and self-esteem so that you can raise your expectations and improve your performance. And if you keep making the same mistake over and over again, remember, you have just been at the effect of a habit trigger; and if you jump on yourself for making that mistake, you are just aggravating the problem.

BE CAREFUL WHERE YOU SET YOUR THERMOSTAT

The reason our reality map is so important, especially our self-images and self-esteem, is that our reality map works like a thermostat. If you want to raise the temperature in a room, you turn up the thermostat. You don't build a fire in the middle of the floor. Trying to improve your performance without raising your thermostat

What it lies in our power to do, it lies in our power not to do.

ARISTOTLE (384–322 B.C.)
Greek philosopher

is like building a fire. It may work for a while but it sure isn't the easiest way to do it. You see this often with people in the area of making money and you see it again with another common American problem, losing weight. You have an image of yourself and you consistently do things to live up or down to that image.

People have a picture of themselves. Let's say they weigh 180 pounds and they would like to weigh 160, but the mental picture they have of themselves is at the heavier weight. So they diet and diet and try to lose the twenty pounds. Maybe they even succeed or at least get most of it off. But since they haven't changed their mental thermostat, they still see themselves at that heavier weight. So within a short time, they pop right back up. How do you change your weight? How do you change your income? You do it by changing your thermostat. How do you change your thermostat? You do it by becoming conscious of the way you talk to yourself about yourself.

You can do it with five words — PUT YOURSELF UP OR SHUT UP. This means that when you are talking to yourself or to anyone else you should find a way to put yourself up or put them up or don't talk at all. My mom used to say, "If you can't say something good about someone, don't say anything at all!" Write yourself this message and put it up where you can see it and practice it. Every time you find yourself jumping all over yourself for a mistake you made, block that criticism with the words PUT YOURSELF UP OR SHUT UP. Change that criticism around. Recognize you have made a mistake. You have learned something from it and the next time you will do better. Get started on your conscious mind today. Get into the habit of putting up or shutting up.

He who undervalues himself is justly undervalued by others.

WILLIAM HAZLITT (1778–1830)
English essayist, critic

D o you find it easy to put yourself up? Or do you find that all those years of conditioning make you feel a little self-conscious and a little silly every time you gave yourself a thumbs up or a pat on the back? Don't let those years of negative conditioning get in the way of doing something positive about your future. Don't be a pike surrounded by glass walls. One of those walls is that you are not worthy of praise and you shouldn't praise yourself. Don't let that glass wall stop you. It does not exist. It is just the echo of past training. Nobody likes a braggart, it's true, but we are not asking you to brag about yourself to yourself or to other people. We are simply asking you to recognize the true value of your own accomplishments; a very important step if you are going to walk *The Lazy Man's Way to Riches* and success.

Isn't today a wonderful day? Don't you feel full of energy and enthusiasm on a day like today? What's that? You don't think it is such a hot day? And you're not full of energy and enthusiasm? Why not? So the weather outside isn't the greatest, what difference does it make? And why should the weather determine your attitude? And if you're not exactly bubbling over with energy and enthusiasm today, why not? Who determines what kind of a day it is for you? Who is responsible for how you feel? The weatherman? The alarm clock? Your spouse or any other family member who happened to get up on the wrong side of the bed? Or maybe it is the morning news broadcast with its unbroken chain of disasters. Just who is the most influential person in your life? Here's a flash for you — YOU ARE. And you are the one who determines what kind of day today is going to be for you. What if you are one of those people whose bones ache in a certain kind of weather? Well, then they will ache. But you still have the choice between focusing on your aches and pains and letting that destroy your day or focusing on living today to

One of man's greatest failings is that he looks almost always for an excuse, in the misfortune that befalls him through his own fault, before looking for a remedy—which means he often finds the remedy too late.

CARDINAL DE RETZ (1614–1679)
French prelate, writer

210

the fullest extent, accomplishing and advancing toward your goals. Our minds are amazing. When you concentrate in one area, you tend to block out other things. Focus on your aches and pains and they will get worse. Focus on the woes of the world and you can easily get depressed and tired. Focus on your purpose and where you are going in life, reinforce your plans with some activity, and the aches and bad news will fade into the background.

Your moods and feelings are the direct result of the thoughts on which you choose to dwell. You have the choice, so you are responsible for the way you feel and what kind of a day today turns out to be for you. You cannot control your environment, but you are absolutely the only one who controls how you react to your environment. There are several things you can do to make it easier for you to focus on the excitement of the day, instead of the negative aspects.

START YOUR DAY EARLY

Actually, your attitude toward today started yesterday with the instructions you gave yourself about today. You probably were not aware of them. If you worked long hours yesterday or stayed up too late you may have told yourself, "I'm going to be exhausted tomorrow," and sure enough you were. Or maybe on last night's weather report you heard that today was going to be cold and damp and you told yourself, "That kind of weather always makes my joints ache." And sure enough, it does — and they do.

It is a fact of life and an essential part of *The Lazy Man's Way* to realize that you control the power of your mind. What you plant in your mind about yourself you will experience whether it be physical — "I always catch a cold about this time every year," or emotional — "Rainy days get me down," or mental — "I know I can't figure this problem out." Your mind will respond. Joe used to say that more

With most men, unbelief in one thing springs from blind belief in another.

G. C. LICHTENBERG (1742–1799)
German physicist, writer

The highest possible stage in moral culture is when we recognize that we ought to control our thoughts.

CHARLES DARWIN (1809–1882)
English naturalist

people catch colds as a result of the five o'clock news and TV commercials shouting that this is the flu season than for any other reason. He knew that what you plant in your mind about your emotions is the most important factor in determining how you feel. Your mind, particularly the part of the mind we refer to as the subconscious mind, has tremendous power over you. It can make you wealthy or keep you in poverty.

RESPONSIBILITY — YOU ARE IN CONTROL

To sum it all up, you are responsible (response-able). You have the ability to control your responses to any situation. Fortunately, the subconscious does only what it is told. Fortunately, you are in control of this mighty power because you, the conscious you, can totally control the instructions the subconscious receives. That's the good news. The bad news is that you do not always pay attention to the kinds of instructions your subconscious receives either from you or from others, without your consent and that results in actions of habit we talked of earlier.

For example, have you ever found yourself getting angry with someone over something that wasn't all that important and then wondering afterwards why you made such a fuss? Have you ever found yourself in a situation where you knew exactly what should be done and yet couldn't make yourself do it? And afterwards you wondered, "Why couldn't I have just done it? It would have been so easy."

It is extremely important for you to take control of the way your subconscious is programmed. In fact, it is the single most important secret of *The Lazy Man's Way to Riches* and you can do it with Daily Declarations, Awareness and Super Suggestion. You have already begun part of this.

Rich people live on what they earn and save a little regularly . . . poor people spend everything they earn . . . bankrupt people spend everything they earn and borrow to live.

ED FOREMAN (B. 1933)
American entrepreneur, engineer, author, speaker, seminar leader, member of U.S. Congress

God helps those who help themselves.

ALGERNON SIDNEY (1622-1683)
English politician, author

PLANT THE SEEDS OF SUCCESS

Remember we asked you to write the following declaration.

I ____(Space for your name)____ accept that *everything changes, including myself. I am free of all past limiting attitudes.*

That statement is what we call a Daily Declaration. Suppose I am trying to plant in my mind the firm belief that I use my time efficiently. And let's suppose that at the present I do not use my time as efficiently as I would like. I might design an affirmation like this:

I, _____, (always use your own name in your affirmation—it gets your attention) use my time efficiently. I plan and perform my activities so that, whether at work or at play, I always make the best use of my time.

PLAN POSITIVELY

Notice a couple of things. I used positives. I didn't say I am not disorganized. I talked only in terms of the result I plan to achieve. And I talked as though the result is already true. After all, I am not trying to build the attitude that I will become efficient. I am trying to reinforce the attitude that I am efficient. When I've planted this affirmation enough times, cultivated it with the Awareness principle, which I will talk about shortly, and nurtured it with the Super Suggestion process, I will soon become exactly the kind of person that I have described. This is because that is what I believe about myself and I always behave consistently with my beliefs. Furthermore, I won't have to think about it — it is automatic and therefore easy. Notice I did not have to spell out all the little things that go into being efficient. I simply have to develop the attitude that I am efficient and my subconscious takes care of the rest.

Your next step is to apply the Daily Declaration

The mind is like a clock that is constantly running down and must be wound up daily with good thoughts.

FULTON JOHN SHEEN, BISHOP (1895–1979)
American religious leader, author

Man is not a being who stands still, he is a being in the process of becoming. The more he enables himself to become, the more he fulfills his true mission.

RUDOLPH STEINER (1861–1925)
Austrian philosopher

Freedom is the will to be
responsible to ourselves.

FRIEDRICH NIETZSCHE (1844–1900)
German philosopher

process to an important concept. The concept of "Response-ability." The ability to control your responses. Make several copies of the following declaration.

> *I, _____ , (always use your own name in your affirmation — it gets your attention) accept response-ability. I know that I have the ability to control my response to any situation.*

As usual, tape them up where you will see them frequently. On your bathroom mirror, on the dashboard of your car, your refrigerator door, inside the most used drawer of your desk at work. Each time you see this declaration, repeat it aloud with as much conviction as possible. Try to do this 25 times today. And by the way, before you go to bed tonight, make an affirmation about how you are going to feel tomorrow. Start taking charge of your responses immediately. What you plan for yourself tonight, you will feel tomorrow.

TURN YOUR "HAVE-TO'S" INTO "CHOOSE-TO'S"

Today is another beautiful day, isn't it? A day in which the whole world can change for the better, especially for you. Today is a day you can look forward to with energy and anticipation. Of course, as the day progresses and challenges arise, as they usually do, it gets a little tougher to believe. I can just hear you say, "I knew he wasn't telling the truth. He said I could make some Daily Declarations and my whole day would be better. Now look at this mess. Maybe it works for him, but I will bet he doesn't have the problems I have." And so on. No, I don't have your problems. I do have my own and Joe had his. But he taught me that problems are not necessarily something to be avoided. You see, our problems are *teachers*, when we learn to look at them correctly. And our problems are also the source of opportunity. That is because problems generate needs; and anywhere there is a need, there is an opportunity to provide a product or service to fill that need — that means opportunities to make money. Besides, the challenge of new problems every day keeps us alive, keeps us developing our minds, our talents and our skills, keeps us stimulated. There is nothing quite like the feeling of accomplishment you get when you take on a challenge and successfully handle it. So, when you encounter a new problem, welcome it. It is an opportunity.

While you need new challenges to help you develop and to provide you with opportunity, what you don't need are the same old problems coming back day after day after day. Life is constantly handing you new ones and if you can't dispose of the old ones, the burden begins to overwhelm you, then you really have a problem. So what do you do when you run into an old problem today? Welcome it; treat it as a new opportunity, one you have

From error to error one discovers the entire truth.

SIGMUND FREUD (1856–1939)
Austrian psychoanalyst

A wise man will make you more opportunities than he finds.

SIR FRANCIS BACON (1561–1626)
English philosopher, statesman, essayist

A thought is often original, though you have uttered it a hundred times. It has come to you over a new route, by a new and express train of associations.

OLIVER WENDELL HOLMES, SR. (1809-1894)
American physician, professor, man of letters

Character—the willingness to accept responsibility for one's own life—is the source from which self-respect springs.

JOAN DIDION (B. 1934)
American writer

Behold the turtle. He makes progress only when he sticks his neck out.

JAMES BRYANT CONANT (1893-1978)
American university administrator, diplomat

never seen before. At least, the you of today has never seen it before, because you are changing. You are not the same person who battled this problem day after day without success. You are someone who can take a fresh look at it. You can work through the problem/opportunity because you now know who is responsible for the recurring problem — namely you. And you are someone who already knows the solution to any problem — it is locked inside you. Locked for the moment behind glass walls. But you know the solution is there; and like our friend the pike, you are probably overlooking it because it seems to be out of reach. You are going to find out how to remove some of those glass walls and get at the answers you need.

Let's talk some more about responsibility. Who is responsible for your problems? Especially the ones that keep recurring in your life. Your parents? Your spouse? Your kids? Your boss? Your creditors? The economy? Some oil company? The government? God? If that is the case you are in real trouble because you have little or no control over any of those entities. The only person over whom you really have any consistent and total control is *you.* So if you are going to work through your recurrent problems, you are the only tool with which you can really work.

BEWARE OF FROZEN ATTITUDES

It has been my experience, both in my own life and in the lives of all the people I have worked with, that at the core of every recurring problem there is a frozen attitude. It is locked in a position that guarantees the problem will occur again and again and again. Invariably, in my own life, I found that the old problems I consistently faced were the result of mental blocks, blocks that kept me from even seeing, let alone doing the obvious things that would solve my problem. One such frozen attitude you are already working on. That's the attitude that tomorrow will be no different from today. You are addressing that attitude with the knowledge that everything changes and that you can take control of that change. Another source of recurring problems is buried in what you call the Fear of the Unknown. Many people would rather keep a problem around that has been there for a while than solve it and have to face some new problem that might be worse.

"HAVE-TO'S" ARE "HATE-TO'S"

And finally, many recurring problems are the result of what you call the "have-to's." Time after time in advising someone with a recurring problem, Joe heard the words, "I can see that Action 'A' is the way to solve my problem but I HAVE TO DO 'B' instead." Let me give you an example. A long-time friend went to Joe for advice about his continuing problems on his job. It was quickly obvious to Joe that he *hated* the work he was doing. When Joe suggested this, his friend agreed that a career change was the solution to his job dissatisfaction. But then he said, he "had to" stay in his current job because he had invested so much time in getting to his current level. He couldn't start over. "Besides," he said, "I have a family to support. If I went into something else, they would have to give up too much. I cannot do that to them." What a string of "have-to's" and what a ducking of responsibility. The solution to his problem was obvious, but it was behind a whole lot of glass walls. You might say, "Now wait a minute. Are you saying this guy did not have an obligation to his family? He has to support them." Sure he has obligations to his family — to love and to cherish and to support them — Yes. But to maintain some arbitrary standard of living for them if it means sacrificing his health and happiness? No. Besides, he never asked them what they wanted. He just *assumed* their lifestyle was more important to them than he was. He had put himself in a box because he really didn't understand the difference between "have-to's" and

The road to success is dotted with many tempting parking places.

ANONYMOUS

You don't get to choose how you're going to die, or when. You can only decide how you are going to live, now.

JOAN BAEZ (B. 1941)
American singer, political activist

"want-to's." When it comes right down to it, there are very few "have-to's" in life. In fact there is only one. We have to die eventually, and except for that, there are no others.

"WANT-TO'S" ARE "CHOOSE-TO'S"

What our lives are really full of are not "have-to's" but "want-to's." You might want to call them "choose-to's." We choose to do certain things in order to produce certain results or to avoid certain kinds of consequences, but it is still a choice. Are you thinking, "Aw, come on, you're making a mountain out of a mole hill." What is the difference if I think I "have-to" do something instead of thinking I "choose-to?" There is plenty of difference. When you think you have to do something, you have no motivation to look for an alternative or even to investigate why you have to do this thing. You put a very high glass wall between you and some of the things you desire. When you realize that you always have a *choice*, you are mentally open to other alternatives and you will be astonished at the difference that makes. Saying you "have-to" do something is a way of ducking responsibility, that someone or something is making you do it. Realizing you are choosing to do it makes it a voluntary act and places the responsibility squarely on you, which is where it belongs and where you want it. When you choose to be responsible you can do something about it. But when you transfer that responsibility onto someone else, not only are you powerless, but eventually you will come to *resent* the person to whom you have given the power. In every recurring problem the major obstacle to the solution of that problem is generally one or more "have-to's."

Pick a problem in your life that is forever popping up to bother you. Write down the nature of that problem. This is extremely important. Often just writing down the problem will put it in a different perspective. Then try to identify the "have-to's." Force yourself to consider the

If you look at life one way, there is always cause for alarm.

ELIZABETH BOWEN (1899–1973)
Anglo-Irish novelist

"have-to's" as "choose-to's." Accept the truth that your problem does have a solution and that the solution will come to you once you have eliminated the "have-to's." Consider the following Daily Declaration:

> *Every problem in my life has a positive solution. I now accept the responsibility for these problems and their solutions.*

It is a vital step on the road to your Riches as it helps establish a new perspective — a new and positive way to take control of your thoughts and ultimately your life. The adoption of this perspective is so important that I selected my personalized license plate on my car — CHOZEWELL — to remind me of it and is a vital step in the growth of all mature people.

Has it occurred to you as you have gone through the steps in *The Lazy Man's Way to Riches* that there is a lot of work involved and that some of the steps are not all that easy? You're right. It is a lot of work *in the beginning*, because you have a lot of changes to go through and that does take some effort. You will be glad to know that it gets a whole lot easier from here on out.

CHANGE YOUR ATTITUDES

We are going to talk about the second of the three tools that are necessary to permanently change your attitudes. The first is Daily Declarations, which involves your conscious mind and the decision to change. The second is called Creative Self-Awareness or simply Awareness. It involves becoming so aware about what you say to and about yourself that you are constantly building yourself up, instead of tearing yourself down. Remember the story about Pat Collins and post-hypnotic suggestions and how they need to be reinforced frequently in order to have any lasting effect? In Chapter 7 of Part 2 you started looking for examples of self-limiting post-hypnotic suggestions in your life and for statements you make that reinforced these mental blocks and barriers. Well, that was your first step toward becoming aware, of really focusing on you and the power you have to affect your behavior either positively or negatively. You probably made some interesting discoveries. Did you find that a lot of your statements were self-limiting? That they reinforced your mental blocks? When I first started utilizing these concepts I was amazed at how much I put myself down in my own speech and in my own thoughts. In looking for reinforcement of self-limiting ideas be careful of the hidden and implied reinforcements. Things like, "There I go

Self-love, my liege, is not so vile a sin as self-neglecting.

WILLIAM SHAKESPEARE (1564–1616)
English playwright, poet

It is doubtless a vice to turn one's eyes inward too much, but I am my own comedy and tragedy.

RALPH WALDO EMERSON (1803–1882)
American poet, essayist, philosopher

again," when you have made a mistake or "I always do that." Questions are important too. "Why can't I do that?" or "Why am I so clumsy?" "Why can't I learn?" Statements that imply a feeling of envy or jealousy are also self-limiting. "I wish I could do that" or "What does he have that I don't?" It really takes a determined individual to dissolve all the self-limiting statements that he or she makes.

For a long time, one goal Joe had trouble achieving concerned his weight. One of his goals was to get his weight down to 170 pounds and keep it there. For the longest time he didn't realize what was holding him back. Finally he became aware that he was actually programming himself to be overweight. Time and time again he would use statements like "It is really hard for me to lose weight. I just can't do it." or "Every time I eat something sweet it sets me off on a craving." You really have to be careful with the things you say to and about yourself. From now on you will have a continuing assignment to recognize and eliminate self-limiting statements from your speech and thoughts.

Take charge of your thoughts. You can do what you will with them.

PLATO (428–347 B.C.)
Greek philosopher, prose writer

FILL THE EMPTY SPACES IN YOUR MIND

Because it's important to continue your effort to become conscious of how you talk about yourself and it's hard to develop a new habit, we are going to reinforce the importance of this tool. I want you to become extremely self-conscious. That may surprise you. I don't mean to say that self-conscious is being worried about how you look and act but rather to be self-aware. Aware of your power statements, the "I am's," the "I can'ts," the "I haven'ts," and so on. These are the statements that reinforce your limiting attitudes. Unfortunately, you can't just eliminate a whole bunch of sentences like this from your daily routine. It leaves a lot of empty space. Learn to fill that empty space with positive self-supporting statements.

To enter one's own self, it is necessary to go armed to the teeth.

PAUL VALÉRY (1871–1945)
French poet, critic

Instead of saying "I can't do that" or "I am not good at that," say "I have never done that, but I am sure I could learn to if I want to." Instead of saying, "I have a poor memory" say, "My memory is constantly improving." Instead of saying, "I can't afford it" say, "I am accumulating all the money I need for this or anything else that I want."

STOP LAUGHING AT YOURSELF

Another area of real importance that many people overlook is what I call the "Ha-Ha Put-Downs." Many people have developed a defense mechanism against the fear of criticism and rejection. This defense is to make fun of themselves before anyone else can. These people will pick on areas where they feel insecure about themselves such as their looks, their weight, their intelligence (or what they think is their lack of it). They think that if they laugh about these things first, then others will laugh with them and not at them. The only problem with this is that our subconscious mind has no sense of humor. It treats those disparaging things we laughingly say about ourself as deadly serious and reinforces the very insecurities we are trying to hide. If you have fallen into this trap of laughing at yourself, you are probably going to experience considerable conflict at the idea of trying to change what you are doing. Most people who do this have come to rely on this part of their personality as a way of being accepted by others and it is scary to think of giving that up. Maybe you choose not to give it all up at once, but if there is an area of your life that is distressing to you and you find yourself making jokes about it, realize that the condition will never change as long as you keep reinforcing it.

If you really do put a small value upon yourself, rest assured that the world will not raise your price.

ANONYMOUS

PROGRAMMED BY SELF-TALK

Just like everything else in life, you have a choice and you have to live with the consequences. In making your choice about changing your self-talk there is a very important fact of life I would like you to understand. Other people will react to you the way you tell them to. What you do, how you act, the way you dress, or the way you introduce yourself tells other people how to treat you. They will, in almost every case, go along with you. If you expect respect and consideration, you will get it. If you expect condescension and laughter, you will get that. If you expect to be ignored, you will get that too. The important thing to realize is that you are in control. You determine how other people respond and you determine how you respond. The voice in your head may be telling you right about now that this is a lot of nonsense. How could harmless jokes and statements about yourself be so important? Let me tell you a story that illustrates how powerful the mind can be when it accepts a suggestion.

PARALYZED BY SELF-TALK

I was told by my mother that none of the men in my family ever lived past the age of 40. Although it wasn't a conscious thought, I truly believed I would only live to age 40. So, I retired at 40, not knowing why. I just had to. My belief acted like an instinct. It drove me, but I didn't understand why. It's as if I had been programmed. My retirement was the beginning of the end for me — or maybe I should say the beginning of the end of the role I was playing that was getting me nowhere — fast. I was just drifting on the currents of life without any purpose or direction. And as the old saying goes, "Idle hands are the Devil's workshop." I became self-destructive.

Then a very significant encounter happened to me while I was vacationing on my boat. I was on a subconscious self-destruction plan and that plan was headed for success. I had no life plan whatsoever. After all, when you only expect to live to 40 and you are now past 40, there isn't any reason to set any future goals or make plans. There's just no future. During one of my perpetual parties on the boat a couple of new-found

Our life is what our thoughts make it.

MARCUS AURELIUS ANTONINUS (121–180)
Roman emperor, Stoic philosopher

Experience is not what happens to a man. It's what a man does with what happens to him.

ALDOUS HUXLEY (1894–1963)
English novelist, essayist, satirist

You are today where your thoughts have brought you; you will be tomorrow where your thoughts take you.

JAMES ALLEN (1849–1925)
American author

As a man thinks in his heart, so is he.

SOLOMON (10th century B.C.)
King of Israel, reputed author of biblical book Proverbs

acquaintances (psychotherapists from New York) gently, but bluntly, pointed out that I seemed to have no purpose or life plan, no goals for my life at all. And they also made the comment that I could live another 50 years or more. "What are you going to do with the rest of your life?" they asked. "The rest of my life?" It was a question I had not asked myself. It wasn't even something I had considered. Wow!

A MAJOR WAKE-UP CALL

This was a major wake-up call. I consulted a doctor for a thorough physical exam. He pronounced me as healthy as I could be. It was at this point that I was confused and terrified. I never realized the incredible power of the belief that I would only live until I was 40. That "belief" had been a map I had followed subconsciously. Amazingly enough, I later found out the true nature of this belief that had charted the course of my life for 40 years. It was absolutely false. Many of my male ancestors lived well into their 90s. I essentially allowed the power of that negative, false belief to nearly destroy my life. I had accepted false programming and virtually believed it.

Dr. Barbara Brown, a leading researcher in the area of bio-feedback, is convinced that we have the ability to control the activity of our system right down to the cellular level. The only thing that stops us from learning how is that we cannot measure the effects of our thoughts accurately enough. How do you form your reality map? How much of your concept of reality is not really true? How accurate are you in evaluating your limitations and insecurities. I was way off in mine If you want to change your mind, you have to change what you tell yourself is true. You've seen how Super Suggestion speeds up the process tremendously. But Super Suggestion is just part of the process. You need to involve your *conscious* mind through the use of the Daily Declarations and through constant attention to your self-talk. Try to turn the limiting self-talk you do into a *self-expanding* statement.

TAKING CHARGE OF YOUR MIND

Now you are going to explore how to use the tools you have been learning about to start *eliminating* some of the really tough roadblocks on your way to Riches. There is no question that the conflicts caused by the unnecessary fears we talked about stop more people than anything else. Fear of criticism, rejection, failure and success lock us in a vise preventing us from following through promptly and thoroughly on the good ideas we have. They make every bit of real progress a real struggle. A struggle with ourselves. I call this struggle "The 2000 Pound Telephone"; because when you have this problem, the telephone seems to weigh 2000 pounds when you have to make an important call. Earlier we talked about the unnecessary fears and how they grow. We saw how fears can become conditioned reflexes causing emotional distress, even physical upset. Now we have the tools to attack these fears, both in our conscious and our subconscious minds.

WHAT'S BUGGING YOU?

Back in Part 1 Chapter 3, we asked you to write down your burning desires. And I have also asked you to examine your fears of success. By now your exercises have started developing your awareness of your feelings, so the process you are going to go through now will be fairly easy for you. The first thing to do in releasing yourself of any conflict is to get in touch with your conflict by bringing it out into the open. You did some of that when you wrote down the pros and cons of achieving your desires. You did it again when you evaluated your attitudes toward success. Now that you understand more about these fears, go back into the pro and con process and see if you can come up with any additions to your list. Search yourself and be

There is no terror in a bang, only in the anticipation of it.

SIR ALFRED JOSEPH HITCHCOCK
(1899–1980)
English-born American film director

Life hardly ever lives up to our anxieties.

PAUL MONASH (B. 1917)
American television producer, writer

Hope is brightest when it dawns from fear.

SIR WALTER SCOTT (1771–1832)
Scottish novelist, poet

We have more ability than will power, and it is often an excuse to ourselves that we imagine that things are impossible.

FRANÇOIS DE LA ROCHEFOUCAULD (1613–1680)
French writer

brutally honest. Don't try to edit anything. Just get it all on paper. A good technique is to keep asking yourself, "What else bothers me?" until you have run out of things. Once you have all your obstacles and doubts down on paper, an interesting thing may happen. Some of your obstacles won't look as bad written down as they do when they are floating around in your head. We all have the ability to enlarge our problems tremendously with our imaginations. Writing them out helps to *see them clearly and reduce them to their proper perspective.* But some of your obstacles will not melt away. These take more effort. Both consciously and through the power of Super Suggestion.

Your next step is to exercise your greatest gift. Look at what you have written and decide whether you're giving up your freedom of choice by treating some things in your life as "have-to's" rather than "choose-to's." If you need to, go back and review Chapter 5 of Part 3 for a refresher on this process. The next key step is to remove the obstacles that are rooted in fear of *criticism* and *failure.* Often these are stated in terms of what will happen if you try and fail. In other words, your expectation is not success but failure.

LOOKING AT HIDDEN CONFLICTS

Joe's friend Dick Johnson tells how Joe helped him see the kinds of conflicts generated by his unnecessary fears:

> *I had an excellent job in the Aerospace industry. Good prospects for advancement. The only problem was my heart wasn't in it, even though I had a Masters degree in Mathematics and had worked for almost 15 years to attain my position. I really liked working with people better than figures. I am a hard worker, but I hated a regimented schedule. The idea of turning 40 years of my life over to a boss really distressed*

me. I wanted the freedom of being my own boss.
Joe suggested that I write out the pros and cons
of changing careers. So I did. I wrote out both
sides of my dilemma — my feelings about my job
and current career and my feelings about the
alternate option I was considering. After I had
written out my feelings, I told Joe it hadn't helped
me out a bit. I was still unable to make a
decision. When Joe looked at what I had written
he wasn't surprised. Everything I had written
about both options was negative. About my
current career I had expressed all my frustration
and boredom. About my alternative choice I
wrote of the uncertainty and the lack of security,
of starting at the bottom and giving up all the
training and experience I had worked so hard to
attain. Of course, I was paralyzed. In my own
mind both choices were totally unattractive. I
had actually managed to turn the positives such
as freedom and working with people that
supposedly were attracting me to the new career
into negatives — insecurity and giving up my
training in the area I didn't like. When Joe
pointed this out to me I began to re-orient my
thinking. With the aid of Super Suggestion I
started working on my fears and my goals.
Within a short time I made my career change and
I did struggle at first, but I knew where I was
going. Soon I was earning twice the income of
the job I had left and within three years we were
able to buy a beautiful home in the Colorado
Rockies. Within five years I had increased my
net worth more than twenty times over what I
had accomplished in the previous fifteen years.
Even more important, my life improved in every
department. Free from the career I hated, my

*Change is not made without
inconvenience; even from worse
to better.*

ROBERT BROWNING (1812–1889)
English poet

*If one advances confidently in
the direction of his dreams, and
endeavors to live the life which
he has imagined, he will meet
with a success unexpected in
common hours.*

HENRY DAVID THOREAU (1817–1862)
American essayist, naturalist, poet

emotional outlook, my energy, and my health all improved. I feel like I am hardly working because I enjoy myself so much. I feel ten years younger and every day of my life is an exciting adventure for me.

So one important key to resolving your conflicts in this area, is building your expectations of success while at the same time understanding about hidden fears of what success can mean. Now let's concentrate on dealing with your fears.

On the conscious level you can help this process by reading biographies of successful, happy people. You will experience their feelings of success and will realize that even the most successful people have human failings and make lots of mistakes. In this way you can begin to build the feeling that if they can do it, so can you. You will realize, at least on the conscious level, that success in itself is not something to fear, and that successful people have had to overcome the same fears and challenges that you face.

Finally, to deal with the useless fears, you have to get on the level where they do the most harm — the subconscious mind. And we do that through Super Suggestion. Remember back in Chapter 2 of Part 3, we talked about how your reality map was formed. Some of your map is a result of conscious choices you have made, but there is another way information gets in. *Vividly imagined* events can also become part of your map, bypassing the conscious mind completely. With this book you are learning how to use your *imagination* to change your reality map in four important ways: by reducing the strengths of the useless fear, by increasing the belief in the attainment of your goals, by improving your self-images, and by building your self-esteem.

The only reason they come to see me is that I know that life is great — and they know I know it.

CLARK GABLE (1901-1960)
American actor

REHEARSING SUCCESS

Can you imagine a football coach spending several hours a day having his players practice fumbling? Can you image a baseball player practicing striking out? Do you see any sense at all in a person spending hours each day practicing failure? And yet that is exactly what most of us do. We spend a substantial part of every day rehearsing failure. Take the salesman who mentally visualizes rejection before he picks up the phone. Or the person who has a speech to make who constantly worries about forgetting his talk. Or the businessman who, under the impression he's being conservative, constantly worries about every conceivable disaster that could occur. All of them are practicing in their imaginations. Practicing failing before they have ever given themselves a chance for success. Therefore, they are guaranteeing that the thing they are most afraid of will happen to them because what you practice and think about mentally, you will do.

When the mind is thinking, it is talking to itself.

PLATO (428-347 B.C.)
Greek philosopher, prose writer

YOUR SUCCESS MACHINE

Your mind is an incredible success machine. Whatever you program it to do, it will accomplish. Mentally rehearse and practice success and your mind will figure out a way to do it. Mentally practice failure and your mind will figure out a way for you to fail. It is very accommodating. What you tell it you want is what you get. The power of mental rehearsal has been known for some time. Championship athletes have used this technique to improve their performance and some, not understanding what they are doing, have used it to degrade their performance. Recently an article in the *Los Angeles Times* described the astonishing experience of an American psychologist who also happened to be a weight lifter. He

We become what we habitually contemplate.

GEORGE WILLIAM RUSSELL (1867-1935)
Irish poet, dramatist, editor

What we are is what we have thought for years.

GAUTAMA THE BUDDHA (560–480 BC)
Indian spiritual leader, founder of
Buddhism

was intrigued by the tremendous progress of the Eastern European countries in sports in general and at an international conference he had an opportunity to talk to some leading German scientists about how this was being achieved. They performed a demonstration for him. His personal best in the bench press was 300 pounds. They asked him what he would consider to be a significant improvement and he said even ten pounds more would be an outstanding improvement. Using a technique virtually identical to Super Suggestion they taught him how to use his imagination to experience lifting a much heavier weight. Within an hour he bench pressed 365 pounds, a 20% increase in just one hour. That is phenomenal. You say you don't want to be a weight lifter or football star. "What does this have to do with achieving your goals?" Just this: The same techniques will work in every aspect of your life. As part of the same demonstration, the American psychologist also worked on imagining himself to be an excellent writer, an area in which he was not particularly good. The results astonished him. People who had no idea what he was doing began complimenting him on his writing skills and how they had improved.

MENTAL REHEARSALS

As a member of Toastmasters International and several other speakers' organizations, as well as in my business and presenting our seminars, I am frequently called upon to make speeches. The audiences vary in size from small groups to several thousands in our seminars. Of course, I want to be at my best during these talks, so I rehearse. Not by writing out my speech and practicing it. In fact, I don't write out my speech at all. I make a few notes about the ideas I want to get across and then program my subconscious to do the rest. I mentally rehearse the feeling of giving a good talk, of being articulate and having a constant flow of ideas. I visualize the happy response of the audience, their enjoyment and enthusiasm so that I approach the date of the talk with anticipation of success and my subconscious knows that it must produce the desired results. So when I am actually in front of the audience, I get the results I rehearsed. I am usually surprised at some of the things I say. Some of my best ideas have come out during a speech — ideas that my conscious mind had not fully formed. By the way, if you are ever lucky enough to see Tim Timmons in person, do so. He is one of the finest speakers I have ever heard and I've never seen him write out a speech either — just an outline.

You can use your subconscious mind in the discovery and development of business ideas. It is extremely important to grasp the idea of mentally rehearsing success as well, when you begin to develop your ideas. One of the tragedies of the way you were raised is that most of you are conditioned to expect disappointment and failure. "Don't count your chickens before they are hatched" is a perfect example of the negative programming you constantly receive. As a result you learn to dread the future rather than anticipate it and you find it too easy to rehearse failure and extremely difficult to rehearse success. Remember the self-defeating self-image cycle in Chapter 3 of Part 3? The only way to increase your performance is to raise your expectations — in other words, to rehearse success. Are you thinking, "But I can't rehearse being successful when I am not. How do I pretend to be successful, when the reality is I have nothing going? And, besides, if I get my hopes up and it doesn't work then I will really be disappointed." So what! Disappointment is hardly ever fatal. In fact, it is rarely even dangerous. Yet, we let the fear of disappointment rob us of one of the greatest sources of energy we have — anticipation. Have you ever watched a child as Christmas gets closer and closer? When does Christmas really start for a child?

The mind is a strange machine which can combine the materials offered to it in the most astonishing ways.

BERTRAND RUSSELL (1872–1970)
English philosopher, mathematician,
social reformer

Don't be afraid to take a big step if one is indicated. You can't cross a chasm in two small jumps.

DAVID LLOYD GEORGE (1863–1945)
English politician, statesman

Sometime between late October and early November they usually start getting excited. They begin looking forward to that exciting time. They begin dreaming. Their behavior starts to improve. They may start doing a lot of chores around the house because they want extra money for Christmas presents. They have more energy than usual because they are excited. Then Christmas Day arrives. The gifts are opened and in just minutes it is all over. But was Christmas just those few minutes on Christmas morning or was it those weeks of excitement and anticipation leading up to it? If you don't learn to anticipate and rehearse success, you rob yourself of the energy and determination that you need to be successful. After all, how much effort will you put into a project if your mind is telling you it is going to fail. How heavy will the telephone be, if in your mind you are already rehearsing a "NO" on the other end? Rehearsing failure puts tremendous roadblocks in your Road to Riches. You can remove those roadblocks using the three basic tools I have discussed: Daily Declaration, Creative Self-Awareness, and Super Suggestion.

What you are going to do in this next step closely resembles the rehearsal period an actor goes through in preparation for a play. Have you ever wondered how an actor can laugh or cry on cue? Do they actually think what they are doing on stage is real? Hardly. But through hours and hours of rehearsal the actor behaves as though the play were reality. He uses his imagination to explore how the character he is portraying would respond if the situation were real and most importantly, he builds a conditioned reflex or rather a whole set of conditioned reflexes that take over when he is on stage. The situation in the play triggers feelings — anger, tears, joy — and the actor experiences and projects these feelings automatically without having to think about them, whenever the proper cue occurs. You see, the actor is doing his own version of

Dr. Pavlov's conditioning by practicing cue response over and over again. That is just what you are going to do. Only, instead of rehearsal, you will be using the three powerful tools — Daily Declaration, Creative Self-Awareness, and Super Suggestion.

You will draw to yourself that which you most persistently think about.

ROBERT ANTHONY, Ph.D. (B. Withheld by request)
American psychologist, writer

Nothing vivifies, and nothing kills like the emotions.

JOSEPH ROUX (1834–1905)
French priest, writer

If you were starting out on a long hike and you personally had to carry every bit of your baggage, how much time would you spend making sure you got rid of all excess baggage before you started? Wouldn't it be worth the time in the beginning to pack carefully so you wouldn't be burdened every step of the way? *The Lazy Man's Way to Riches* is a journey. A journey that will last the rest of your life. Doesn't it make sense to dump your excess baggage now? Because, believe me, if you don't, it will drag you down every step of the way and wear you out before you achieve everything you want. Oh, you will make progress, but it will be a lot tougher. What kind of excess baggage am I talking about? The kind we all carry into every new venture — the negative emotions and fears that act like a brake on our tremendous potential, making every step forward a tremendous effort. I have already discussed the fears of criticism, rejection, failure and success and how to get rid of them. Now I want to talk about some emotions that are not such *obvious* obstacles but can be even bigger roadblocks than these fears, especially since you probably will want to hold onto them with a vengance and deny that they are holding you back. Believe me, they are among your worst enemies. What are these emotional roadblocks? Envy, jealousy, greed, revenge, bitterness, resentment, hatred, prejudice, guilt. Get the picture? You may say, "Now wait a minute, what do these emotions have to do with success? I am not bitter about much, but believe me I have a right to be." Do you have any of those thoughts? Are you cherishing thoughts of *revenge* for some wrong that has been done you? Are you a little *bitter* at the hand life has dealt you? Are you a little *envious* of the person whose old man left him a million dollars? Do you feel like you have a right to those feelings? Well, you are welcome to hang on to them, and I can tell you right now they are excess baggage and eventually will wear you right into the ground. You may go on and achieve some of the good things of life, and you pay a much higher price than the person who is willing to spend a little time to drop some of the excess baggage of the negative emotions.

LET GO OF THE ESSENTIAL DEAD WEIGHT

I can just hear some of you saying, "Now, are you telling me I have to be a saint to walk *The Lazy Man's Way?*" No, or none of us would ever make it. I am suggesting that you can make your progress a whole lot easier by letting go of some emotional dead weight. Let's take a look at these negative emotions. The first set — bitterness, revenge, resentment, hatred, and guilt — are all leftovers from the dead past, and there is one absolute fact about the past. *It can't be changed* and these feelings ruin your precious "now" time — the only time you really have to work with. Every minute spent wallowing over a past wrong or beating yourself for a past mistake is wasted time and wasted energy. Thoughts of revenge do nothing to the person or persons you think wronged you. *They only harm you*, distorting your view of life in the present and preventing you from focusing on where your life goes by keeping you looking over your shoulder all the time.

And what good does it do to continue feeling guilty about a serious mistake you may have made that hurt you or someone else? Do what you can to repair the damage, learn the lesson of your mistake, and then *forgive yourself* and go on. Remember, unlike the past, you can change the future. You are not the same person who made that mistake. Chances are the mistake was made because you didn't or couldn't possibly predict the consequences of your actions. Or maybe you were simply acting out some post-hypnotic suggestion. But you are treating yourself as

A brave man thinks no one his superior who does him an injury; for he has it then in his power to make himself superior to the other by forgiving it.

ALEXANDER POPE (1688–1744)
English poet, satirist

How unhappy is he who cannot forgive himself.

PUBLILIUS SYRUS (1st Century B.C.)
Latin poet

though you deliberately set out to cause harm. I am not saying you are not responsible for your actions. You are. Everything I have told you in these chapters should make it clear that I do believe in personal responsibility. So accept your personal responsibility. Do what you can to correct the problem. Forgive yourself and go on. Wallowing in guilt is not accepting responsibility. It is usually a way to avoid living in the here and now.

But what about envy, jealousy, and greed? These are rooted in insecurity and low self-esteem. Why envy someone else's possessions? You can easily get your own *The Lazy Man's Way.* Jealousy? It is probably the most destructive of emotions. Certainly it destroys the love that it is supposedly trying to protect. And once again, it is a symptom of insecurity and low self-esteem. The solution is not in restricting someone else's behavior, it is raising your own concept of yourself. And how about greed? The person who is truly greedy, who can never get enough money or power or whatever, really has a problem. His life is out of balance and he is attempting to make up in one department for what he is lacking and really needs in another department. If you feel that you can never get enough money to satisfy you, you are right. Because you can never get enough of what you don't really need. It is not the money you want and need. Money has simply become a symbol for love or respect or acceptance. Stop wasting your energy, sit down and look at yourself, and go after what you really want.

HOW YOU CAN LET GO

Now, how do you get rid of all this excess baggage? Now, don't worry, you don't need seven years of psycho-analysis. You simply have to work on removing these emotional drags every single day. How? By using the tools you have been learning in these chapters. Your emotional reactions are simply a product of your attitudes, and your attitudes can be changed, *if you really want to change*

Begin somewhere:
you cannot build a reputation
on what you intend to do.

LIZ SMITH (MARY ELIZABETH) (B. 1923)
American journalist

them. After all they are just your attitudes, they are not carved in stone, so just change those that don't work for you. That may be the hard part where these emotions are concerned. (Giving them up, releasing those feelings of revenge, that bitterness.) "You mean I have to let that so-and-so get away with what he did to me?" No, you don't have to, but everything will be a lot easier for you if you do. And not only let that so-and-so get away with whatever it was, but *forgive* that so-and-so as well. Simply release all feelings of anger, bitterness, and revenge, no matter how justified you think they are. And while you are at it, forgive yourself as well for all your past mistakes. Let go of your past and go on with your life; it's a choice you make. It's a conscious choice.

TAKING YOUR EMOTIONAL INVENTORY

You're already working on any feeling of jealousy, envy, or prejudice that you may have, because you are building your self-images through Super Suggestion. The better you feel about yourself the less you will need these drags on your energies. Begin by taking an inventory of all your negative feelings. Write down all the people at whom you are angry, the ones whom you feel have wronged you, the ones you feel you hate and why you feel that way. Write down the names of people of whom you are envious and why. Add any jealousy you are feeling and all the people, races or organizations you have prejudice against. And finally, write down any reasons you feel guilty. Get it all out — all of the garbage. Be totally honest.

No one will ever see this list but you. When you are sure this list is complete, very carefully burn your list and, as you burn it, realize that all the feelings that you put down on your list as you were writing it are burning up too. Release them and let them go up in smoke. This is more than just a symbolic act. In *writing* your feelings down you release some of the pent-up energy behind your

Forgiving is the answer to the child's dream of a miracle by which what is broken is made whole again, what is soiled is again made clean.

DAG HAMMARSKJOLD (1905–1961)
Swedish statesman, U.N. Secretary
General

The ineffable joy of forgiving and being forgiven forms an ecstasy that might well arouse the envy of the gods.

ELBERT HUBBARD (1856–1915)
American businessman, writer, printer

emotions. You also realize how silly some of them are. At least, that has been the experience of hundreds of thousands who wrote down all their grievances. If you do this exactly, you will be amazed at how good you feel. You may find that some of your suppressed grievances still hang around. After all, these emotions can be deeply buried in your subconscious. That is why I have given you a Super Suggestion exercise in Chapter 9 of Part 1 to help you in this area. It is no exaggeration to say that using this exercise regularly can be one of the most important steps you will ever take along the way to Riches in every aspect of your life. Remember the good feelings that come from letting go of these emotions and use them to beat back any of those downer emotions that try to come back. And work with the Super Suggestion exercise frequently as you look at what you want to start dumping.

MAN DOES NOT WORK FOR BREAD ALONE

You have just talked about getting rid of the excess baggage, habits, downers and emotions that sap your energy and divert your attention from your *chosen direction*. Now I want to give you some ideas on how to avoid taking on new downers by making the best out of all your relationships with others.

SUCCESS DOESN'T HAPPEN IN A VACUUM — NO LONERS

When you study the lives of successful people, you rarely find a loner — someone who did it all on his or her own. In fact, it's hard to think of a single one. Success is a cooperative effort, especially when you do it *The Lazy Man's Way*. Money-making ideas nearly always need the financial and emotional support, the advice, the talent and the skills and labor of others to blossom and grow. To turn your ideas into reality it will greatly facilitate gaining the enthusiastic cooperation of others. Some people think you can get others to cooperate through manipulation, and a lot of people try this. To me the major problems with trying to manipulate people are: first, you can't feel good about yourself if you are not completely honest with people, and second: as Mr. Lincoln said, "You can't fool all of the people all of the time." Eventually your manipulation is discovered and the people you have used tend to get downright hostile. With all the internal challenges and fears you have to overcome, the last thing you need to do is to make enemies. Perhaps you are thinking, "Wait a minute, you just got through saying that I need people to make my projects go and now you say I can't use people." You can use people, *but only with their knowledge and consent and in a "win/win" setting.* You can gain the enthusiastic cooperation and support of everyone you need to make your ideas productive. It is

When you make a world tolerable for yourself, you make a world tolerable for others.

ANAIS NIN (1903–1977)
French-born American novelist, dancer

Long-range studies imply that doing something with other people, especially something for them, is the most powerful of all stimuli to longevity and health.

JON POPPY (B. 1942)
American health columnist

very simple. Help people get what they want and they will help you get what you want. Help enough other people to get what they want out of life and your success is assured.

GIVE PEOPLE WHAT THEY WANT

So, what do people want? Of course, it varies. For some it might be a job with a decent wage. If development of your idea requires that you have employees, remember, you get what you pay for. Always pay a fair price for the job you want done and hire someone whose skills, abilities and interests match the job. It's better to have someone in every position who has to stretch a little to accomplish the job than have someone whose abilities are not fully used. If your cash is short, offer profit sharing and performance bonuses as incentives. Do not fall into the trap of believing that money is the only thing your employees require or even the most important thing. Sure, money is a necessary part of our lives, but haven't you heard about the thousands of people who leave excellent paying jobs each year to work for less because they are looking for something else. That something is called *satisfaction*. Satisfaction is a basic human need that has nothing to do with money. When you ask these people why they changed careers they often mention their desire to make a contribution or to do something meaningful. Many said they felt like they were just lost in a big crowd — that nobody knew or cared what they were doing. Others talk of a desire for more freedom or more independence. What these people are expressing are fundamental human needs for appreciation, recognition and opportunity for personal development. How many times have you seen people work at low-paying jobs because they knew their efforts were valuable and necessary. (Nurses, teachers, devoted secretaries, and the key man in a company who gives 40 years of loyal service.) These people are working for something other than financial gain and they accept less in the financial

Happiness is mostly a by-product of doing what makes us feel fulfilled.

DR. BENJAMIN SPOCK (B. 1903)
American physician, writer

department, because they feel needed or important or valued. Don't ever make the mistake that people can be bought. Give value for value, but go an extra mile and give appreciation and recognition as well. You get a lot more than just an employee in return.

GIVE AWAY MORE THAN MATERIAL THINGS
The importance of intangibles such as appreciation and recognition and respect go far beyond the employer/employee relationship. It extends to your family, your day-to-day associates and all your business dealings. People want to be around you and support you in your efforts in *direct proportion* to how good you make them feel about themselves. This doesn't mean you should falsely flatter people or be insincere; that is manipulation and it always rings false. Find some quality that you admire in each person you meet and especially each member of your family. Do the same with all your close associates and praise them for their good qualities. Look for ways to show your appreciation, not for what they do for you, but for what they are, and offer your appreciation freely without expecting anything in return. Don't worry, you will get results. Remember, it's best not to tie your appreciation to any specific favor or other return. If not given freely, it is meaningless. A short note expressing your feelings is usually much more meaningful to the person than a 15-minute eulogy. Suppose you receive the following letter from a friend or a member of your family:

> *Dear Bruce,*
>
> *Just a short note to tell you how much I enjoy your friendship. You are the kind of person that is a pleasure to be around. Let's get together soon for some good conversation.*
>
> *Regards,*
>
> *Richard*

*Everybody forgets the basic
thing; people are not going to
love you unless you love them.*

PAT CARROLL (B. 1927)
American actress, comedienne, Emmy
and Tony award winner

*Never lose sight of the fact that
the most important yardstick of
your success will be how you
treat other people — your family,
friends, and co-workers, and
even strangers you meet along
the way.*

BARBARA BUSH (B. 1925)
American First Lady

What is your first thought? As a human being with negative training, your first reaction might be, "Hey, how much does he want to borrow?" If you realized that the note is simply what it appeared to be, a sincere expression of appreciation for you as a person, then what would your first thought be? "Wow! What a terrific person this is to write me such a nice note." Wouldn't you like people to feel that way about you? Just show them a little appreciation and you will be pleasantly surprised with the results.

APPRECIATION — IT'S AN ART

A woman friend of mine tried this approach with her mother whom she had resented for years — she actually found it difficult to be around her. Most of this tension was a result of misunderstandings during her childhood. But the resentment carried on into adulthood and, as a result, their contact as adults aggravated the problem. One day, having learned the principles we have been talking about, she had a floral arrangement sent to her mother with the message "You are loved." Her mother was deeply moved and when she called to say "thank you," the years of friction started to turn into a warm relationship that "enRiches" both of their lives. Make a list of the people who are important in your life — your spouse, your children, your family, friends and business associates. For each one, make a list of all the qualities you appreciate about that person and then write a short note expressing that appreciation. Not for the things they have done, but for what they are. Don't flatter them; be honest and objective. Now, this may take a little more time than most of your steps, but it will be worth it. And you probably won't have time to do it all in a day. Make a habit out of it. Start with those closest to you. It will be easier and you will feel less embarrassment. Don't cop out with, "I don't have to tell my family how I feel. They already know." If that is the way you think, they probably *don't* know, because it is probably difficult for you to show your feelings. We are all a little insecure and we all need reassurance from time to time, so even if you think they know, tell them anyway. If you are afraid they will think you have gone crazy, I have given you a little paragraph to insert in your note, so they will understand what you are doing. You don't have to use it, but if it helps, go ahead and do it. Here it is:

> *Dear Suzanne,*
>
> *I am in the process of going through a course in self-development and improvement. Each day I have have an exercise to complete. Today I'm to write a note of appreciation to someone I care for. I chose to write to you because of all the things I appreciate about you. This isn't a thank you for past favors; it's a thank you for all the things our friendship has meant to me.*

For some of you, this may be the hardest step on *The Lazy Man's Way*, but don't skip it no matter how hard. Remember, what you freely give in this world always comes back multiplied many times over.

By now, if you have faithfully followed the steps in this book, you have papered the surfaces around you with lots of messages and reminders; and it must be getting pretty cluttered by this time. So to make things a little easier and neater, you are going to introduce a concept that will take care of this clutter and at the same time helps you get the necessary reinforcement that you need every single day to remind you of the habits you are changing.

After you have been looking at the messages for two or three days put them on little 3 x 5 file cards. They fit into most pockets and handbags. Three times a day make a practice of reading through these file cards one at a time, taking a moment to think about the meaning of each message. This way you continue to get the reinforcement. From now on when we ask you to put up something on the bathroom mirror or on the dashboard of your car, go ahead and do that for several days and then transfer it to a file card. Once again, what I am trying to do is get maximum saturation of all of your senses in this process of changing.

BOOK TWO

Turning Dyna/Psyc into Dollars

□

THE WORLD'S MOST EXCITING BUSINESS

CHAPTER I OF BOOK TWO

You've come a long way on your journey to Riches and have been exposed to all kinds of wonderful principles, ideas, and suggestions. What can you do in a practical sense with all of this information? Turn it into dollars, lots of dollars — just like Joe did. No matter what your gender, age, interest, talents, needs; there are all kinds of ways to make it happen for you. In BOOK TWO, Joe shares with you all kinds of wonderful information to make your dreams come true. He felt passionately about the subject and shares that with you next; particularly his specific passion . . . what he called The World's Most Exciting Business.

I'm going to tell you about the most exciting business in the world. It's just about the last frontier for the "little guy." It's a business you can start in your garage or bedroom, right in your hometown. And, if things go right, you can build a national — even a worldwide — business almost overnight.

It takes very little capital to get started; and if you play your cards right, it's self-financing. You can have thousands of salespeople working for you — some on a straight commission basis. In other words, you pay them only for what they sell, so your profit is assured.

GET INTO A GROWING BUSINESS

It's called the Direct Response Business. And probably no other business has so many people who started from scratch and became millionaires. You know some of the giants: Sears, Montgomery Ward, Dell Computer, Spiegel, Fingerhut, Sharper Image, Nieman Marcus, Victoria's Secret; and I'm sure you could list a dozen more household names. And there are thousands of less familiar names who are raking in the profits from what

No matter what your gender, age, interest, talents or needs, what you're about to learn can make all your financial dreams come true.

It's one of the last frontiers where — starting with very little capital — you can build a worldwide business almost overnight.

It is probable that in no other business have so many people who've started from scratch become millionaires.

Barron's, the financial journal, described the direct response business as — "the fastest growing business in America." Now a 30-billion-dollar-a-year industry in the U.S.A. and perhaps three times that worldwide.

The greatest thing is that you can be, if you pick your spots, on an equal footing with the giants. The discounts they get, through buying power, can be relatively insignificant, and you can more than offset their advantages by "cutting corners." What's more, because you don't have to filter your profits through layers of people and acres of overhead, you can act more quickly and efficiently.

A BUSINESS WHERE CUSTOMERS ALWAYS WIN

Here's why the Direct Response Business is growing — and will continue to grow. It offers your customers convenience. It's a lot easier to clip a coupon, make up a check, and stick it in the mail box, or simply call or fax your order and pay by credit card than it is to drive to a store, find a parking place, and try to get a clerk's attention.

It's convenient, it's efficient, it's very competitive, and almost anything can be sold using these methods.

It's efficient. Most stores have to pay clerks to stand around during the slack hours, just so there'll be enough — or almost enough — to handle the peak periods. In the Direct Response Business, you can spread your workload throughout the day, getting maximum production from every employee.

Customers save by reduced handling costs. The average product has to go through the hands of wholesalers, distributors, and jobbers before it even reaches the retailer. Each one takes his cut — and adds to the cost. And the retailer has to take a good chunk just to cover the cost of prime real estate, to say nothing of a whopping investment in fixtures; and there's the cost of merchandise that's damaged as it's shipped, reshipped, and shipped again. Those are just a few of the costs that are eliminated or reduced in the Direct Response Business.

That's why almost anything you can name is sold, using Direct Response methods, and more items are being added every day. Here are some estimates on sales volume — the number of units sold — in various categories. The figures came from the trade magazine *Advertising Age:* Kitchen appliances — 6,100,000; Tools, under $30 — 5,200,000; Tools, over $30 — 1,600,000; Watches under $40 — 2,500,000; Watches, over $40 — 1,000,000; Luggage sets, under $30 — 2,200,000; Tableware sets, under $30 — 1,600,000; Vacuum cleaners — 1,200,000; Radios, under $80 — 1,200,000; Cookware sets, under $40 — 950,000. And those figures do not include sales from catalogs.

Here's more proof that Direct Response is a growing, multibillion-dollar business: Ninety-five of the major corporations listed on the New York Stock Exchange chalk up an important part of their sales using Direct Response techniques. And some of the biggies — General Foods, General Mills, ITT, and Avon — are now into it.

But don't let the size of the competition scare you off, because, unlike any other kind of business I can think of, in the case of the Direct Response Business, your smallness is an *advantage.* Your direct, personal control — and your low overhead—work for you. The president of some corporate octopus is not going to go into the business. He's going to have to hire and pay experts, who are going to hire other experts — all in the hope that they'll know what they are doing. And they'll make mistakes because they're not spending their own money — and never have. They'll have monstrous expenses I'll show you how to avoid. Not the least of which are advertising agencies that take 15 percent off the top. The discounts that are available in the two most important areas — advertising and mailing costs — are available to anyone. In fact, I'll show you how you can pay far less for your advertising

Though it's a growing multi-billion-dollar industry, your smallness is an advantage.

I'll show you how to slash your ad costs and, in fact, how to pay far less than what the Big Boys have to pay simply because they are big.

than the Big Boys pay using identical media (including radio, TV, and newspapers) simply because they are big. What's more, if you mail 200 letters, the Post Office will give you a 40 percent discount.

Furthermore, in the pages that follow, I'm going to share "trade secrets" that cost me, literally, hundreds of thousands of dollars to discover — information that has never been published before.

I believe I've read just about everything that's been written about this business. I can only conclude that the authors didn't know what they were talking about, or didn't know enough, or wouldn't tell what they knew.

I'll hold nothing back. Follow my advice, step-by-step, and you may end up with more money than you ever dreamt was possible.

As for me, I'm not going to hold anything back. If you follow the procedures I'll outline, step by step, you can have any degree of success you really want; anything from a comfortable "second income" to more money than you ever dreamt was possible.

Why am I willing to do this? Well, because you paid me for it. The amount of money you spent may be a ridiculously low figure for the value of what you're about to receive, but I think that there are a hundred thousand like you. And fifteen dollars times a hundred thousand people is one million five hundred thousand dollars. So I'll make a lot of money doing what I like best. As for you, you've already had your first — and most important — lesson in the Direct Response Business.

YOU CAN HAVE A LOT OF FUN . . .

AND MAKE A LOT OF MONEY . . .

GIVING PEOPLE WHAT THEY WANT . . .

AT A REASONABLE PRICE.

TECHNIQUES FOR GETTING UNUSUAL IDEAS

CHAPTER 2 OF BOOK TWO

The Direct Response Business can be divided into these five major categories: Radio, TV, Newspapers, Magazines, and Direct Mail. But these are really only the means you use to tell people about what you have for sale.

I've used them all successfully. I'll tell you how you can, too.

There are other methods of communicating — and making sales — that require no investment, and I'll tell you about those, too. And what may be the greatest method of making sales is just aborning. It's cable television, and many of the stations are so hungry for business that they'll sell for you on a commission basis. Which means that you'll end up with a small but sure profit.

WHAT ARE YOU GOING TO SELL?

The first thing you're going to have to consider — and it's really the hardest part of the problem — is what you're going to sell.

The best thing to sell is something unique: a better product, a greater service, at a lower price. What you're looking for could be any one of these or could include all three. The crucial element is that people should have to come to you when they want it.

So first make a list of what you enjoy doing and do better than most people. Are you a great cook? Are you a genius at fixing things around the house? Are you a sharp poker player? Does everyone admire the way you refinish furniture? Is there something special you know about attracting people of the opposite sex? When you're on a fishing trip, are you the one who usually ends up with the biggest catch? Are the parties you give the ones that

Radio, TV, newspapers, magazines, and direct mail — I've used them all successfully. I'll show you how you can, too.

The best thing to sell is a better product, with greater service, at a lower price.

JOE KARBO (1925–1980)
American entrepeniur, author, television personality

We all do something better than most, and a million-dollar direct response business has probably already been built on it — but there's plenty of room for competition.

Even if you're just a little bit better than average — that still leaves you with a potential market of over one hundred million people in the U.S. alone.

people talk about? Do you get a kick out of meeting new people? Are you the one person in the neighborhood everyone tells his troubles to? Are you the guy people call for advice when they're having trouble with their cars? Are you a whiz at math? Can you make people laugh? Do you know how to butcher a cow? Do people admire your garden? Do you have a good memory?

A million-dollar Direct Response Business has been built on every one of these, and there's a lot of room for competition.

Start your own list. Use those that are applicable from the examples I've given and add your own — things you do better than most people. Notice I didn't say "better than anyone." You just have to be better than average. Because if you're just a little better than only half the people in this great country and they want some skill, product or service that you can do better or more easily than they can, that's a market of more than one hundred twenty five million people. Surely those are enough prospects to start with here at home. Let's not forget the people in Canada, The European Common market, Asia, South and Central America, Oceania, (Australia, New Zealand, etc.) and the Peoples Republic of China, and the new consumers in The Commonwealth of Independent States (the former Soviet Union).

When you've completed your list (and if it's not a long one, work harder on your ISI), try mixing it up to produce an unusual combination. For example, if you can make people laugh and you're a great fisherman, you could make a good living as a guest speaker at service club meetings — or writing for *Field and Stream* — or printing signs and cards for the tourist trade of fishing resorts — or . . .?

Or if butchering a cow and throwing great parties are the two things that really turn you on, maybe you could go into the business of catering barbecues for organizations —

or you could set up a "party plan" for selling meat wholesale — or . . . ?

SELL AN IDEA OR A PLAN

Anyway, you get the point. Fool around with it. Have fun. And keep in mind that you don't have to sell a product. You can sell an idea or a plan; a way to do something better, or faster, or cheaper. There are a lot more people who got rich selling cookbooks than running restaurants. Paper is cheaper than plastic. And people will pay you well for a good idea — any idea that will make them healthier or happier or stronger or sexier or richer. Certainly, as you've gone through life, you've learned *something* that other people would like to know — and will pay you to find out.

Another way to get ideas is to use Creative Unhappiness. Make notes of the things that bug you: long lines in the supermarket, a gadget that won't work, surly waiters, paperback books that are printed too close to the margin, cluttered TV commercials, the kids leaving the lights on in every room of the house, your spouse snoring, cleaning up after the dog, dripping faucets.

Remember that the things that annoy you bother other people too. And, if you can find a way to get rid of some petty annoyance, people will be glad to pay you for your solution.

TURN WORRY INTO WAMPUM. If you have a serious problem, attack it. Don't just let it whirl round and round in your head, making you miserable and robbing you of sleep. Look at it as a challenge — an opportunity — because it is. When you figure out the answer, you could have a profitable business on your hands.

Let me give you an example:

When I was head-over-heels in debt, I knew that there were two things I could do: (1) Declare bankruptcy or (2) Work my way out. The first alternative would be a "legal"

Keep in mind, you don't have to sell a product. You can sell an idea, a plan, or a better, faster, cheaper way of doing something.

I had a problem. I was head-over-heels in debt, yet I couldn't declare bankruptcy. So I found out everything I could about getting out of debt. I even interviewed four lawyers and a judge.

solution to my problem, but, in my eyes, it would not be an honorable one. My creditors had "loaned" me money in good faith. If I didn't pay them back, I would be betraying that faith. I'd given my word and I wouldn't break it. It was as simple as that.

TAKE PERSONAL AND FAMILY INVENTORY

But I also had an obligation to my family — to house, clothe, and feed them decently. Not luxuriously — just decently. So, obviously, any repayment program would have to take that primary obligation into account. It had to be something we could live with — and for a long time — because a $50,000 debt wouldn't be repaid overnight. (It took us eight years.)

So I started to find out everything I could about getting out of debt. I interviewed four lawyers and a judge to find out what my legal rights were — what my creditors could and couldn't do.

My wife and I inventoried the material things we had and the qualities of our life that were essential to us as individuals and a family. We decided which were important to us and which we could do without. We discovered, of course, that the things that were truly meaningful to us — the beach, the parks, the forests, the museums, reading, the picnics, and good conversation — were all free. The other things we enjoyed — an occasional evening at the theatre, a dinner out — could be budgeted and the pleasure actually enhanced. It was more fun to find "bargains" in these areas: the rundown movie houses where you could see a good feature for two dollars, the offbeat storefront restaurants where you could get an excellent meal for less than five dollars. (Someday I'm going to write a book, *The Gourmet's Guide to Budget Restaurants*. There are hundreds of them in every large city. Why don't you write one for your town?)

As we compiled our list of all the things we had to

have — including shelter, utilities, furniture, food, transportation, clothing, medical and dental care, etc. — we researched how to get the most for our money. Incidentally, Christmas is not an "Emergency." It happens every year and has to be saved for — in advance.

SET UP A BUDGET

When we finished our list of essentials, we made up a budget, allotting the necessary money for each thing, including an Emergency Fund, a Savings Fund, and one called "We're Just Human Beings." The last was a small amount set aside so we could buy or do something "foolish" (and human) once in a while.

USE THE ENVELOPE METHOD OF ACCOUNTING

Then we made up envelopes for each category and put the necessary cash in an envelope every week. There are two important elements in that preceding sentence: "cash" and "every week." "Cash" because you can see it and touch it. It's real — and much easier to keep track of than a bank balance. "Every week" because when you provide for your monthly payments on this basis, it's a lot easier than having to come up with a lump — and $4\frac{1}{3}$ times larger — sum at the end of the month.

The rules we set up were: (1) You couldn't "borrow" from one envelope if you developed a shortage in another. (2) If you had an overage, it had to go into the Emergency Fund or the Savings Fund. (3) We bought nothing on credit.

Because when you buy on credit, you usually can't make as good a "buy" and you have to pay for the money you're borrowing. That meant we had to anticipate our needs for major purchases and/or repairs, furniture, appliances, a car, whatever — and budget for them in advance so we'd have the money when we needed it — by setting it aside every week.

I set up a budget I could live with. One that would allow me to take care of all of the family bills, as well as a small amount set aside so I could even do something "foolish" once in a while.

Each of the kids had his/her own envelopes: for "School Expenses," for example, for "Snacks" (this kept us from being "nickeled and dimed" to death), for "Clothing" (this kept us from being nagged for the faddish clothes that "all of the other kids" had. If they really wanted it, they could buy it — and figure out what they were going to do without).

The most pleasant by-product of all this planning was that it brought us closer together as a family. The kids actually felt more secure, more a part of the action. And we think they learned valuable lessons about money — where it comes from and where it goes. All of us derived more pleasure from the things our money bought because we were in control. We didn't have to make dozens of little decisions every day.

Could we — or couldn't we — afford this or that? We could afford anything we really wanted as long as there was enough money in the envelope — and we had decided what we could do without. In simple terms, we could have steak for dinner any day of the week, but it would mean some corner cutting on the other six days — and occasionally, it was worth it.

The Budget Plan eliminated most of our careless "impulse buying." In other words, it stopped us from buying a lot of things we didn't really want or need. We didn't just "buy" things; we *shopped* for them. And it was fun — pitting our skills against a whole world of businessmen who were bombarding us with advertising, sometimes trying to mislead or cheat us, always anxious to separate us from our money.

I found out that setting up a Budget Plan and making it work is crucial. Dun and Bradstreet, the credit reporting firm, says that over 90 percent of all businesses fail within five years after they've opened their doors. Most of these failures have one thing in common — they *don't keep good records*! And, without records, they don't know what they're doing, where they've been, where they are, or where they're going. I think that most family finances fail or stay in hot water for the same reason.

These are some of the other things about getting out of debt, staying out of debt, and having more money to spend that my research uncovered:

How you can make yourself judgment — and attachment — proof.

How you can have thousands of dollars in assets that creditors can't touch.

How to use the little-known Law of Debt Relief to protect what you have (your home, car, salary, possessions) from grasping creditors.

How to pay off debts — on your terms.

How to avoid bankruptcy — by preparing for it.

Why there are certain old bills you'd better not pay — or even acknowledge.

Why not owing *enough* money can be worse than owing too much.

How to beat a greedy merchant out of excessive interest charges and even collect damages.

Where to get *free* legal advice.

How to win a lawsuit.

Which creditors to pay *first*. (The ones who are bullying you probably have the least chance of collecting.)

How "going bankrupt" may actually *improve* your credit rating!

Where you can legally deposit your savings so they're

I found out some very interesting things in this process, such as: how to make myself judgment proof; how to pay off my debts — on my terms; where I could go for free legal advice; and how going bankrupt could have actually improved my credit rating!

probably safe, even if you do go bankrupt.

How and where to borrow at "wholesale" rates.

How to get your hands on money you may not know you have.

All of these things, and a lot more, are perfectly legal — and honorable. They are based on laws and facts that the Easy Credit Merchants, Finance Companies, and Collection Agencies hope you won't find out about. But an honest man can use this information to pay off his bills in an orderly fashion without living in fear or being sick with worry.

Which brings us back to the original point: How to turn Worry into Wampum. When I'd worked out a plan for getting us out of debt, I realized that there had to be a lot of people in the same boat. So I wrote a book entitled *The Power of Money Management.* I then wrote an ad, headlined "Get out of debt in 90 minutes — without borrowing." (The 90 minutes referred to the legal steps you can take, with or without a lawyer, that stop creditors from badgering you.)

Some newspapers and magazines refused to publish the ad. (The Easy Credit Merchants and Finance Companies are big advertisers.) The Bar Association investigated the ad and the book — and cleared both — somewhat reluctantly. (After all, lawyers have to make a living, too.)

The net result was that I sold over 100,000 copies.

In solving my own problems — and sharing the solution — I made a lot of money and, not so incidentally, helped a lot of other people with debt problems.

So I'm going to hand you a great opportunity. Make a list of your worries. Pick your biggest, meanest Worry. Then make a list of alternatives — the ways the problem might be solved. Next, gather all the information you can about the possible solutions. Usually, at this point, the

I then realized that there were probably a lot of other people in the same boat I was in. So I wrote a book, The Power of Money Management, *and the net result was that I sold over 100,000 copies!*

Solving a problem, and sharing your solution with others, not only helps them, but can make you a lot of money in the process.

answer will be obvious. If it's not, or if you don't like the answer, simply turn the problem over to your Subconscious Computer.

When you get your solution — and you will — you could be on your way to getting rich. First, because you'll have proved to yourself how easily you can rid yourself of your own worries. Second, if it was a really Big Worry — one that a lot of other people share — they'll be glad to pay you for telling them how to solve it.

TURN WORRY INTO WAMPUM

If you don't have any worries of your own, here's a list of subjects that other people are concerned about. They represent a compilation of the questions (almost 300,000) sent into the research division of the *Encyclopedia Brittanica*. The list is in order of most popular reports requested through December 1991 and the greatest number of questions. They are:

Establishing a Small Business, How to Prepare a Business Plan, Recycling Trends and Potentials, Debate Over Capital Punishment, Acid Rain, Euthanasia, Abortion Issue, The Right to Die, Ocean Dumping, Water Pollution, Animal Experimentation, Garbage Crisis, Child Abuse, Adolescent Suicide, Effects of Marijuana, Ozone Depletion, Air Pollution, AIDS as a Public Health Problem, Tobacco Smoke, the Effects of Cocaine.

That's what other people are worrying about. I think it's obvious that millions of dollars are already being made, providing some of the answers. But I assure you that they haven't scratched the surface. So go to it — pick a worry you really like — and get rich!

When you're problem-solving, don't overlook the obvious. The best answers are usually brilliantly simple. Don't fret that "It's so obvious that someone else must have thought of it," with the inference that "It's so easy;

There are plenty of problems that still need solving. Just because someone else may be making millions from their solution, there's still plenty of room for yours.

Don't overlook the obvious. Just because your solution may seem so easy — so obvious — it still doesn't mean that anything has been done on it.

Though ungrateful, broke, and mad, I had an idea for making money in the surplus business. It suited me well; I didn't need to buy anything until I had a customer.

something must be wrong with it." Chances are that someone else *did* think of it . . . and abandoned the idea for that very reason. Don't make the same mistake.

UNGRATEFUL — BROKE AND MAD

Let me tell you about a modest, personal experience with the danger of overlooking the obvious.

When I got out of the service, I was 20 years old, married, had one child. I went over to UCLA to enroll and saw the long lines of students queuing up in front of the Registrar's window. I decided that 2 years, 9 months and 13 days of waiting in line for food, haircuts, supplies, and the latrine had been enough. I wasn't going to wait in line for an education. I was going to get a job.

But I found out there wasn't really a big demand for ex-Third Class Pharmacist's Mates with a high school degree. The only job I was offered at what we called the 52-20 Club (because for 52 weeks an unemployed veteran could draw up to $20 a week) was as a Roller Skate Assembler. It paid $35 a week for a 48-hour week. When I turned it down, the 52-20 man told me that I was ungrateful and cut off the $20 a week.

Now I was not only ungrateful, I was broke. And I was mad. For years, an older friend of mine had been telling me about all the money that could be made in the surplus business. Not War Surplus, but the surplus goods acquired by manufacturers and businesses. Things they'd sell cheap because they couldn't dispose of them through their normal channels. You didn't have to have any capital, he said, because you didn't buy anything until you had a customer.

Well, I was scared — but desperate. So I took a streetcar into downtown Los Angeles. The first big building I saw was the May Company Department Store. I went up to their Purchasing Office. I told the lady that I was in the Surplus Business — did they have anything they wanted to sell? She thought for a moment, then said there was one thing. The May Company had about 20,000 small cardboard shipping cartons. It seemed that during the War, the government had specified that all packages sent overseas to servicemen had to be shipped in this kind of a carton. Now, with the war over, nobody was buying them. Would I like to make her an offer?

I swallowed hard and told her I would have to call my "associate," who was our company expert on shipping cartons. In a daze, I wandered out of her office and into a phone booth. I held the phone book dumbly in my hands. Who would want to buy 20,000 shipping cartons that weren't being used to mail packages overseas any more? The one obvious answer was a "paper jobber," who would sell them to small manufacturing companies for their shipping needs. But surely the Purchasing Office lady would have thought of this outlet. It was too simple. There must be some reason the paper jobbers couldn't use them.

But, out of sheer desperation, I looked in the Yellow Pages and found the largest ad. (It turned out later to be a very small company.) Sure enough, a line in the ad assured me that they bought and sold cardboard cartons. I called them, described the carton the best I could, and asked what they'd pay for 20,000. The man told me one-and-one-half cents a piece — $300 for the lot. I thanked him and told him I'd let him know.

I went back to the Purchasing Office and told the lady I'd pay her $250. She accepted the offer. I was in the surplus business and I had made $50 the very first day — the equivalent of a week-and-a-half's pay as a Roller Skate Assembler.

Most important, I'd learned my lesson: Never Overlook the Obvious. Sure, the Purchasing Office lady could have made the same phone call. However, she had a lot of other things on her mind — and it wasn't her money. But I was

By using the obvious — most simple — solution, I was able to earn in one day what would take a week and a half at a normal job.

concentrating on that one little problem — and it was easy money if I could solve it.

I did find out later what the boxes were really worth at "wholesale" — about a nickel a piece or $1,000 for the lot — and about $2,000 at "retail," and that they were easily saleable because there was a paper shortage. No matter, my business career was launched — and I'd learned a lesson that would profit me a thousandfold.

The windup on this story is that in less than six months we moved out of my in-laws' house into a handsome apartment, paid cash for a brand-new car, and had *four years'* income in the bank. All because it occurred to me that if the May Company had a large inventory of these "obsolete" boxes, the same must be true of every major department store and dime store in the country. I didn't have the capital, so I had to buy one batch, sell it, and then parlay the profits to buy a bigger batch. Storage space was scarce and expensive so I rented private garages in my neighborhood for next to nothing. It was slow and a lot of hard work. But it sure beat assembling roller skates.

Incidentally, there's still a lot of money to be made in the Surplus Business (only now it's called "recycling"). Is it something you'd enjoy doing? The only basic it requires is imagination.

IMAGINATION — THE KEY TO ALL SUCCESS.

Which brings us to the next point. It's the counterpoint to "Don't overlook the obvious." This lesson is entitled "Don't accept the obvious." To illustrate, I'm going to ask you to change the following figure into a "6" using only a single line:

IX

The bottom line? By applying the obvious solution, in less than six months I was able to get a new apartment, buy a brand-new car, and had the equivalent of four years of income in the bank.

I've provided you this entire page as a worksheet to figure out the answer. Use it and enjoy. When you're ready either with the correct answer or have reached your frustration level, turn the page for the answer.

Here's the answer:

SIX

Simple, wasn't it? But only one out of 500 will get it right. The "trick" is that most people immediately see the "IX" as a Roman numeral, and they're trapped. Or they think only in terms of a straight line, not a curved one. They accept what is "obvious."

In trying to find an imaginative solution to a problem, examine what "everybody else" is doing. Don't assume that, with their wider experience, "they" must be right. They may just be playing "follow the leader." Instead, apply what I call "Operation Zig Zag." Determine what everyone else is doing — and then ask yourself what would happen if you did just the opposite — when "they" zig, you zag.

COME ON DOWN — LOUSY FOOD — BAD SERVICE

Successful restaurant businesses have been built by advertising "Lousy food, bad service" or something to that effect. True, nobody believed the sign or they just had to find out for themselves. But it worked. It got people to try the food and service — at least once.

When I started doing advertising for the Ford agency I mentioned earlier, we looked at what our competitors were doing. You can tell me what it was, because they're still doing it. Everyone was the largest, offered the best trade-ins, practically gave cars away; and if you didn't have enough money to buy a car, they'd lend it to you. On TV, they always sponsored old movies so they could have frequent, long commercials and show lots of their used car "bargains."

They did all this because that was the way it had "always been done" and the techniques had apparently worked very well for some of the car dealers. (Happily, most of the competitors we surveyed at that time have since gone

When searching for an imaginative solution, sometimes by doing the opposite of what everyone else is doing you can come out a winner.

"Lousy food, bad service," the motto for a successful restaurant?

broke. In fact, all except one — which only proves that you can't lose 'em all.)

So how do you go about advertising for a small car dealer, in an inconvenient location, who has a few green salesmen?

TRUTH WORKS WONDERS

Well, when all else fails, *tell the truth* (it works wonders in advertising). In our advertising, we told people that we were a small car dealer in an inconvenient location, with a few green salesmen. Then we also admitted that we were in business to make a profit — at least enough so that we could be around long enough to give them the service they had coming. We didn't show any used cars or quote any "bargain" prices. We shared our feeling that if a car was priced way below the market, it must be because that was all the car was really worth or the dealer was losing money — and why would a dealer add the cost of advertising to the loss he was already taking on a sale — unless he really didn't intend to sell it?

We interviewed numerous customers ("live" so we couldn't be accused of editing) who told how they'd saved money or had a financing problem solved. We guaranteed that we'd do anything within reason and a few things that were unreasonable — to keep a customer happy.

Instead of having many long commercials in one movie, we bought a number of comparatively short commercials in many different kinds of programs.

In other words, where our competitors zigged, we zagged. The whole campaign was directed toward building confidence and believability because we thought that people distrusted car dealers in general. And you have to be trusted if you're going to sell something to anyone. And you have to live up to that trust if you're going to sell them again.

The result: The Ford agency netted over a million

If all else fails, tell the truth in advertising. It works wonders.

By doing the opposite of what everyone else was doing, I helped build a local Ford agency into one of the most profitable in the nation.

Welcome problems, because when you solve them: 1) you rebuild your self-esteem and 2) your solution can become the foundation for an exciting new business.

dollars in the first three years. Moral: Don't accept the obvious.

There are two reasons why you should *welcome* problems:

1. As you solve them, you rebuild your self-esteem. It's powerful help in correcting your ISI. And the knowledge, the skill, the practice in problem-solving you gain as you solve each problem make it easier to solve the next one.

2. When you solve a really BIG problem, in an imaginative way, you could be laying the foundation for an exciting, enriching business.

Problem-solving is an *adventure*. It'll take you places you've never been before. It'll make you see things you've only looked at before. One of the curious things that happens when you start researching your answers is what I call "Tuning In."

"Tuning in" works like this: When you get interested in a subject, you "tune in" to sources of information you would have otherwise missed. Articles in newspapers and magazines, TV and radio programs, the conversations of friends, the sermon at church — all of these things and more — suddenly start coming into your awareness. You get vital input you would not have seen or heard if you hadn't been "tuned in." In my own case, I'm not sure whether the information was there all along and I had missed it — or whether some kind of magnetism I've unleashed is drawing the new material and attracting people who can be of help to me. It doesn't matter. It works.

Selective perception: you buy a new car. Suddenly you notice how many others are driving the very same make.

The correct definition of this phenomenon is Selective Perception. You selectively perceive what your subconscious is searching for. A common experience in "tuning in" or in Selective Perception is when you buy a new car — all of a sudden you notice lots of the same make you never noticed before. Or when you find out you are about to become a parent — all of a sudden you notice babies and pregnant women.

When you're tracking down answers, do it with energy and enthusiasm. Don't be afraid to ask questions. No one will think you're stupid. Remember what Will Rogers, the Cowboy Philosopher, said: "We're all ignorant . . . only on different subjects." Experts are flattered by your interest in "their" subject.

When you make a mistake, make it a WHOPPER. Anyone can make a careless or thoughtless mistake. All that shows is that you weren't paying attention or weren't interested.

But a BIG mistake — one that you've put a lot of thought, heart and sweat into — a mistake that you made after carefully weighing the alternatives and energetically implementing the conclusions. Now, that's a mistake to be proud of.

Babe Ruth held two records: one for home runs and the other for strikeouts. But he isn't remembered for his strikeouts.

I don't know of any advance in science that was made without a whole series of mistakes being made. And what's "science" but a systematized approach to solving problems? Each "failure" brings you one step closer to the right answer.

I know one insurance salesman who used the phone to "prospect." He figured out that for every ten "cold calls" he made, he got nine "No's" and one "Yes." So each "No" was not a rebuff. It was just a step up the ladder. He could hardly wait to go up the nine steps so he could get what he was after — the "Yes" at the top.

My only question is: Could he, with Dyna/Psyc, have raised his expectation say, one "Yes" for every five "No's?"

If you make a mistake make it a BIG mistake. Babe Ruth held records for both home runs AND strike outs!

A few years ago I helped set up a sales training program for real estate salesmen. Through interviews with the most successful salesmen, we had been able to determine what they did to find prospects, make presentations, close sales.

We distilled the best techniques and taught them to the new salesmen. This was a Formula for Success. Because we were able to prove to them that, if they followed our program, step by step, they would get the following results: For every five phone calls they made, they would make one appointment. One out of three people would keep the appointment and two would cancel. One out of three of the people who kept the appointment would visit the property being sold. And one out of three who visited the property would buy.

So all the new salesmen had to do is make 135 phone calls to wind up with one sale. And if the average commission was $1700, that made each phone call — whether the particular answer was "Yes" or "No" — worth $12.60. If they made 30 phone calls a day, worked five days a week, took a two-week vacation, their income for the year would be $94,500!

Success is a matter of viewpoint. The pessimist sees the bottle as half empty. The optimist sees it as half full.

My wife is the most optimistic person I know. I tease her that if she found a pile of manure in the middle of the living room, she'd clap her hands and say, "Oh boy! Somebody gave me a pony."

She bounces out of bed each morning, eager to discover the delightful surprises she knows the day holds.

She knows that everyone loves her and that they delight in her enthusiasm and curiosity. If, infrequently, she meets someone who isn't taken with her charm, she's disturbed, at most, only momentarily. She wonders (if she

Success is a matter of viewpoint. The pessimist sees the bottle as half empty. The optimist see it as half full.

reacts to it at all) what's wrong with *them*.

EVERYBODY IS IN SALES

You may wonder why I dwell so much on salesmen. Because we're all salesmen. When you were a "helpless" infant, you had to occasionally convince your mother that you needed to be fed. When you were a child and growing up you had to use sales techniques on your parents to get what you wanted. You had to "sell" yourself to your lover, your boss, your customers, your friends. The technique was always the same. All you had to show them was that you had something they wanted — even if it was "only" your respect or admiration — even if it was only the self-respect they achieved by doing their duty.

So we're all salesmen — good, bad, and indifferent. And the good salesmen get more because they expect more.

DON'T JUST GET ALONG — GET AHEAD

Don't be afraid to ask "Why?"

It's no accident that children learn most during their first six years— before we start "educating" them and getting them to memorize "facts" instead of youthfully pursuing their interests and satisfying their curiosity.

The two subjects our schools teach best are "Sitting Still" and "Being Quiet." A child can "pass" if he does very little else. Then we wonder why adults are so passive. Why they have so little energy (call it ambition or "get up and go"). Why they accept the "rules" without question.

That's because they've learned their lesson — "That's how you get along" — and they've learned it well.

Well, don't just "get along" — Get Ahead.

The persons who ask "Why? show that they're not just "doing" — they're thinking, and they'll probably find a better way to do it. Business is hungry for Thinkers. They'll shower them with rewards because there are so few Thinkers. Many Doers but very few Thinkers. And all you

We are all in sales. The infant wanting to be fed. The child wanting a toy. The housewife wanting respect. The employee, a raise. The business owner, more customers. And the good salesmen get more because they expect more.

The persons who ask "Why?" show that they're not just doing— they're thinking.

The only things I regret . . . are the things I didn't do.

have to do to be a Thinker is use the magic word. It's "Why?"

Don't be afraid to take chances.

How many people do you know who have starved to death? You won't starve either.

When you've figured out where you want to go — jump. If there's a two-foot chasm between where you are and the next peak, the only way you'll fall in is by taking a timid step.

My father-in-law, in his late seventies, told me something I never forgot. I was a little nervous about having bought our new home. I thought I could swing the payments, but what if . . .

He said, "What's the worst that could happen? You might live in your beautiful new house for a couple of years and then lose it. But you'll have had it for a couple of years, and you can never lose that memory. Isn't that better than never having had it at all?" He paused for a moment, and I could sense that he was looking back on his own life. "You know," he said quietly, "the only things I regret . . . are the things I didn't do."

DAILY BUILD UP

Set aside a definite, prescribed time each day to build your new life. Include your Daily Declarations in the morning when you get up and just before you go to sleep. Time: 20 minutes. Super Suggestion once each day. Time: 10 minutes. Then take a half-hour, an hour — whatever you can spare — to make your purpose and supporting goals a reality. R.S.V.P. — Read. Study. Visualize. Perform.

That's an average of an hour and a half out of your 16 waking hours — 9 percent to discover what you have that other people want. And that 9 percent of your time is probably time that you're frittering away worrying or watching TV or something else that's meaningless. But 9 percent of your life is seven years. And even if you've lived more than half of it, that's three years. Can you think of many problems that couldn't be solved in three years of concentrated effort?

So don't tell me you "haven't got the time." The wisest man I ever knew told me that "Most people are too busy earning a living to make any money." Don't take as long as I did to find out he was right.

Don't be "too busy" earning a living to make any money.

Every newspaper and magazine is crammed with Business Opportunities — and I don't mean the ads or the ones that appear in the Classified Section. Newspapers and magazines report the things that people are interested in and concerned about. Today. Right now.

Every newspaper and magazine is crammed with business opportunities.

SCAN THE NEWSPAPER FOR IDEAS

Here are one day's headlines and some rather obvious products they suggest — most of which could be or are being sold by Direct Response methods.

The ideas are there for the picking. All you have to do is take the time to look for them.

"Free Rides for Elderly"

Senior Citizens have millions of dollars to spend for leisure, gifts for their grandchildren. They're concerned about property taxes, hospitalization costs. How can you help them?

"Sued Firm Agrees to Cancel Subscriptions"

How about a consumer newsletter warning people in your town about rackets?

"8 Day Gospel Convention to be Held Here"

Conventioneers need places to stay and places to go, souvenirs.

"Family of Gang-War Victim Makes Appeal"

So much violence. What about a personal alarm that people could carry?

Here is something for you to think about. I believe it was Emerson who said it: "The creation of a thousand forests is in one acorn."

"Credit Card Fees Deductible"

How about a pamphlet listing overlooked deductions?

"Panel Says Autos Can Meet Smog Goal"

How about lightweight gas masks that people can wear? More serious answer: Natural gas is a practically smogless fuel. It triples engine life and the "life" of your oil and lube jobs. Its only drawbacks are that a car loses about 10% in speed of acceleration and you can only go about 120 miles on a tankful. So who needs to go from 0 to 60 in 9 seconds? Ten seconds is fast enough for me. And there are dual-fuel systems available for about $1500, installed. So you could still go on long trips, using the natural gas for the trips around town that rack up 90% of your mileage. Mileage figures are about the same, and natural gas costs fewer cents a gallon. (It's apparent that I've done some research on this. But I'm not greedy. C'mon in; the money's fine.)

"Traffic Snarled as Drifting Snow Covers Midwest"

Could roads be heated like an electric blanket by "planting" wires when they're paved — and melt the snow?

"48 Meat Plants Called Unclean"

Could you start a maintenance service to take care of this problem for them?

So much for the news. When I look over the ads, I really can't see a thing that couldn't be sold better and cheaper by Direct Response. Even cars are being sold that way, and I'm told that a buyer can save several hundred dollars.

I've told you a few of the ways that you can develop a

There's hardly a thing that couldn't be sold better or cheaper than by Direct Response . . . even cars.

unique product or service. Probably the best ones will crop up when you open up your mind to the possibilities.

For example:

1. We were testing some "invisible" powders that would help trap thieves. That didn't work out the way we hoped. But we suddenly realized that a process we'd developed would make it possible to produce Christmas ornaments that would be shatterproof, glow in the dark, and sell for less than a buck. Through the years we've sold millions of them.

2. I was talking to my best friend. I found out that he had a manuscript telling all about, "How to Build Your Own Swimming Pool for Less Than $500." I arranged to have it published. The booklet cost us about 50 cents and we sold them for $10. The people who bought them got more than their money's worth and we made out all right.

3. One of the newspaper sales representatives who called on me kidded me about what an easy way I had of making a living. He said that he'd like to find something to sell — and get away from punching a clock. I asked him what he liked to do best. He grinned and told me, "Play the horses." I asked him if he was any good at it; he told me, "Yes." So, I suggested that he write a book. I needled him for about two years, but he never did write the book. But he did run into a guy named Larry Voegele, who had a fantastic record of success at picking the winners — and had written a book, *Professional Method of Winner Selection*. I bought the rights, and in our best year we sold 130,000 copies at $10 apiece.

The former newspaper sales representative quit his job and became my associate in a Handicapping

The importance of this process of opening up your mind to new possibilities was best put by Oliver Wendell Holmes when he said, "Man's mind stretched to a new idea, never goes back to its original dimensions."

School. At the Handicapping School (which has since become a home study course), Larry Voegele (The Master) teaches what he knows in a three night course that costs $200. The fellow who introduced us is the Administrator and probably makes more money working from 9 to noon than he did when he was peddling space full time — and has plenty of time to go to the track.

4. My wife read a newspaper article about a new kind of diet plan developed by a doctor. We investigated and saw the possibilities of marketing it. The circulation of that newspaper is over a million.

   But one person who read that article did something about it. The result: the Northwestern Weight-Loss Plan was the largest selling product in its field, and sold for almost 20 years.

5. A client of mine gave me about 200 door-viewers. (You know the things they put in doors so the person inside can see who's outside without being seen.) He'd imported about 500 from Germany; these were the remains and he couldn't seem to sell them. He thought maybe I could figure out what to do with them. At any rate, we moved them out of his warehouse into mine. There they gathered dust for two years.

   One day the shipping clerk told me they were in the way and asked if he should throw them out. Well, I was too cheap to do that, so I called a wholesale hardware company and a couple of retail hardware stores. They all gave me the same story. They weren't interested in an odd lot of what was, at best, a slow-moving item. They already had regular suppliers of "name brand" merchandise. The challenge nagged me, and I finally assigned the

A man to carry on a successful business, must have imagination. He must see things as in a vision, a dream of the whole thing.

CHARLES M. SCHWAB (1862–1939)
American industrialist

problem to my Subconscious Computer. A few days later, driving home, I got the answer.

Why should a door-viewer be installed in just a front door? Why not any door? Or in a fence? Or even a wall?

So, I pulled off the freeway, into a gas station. I scribbled out an ad. I can't say I "wrote" it. It just came to me. (That's one of the creepy things that happens when you use your Subconscious Computer.)

The headline was "Super-Spy Lets You See Through Walls, Fences, and Locked Doors." The ad resulted in interviews on national radio and TV; was reprinted by a *Los Angeles Times* columnist (who hated it) and by *New Yorker Magazine* (who thought it was funny). Most important, it sold over 140,000 door-viewers.

The secret of this business is to milk your winner — and when you lay an egg, cut your loses.

Don't get me wrong. I've had my share of flops. Can you figure out what to do with a game that tests your ESP Quotient? Or some beautiful Christmas cards with a sculptured medallion that glows in the dark? We sold some of these items, but not enough to make it interesting. But someday . . .

The secret of success in this business (or maybe any business) is to milk your winners — and when you lay an egg, cut your losses. If you've taken your best shot, and it hasn't worked, forget it and go on to the next project. Since you can test your potential so inexpensively (and I'll show you how) you can have an awful lot of losers before you can have one winner. And the Winner will make up your losses — and then some.

Here are some more ways to develop a product or service: When looking at something, play "What Would Happen If."

Stretch your imagination. It's a muscle and it develops with use.

Don't become a "distributor" or fall for those "get into the import business" or "buy at wholesale approach."

What Would Happen if . . .

It was larger?

It was smaller?

It was upside down?

It was inside out?

You charged more?

You charged less?

You used it in a different way?

It was made out of a better kind of material?

It was made out of a cheaper kind of material?

S-t-r-e-t-c-h your imagination. It's a muscle and develops with use.

I've told you a lot of different ways you can find a product or service to sell. Now I'm going to warn you about a couple of things I do not recommend.

1. Don't become a "distributor" for some gadget unless you get an exclusive from the manufacturer. Even if you do, be careful. Just the other night, a magazine sales representative told me this true story:

   A small businessman had a modest success selling a wooden chest for coasters for $7.95. A larger firm noticed that the ads were repeated and deduced that it was a success. So he played "What Would Happen If" it was made of a simulated wood and offered for $4.95. Then a larger firm played the same game, produced it out of plastic and sold it for $2.95. Recently, a very large firm produced the same item in a very cheap Styrofoam and is selling it for $1.49.

   Don't be too reassured if the gadget is patented. There are plenty of unscrupulous people who know that patents don't hold up or can be changed slightly. In any event, patent litigation is very costly and it takes a long, long time to get to court.

2. Don't fall for the "Mail Order Courses" or "Get Into the Import Business; Buy at Wholesale" approach. Mostly for the reasons I've already enumerated (lack of exclusivity, etc.). But, even more important, because you'll be paying too much for the merchandise. (I'll go into that at greater length later.) Most of these outfits are primarily interested in charging you for having your firm name printed on a catalog. Then you have to dig up the mailing list (more about that later, too) and pay the postage costs. Any orders that do straggle in result in a sure profit for them . . . and a doubtful one for you.

Besides, if you use the techniques I've described, you can come up with enough products of your own. And they're the best — and most profitable — kind.

There are opportunities all around — and within — you.

Don't forget: "All things come to him who goes after them."

FIRST, MAKE UP YOUR MIND — TO MAKE MONEY.
SECOND, CHANGE YOUR MIND — WITH DYNA/PSYC.
THIRD, OPEN YOUR MIND — SO YOU CAN TRULY SEE WHAT YOU'VE ONLY "LOOKED AT" BEFORE.

You'll soon find the problem isn't coming up with ideas, it's evaluating and following through with them.

If you are faithful in using the principles of Dyna/Psyc for creating ideas, you are soon going to find out that the problem is not getting the idea. It's evaluating the idea and carrying it through to completion. Now, how do you determine whether the idea you have come up with is the right one for you to pursue and how do you launch it successfully?

SHARE YOUR IDEAS CAREFULLY

One of the first things Joe became aware of, when he consulted with people who had read his book, is that most people haven't the slightest idea where to go and who to ask for help in evaluating and developing their ideas. Many times Joe heard people tell about good ideas they had, that were not pursued, because someone gave them bad advice. When a new business idea is born in your subconscious computer, like any newborn baby, it tends to be a little delicate and fragile. The wrong treatment in its infancy can destroy what can become a really tremendous idea. The worst thing that you can do with an idea in its formative stages is to expose it to too many people, especially the wrong kind of people. It never ceases to amaze me how many people will expose their ideas for evaluation to people who are negative and uninformed. The first rule for nourishing and developing your ideas is:

Don't talk about them to your friends, spouse or brother-in-law or next door neighbor unless they have extensive special experience that can be helpful to you or they have already shown that they are successful entrepreneurs and you know from past experience that they are supportive of your ideas.

IDEA KILLER

You have two problems when you expose your ideas and plans to someone else. The first is, unless you choose very carefully, your "expert" may have absolutely nothing from which to base his opinion about your idea, even if he is successful in his own profession. Your second problem is what I call the "Second Crab in the Bucket Syndrome." When you go crabbing you don't have to put a lid on your bucket once you have at least two crabs in it, because as soon as one tries to climb out the other will pull him back. Some of your friends are professional second crabs and they will put down your idea or plans, no matter how good they are. Does that mean you should never seek advice? No. Expert advice can be extremely helpful after your idea has had a chance to develop some substance and you have had a chance to build some confidence in it. Also, when you consult an expert you have to know the right questions to ask. Otherwise, you will not get the answers you need. And in getting expert advice, remember, free advice is usually worth exactly what you paid for it.

BACK TO JOE RE: CREATING IDEAS.

The same gentleman who told me that "Most people are too busy trying to earn a living to make any money" gave me a business maxim I never forgot:

A GOOD IDEA DOESN'T TAKE MUCH MONEY.

It's proved to be true for me. And I'll prove it can be true for you.

You can spend a lot of money on a good idea, but that doesn't make it any better. And all the money in the world won't salvage a bad idea.

The beautiful part of a good idea is that it's self-financing. You can, and should, expand by plowing part of the profits back in. "Seed" or "venture" capital should be small, something you can afford to lose. Not because, as every gambler says, "Desperate money doesn't win."

There never was an idea started that woke up men out of their stupid indifference but its originator was spoken as a crank.

**OLIVER WENDELL HOLMES, SR.
(1809–1894)
American physician, professor, man of letters**

Should you never seek advice? No. Expert advice can be extremely helpful after your idea has had a chance to develop.

The beautiful part of a good idea is that it's self-financing.

Because desperate money does win — sometimes. But you've reduced your odds for success.

I can think of a number of deals that I literally worried to death. Instead of going with my original concept, I kept changing it around, hoping to hedge my bet. I was playing a destructive game of "What would happen if . . .?" The ideas that I worked and reworked failed. No exceptions.

The ideas I've conceived in a white heat and pursued with enthusiasm succeeded 50% of the time. It's been enough to make me rich.

The ones I conceived in a white heat and pursued with enthusiasm succeeded about 50 percent of the time. That's a .500 batting average, and it's been enough to make me rich. Rich enough that when a friend I told you about (the one who made 11 million dollars in this business in eight years) jokingly asked me if I wanted a partner, I could honestly tell him, "No. I don't have any problems that money can solve." And you shouldn't want a partner either. Because you don't need one.

I told you before and I'll tell you again, "You can have everything in the world you really want."

Nothing would give me more pleasure than to see you succeed. And you will — if you do nothing more than apply what you're learning in these pages.

Every successful person uses some of these methods. The most successful use more of them.

And, since you're still with me, maybe you will at least try it. I know it sounds "too easy," but it works! Every successful person uses some of these methods. The most successful use more of them. These successful people may not follow the form, but they surely follow the substance because they couldn't succeed without it.

Dyna/Psyc is a systemized method for releasing creativity. All you have to do is follow the system. That's all you have to do. What have you got to lose?

I guess that two kinds of people will respond to that challenge. The first will be the person who's open-minded enough to admit that he's seen some evidence that the principle works — even in his own life — and the refinements we've offered might make it work better. The other kind of person is desperate, but not without hope. As one man wrote to me, "I'm a truck driver. I realize that the best I can get out of life right now is some overtime. There has to be something better than this." There is. I promise.

But I'm worried about all those people in between. The ones who are saying, "Oh yeah, all that Positive Thinking stuff. I know all about that." Oh no they don't! If they really knew — and put it into action — they wouldn't be in humdrum jobs, or making "some" money, but not enough.

And what you have in your hands is not "just" Positive Thinking. I know. I took the Dale Carnegie course. I read Norman Vincent Peale and Napoleon Hill. And I got a lot out of them. But Dyna/Psyc takes over where Positive Thinking leaves off. Dyna/Psyc gives you everything that Science and Psychology have discovered about the System for Success. Work the System — and the System will work for you.

Maybe you're not interested in the Direct Response Business. I love it, because I think it's one of the last areas where a little guy can get a start, live where he pleases, work when he wants.

But, regardless of whether the Direct Response Business or any other idea appeals to you, I assure you that, using Dyna/Psyc and getting the kind of help you need, the freedom and pleasure of a business of your own can be yours. And you can't say that you "don't know how to go about it" because you now know a lot more than I did when I got started.

> *Dyna/Psyc takes over where Positive Thinking leaves off. You do what you can — Dyna/Psyc will do what you can't.*

EVALUATING YOUR IDEAS

Joe was right. Using the principles of Dyna/Psyc does work! Let's expand on this process in regard to the next step in creating and developing ideas — evaluating that idea. How do you determine whether the idea you have come up with is the right one for you to pursue ?

Believe in your idea. Ask your subconscious computer to help you expand it.

DEVELOP CONFIDENCE IN YOUR IDEA

Develop confidence in your own judgment and the power of your subconscious mind to come up with the details necessary to fill out your idea. That means you must continue to ask your subconscious computer to expand and develop the idea just as Joe did. It also means that you use your conscious mind to collect as much information as possible to feed your computer. This information should be factual, not feelings of doubt.

More enterprises fail because of cash flow problems than for any other reason. Don't commit yourself to large expenditures.

FINANCIAL CONSIDERATIONS

Let's look further at the financial aspects of your idea as we continue our evaluation process. As Joe said, "It doesn't take much money to create an idea." But it is crucial to manage and budget what money you have wisely. Cash flow is the first thing to consider. Good cash flow means that you always have enough in the till to meet current expenses. More enterprises fail because of cash flow problems than because of any other reason. And usually it could have been avoided with a little planning. Don't commit yourself to large expenditures until you know the idea will work. Don't buy the product, until you know you can move it. If you need to secure your position, take a short-term option for as little money as possible. Better still, try to work out an agreement that doesn't cost you anything, until you actually need the product.

The best ideas are the simple ones.

IDEAS THAT ARE SIMPLE

There are three other general principles to keep in mind in evaluating your ideas. The **first** is: *the best ideas are the simple ones.* The cleverness comes in thinking of them. If you find your ideas really complicated and they become even more complex as you try to solve the problems that arise, then they are probably not the best idea for you to go with — especially your first time out. It was Joe's experience that the really good highly profitable, low-risk ideas are always based on a simple concept with only minor variations.

IDEAS THAT MULTIPLY

The **second** principle in evaluating your idea is: *How much leverage will it provide?* Leverage means the ability to multiply your efforts or your money or the value of your time. A good example of leverage on your money is buying your own home instead of renting. Suppose you buy a piece of property for 10% down. If the total value of the property appreciates at least 15% per year, which it has in many areas of the country, you will earn three or four times that much on your investment even after your interest costs. This is because the appreciation is on the total value of the property, not just on your 10% down payment. Multi-level direct sales plans such as Amway and Shaklee Corporation are examples of programs that allow you to multiply your efforts by building a sales organization. The multiple listing approach to real estate sales is another example. You can have hundreds of agents trying to sell your listing. Of course, Joe's baby was direct response marketing: direct mail, magazines, television, radio and newspapers. A good ad in the right place turned Joe into thousands of salesmen making calls. Your idea should provide you some leverage. A good idea must give you leverage on your time, your efforts, or your money. If you can get sufficient leverage on your money and you have some capital to play with, you can live without leverage on your efforts. Don't fall into the trap of building your idea around yourself as the indispensable person unless there is an opportunity for tremendous leverage on the value of your time. Otherwise, you will find yourself worked to death to keep the thing going.

A good idea must give you leverage on your time, your efforts, or your money.

IDEAS HAVE OBSTACLES

Your **third** principle to remember in evaluating your

idea is to be aware of a potential obstacle to avoid, and that is: *too much planning.* I call this the "Green Light Syndrome." If you are in a hurry to get across town, you don't sit in your car in your driveway waiting for all the traffic lights on your route to turn green. There will be times when you should go ahead with an idea, even though there is a potential problem down the road that you haven't completely solved. Remember, you have a powerful tool working for you. Your Subconscious Computer is a tremendous success mechanism. If you program it properly, by the time you reach that problem, it will come up with the answers you need.

FILL IN THE DETAILS OF YOUR IDEA

Assume that the solutions and answers you need actually exist and are available to you.

Now, let's examine how you use your Subconscious Computer to fill in the details of your idea and to solve the problems associated with the development of your idea. The key here is to assume that the solutions and answers you need actually exist and are available to you. Your subconscious takes its instructions literally. If you say, "I can't figure this out" or "This is impossible," your subconscious will take your word for it and not even try to find the solution. So, as usual, you have to be careful of the way you talk to yourself and put your negative input into proper perspective. I found that I had to tell my subconscious to search for the answers I need. I told you how Joe programmed his subconscious to provide him with the advertising approach that made his first million dollars.

There is one final thought. If the idea you are evaluating came as a result of the proper programming of your subconscious, then you can be sure that the additional help you need will be available to you, too. And it is a pretty good indication that the idea has a strong possibility for taking you to your goal. Otherwise, your computer would not have come up with it in the first place.

BRINGING YOUR IDEAS TO COMPLETION

The care and development of a new moneymaking idea is extremely important. Like a newborn child, your new idea is fragile at first. Treat it gently and don't expose it to harsh treatment — such as the criticism of others — until you've had chance to strengthen the idea and develop some confidence in it.

Like a newborn child, your new idea is fragile at first. Treat it gently until you've had a chance to strengthen it.

1. Start by writing out your idea in as much detail as you can. You won't know all the details at first, and get everything you do know down on paper. Break the project down into its major parts — the product itself, whether you are going to buy it or make it, what it will cost you. Your marketing strategies: What market are you going to reach? How are you going to reach that market? What type of approach are you going to make? How are you going to handle the distribution? And so on.

2. Make a list of the questions you need answers to. Identify an area in which you feel you need more information. Try to figure out where you need to go for the information. (By the way, the public library is often an excellent place to start.)

3. Figure out how many and what kinds of people you'll need to get your idea going. Try to identify the people you need and work out the kind of participation that is best for each, such as investors, partners, consultants, and employees.

4. Estimate the amount of money required to get your project successfully launched. Work out a strategy that will generate the maximum amount of progress for the least amount of money. Test your project, marketing approach, and market demand before you make large commitments.

5. While you are doing the above steps, keep asking

Above all else, remember these two things: 1) Ideas are the root of creation; and 2) no army can withstand the strength of an idea whose time has come.

your Subconscious Computer for the answers you need. Outlining your project, asking questions, studying available information will help to load your Subconscious Computer with all the information it needs. Be sure to tell your Subconscious Computer exactly what you want. For example, suppose you can't quite figure out how to finance your project. Each day before your Super Suggestion period, give the following instructions to your Subconscious Computer:

> *There is an ideal way to finance this project that I am becoming aware of. This financing approach is simple and within my ability to work out. The details of this plan are becoming clear in my mind.*

6. Remember that, to really be productive, an idea must provide you with some leverage; that is, a way of multiplying either your money or your efforts or the value of your time. If the idea of leverage is not clear to you, reread the last chapter again.

7. When your plan has taken shape and your Subconscious Computer has given you what you need to get started, *then start.* Don't let your idea die — as many die— because you can't get started. Even if you haven't solved all of the problems you can foresee, get your program moving.

8. Remember that all the best ideas are usually the simple ones. Avoid the "Band-Aid approach." When you are always running into a problem, take the necessary time to gather the information you need and then ask your Subconscious Computer for the best solution. Then act on your solution promptly and effectively.

9. Avoid distractions. Focus on your goal.

SETTING THE BEST PRICE

CHAPTER 5 OF BOOK TWO

The most common (and usually fatal) mistake that the amateur in the Direct Response Business makes is in the area of pricing. He simply doesn't realize how much he has to charge in order to make a profit. The inflexible rule is this: Your selling price must be at least three times your actual cost.

"Actual cost" is defined as:

1. The cost of the product

2. The cost of packaging (materials and labor)

3. The cost of postage

4. The cost of refunds/bad checks

For example, if you're going to sell a Widget, and the actual total cost is ten dollars, your sales price must be a minimum of thirty dollars.

Now using that minimum as a base, how much can you charge for it without running into buyer resistance? That depends, of course, on the item. What do similar or competitive products cost? What's it readily worth to a buyer in terms of what it'll do for them or save them? How important is the problem that your Widget solves?

The price you want to charge is the one that gives you the best return on your investment. And the best way to determine that optimum price is by testing.

TEST THE PRICING

Let's say that you're undecided whether to charge thirty, forty, or fifty dollars. To test, you prepare ads that are identical in every detail, except one — the price.

Then, for this purpose, you divide your prospects into three parts. Let's say that you are going to mail 3,000 letters to people who should be interested in what you're

As a minimum, your selling price must be at least three times your actual cost.

To determine the best selling price you must test.

287

selling. (I say 3,000 because the larger the "sample," the more you can rely on the results.) What you do is mail a thousand letters offering the $30 price; a thousand letters quoting the $40 price; and another thousand giving the $50 price.

Be sure that the only difference between the letters is the price and that they're all mailed at the same time. That's because when a person receives a letter this can have a strong influence on whether they respond to it or not. Furthermore, when you're testing, be sure that the different offers are equally distributed if there's an economic differential within the areas you're mailing to.

The selling price that generates the greatest number of dollars is the one you will most likely use.

When you get the orders, tabulate the results. The price offer that produced the greatest number of dollars is the one you'll probably want to use from then on. (There's another factor to weigh, which I'll go into at the end of this chapter.) However, if the difference in response is less than 5%, you usually go with the *lower* price.

For example, let's suppose you get a 100 orders at $30 ($3000); 90 orders at $40 ($3600); and 74 orders at $50 ($3700). The price you'd set would be $40. First, because the difference between dollar returns on the $40 offer and $50 offer is statistically insignificant. (Statisticians tell us that you have to allow for a 5 percent "error.") Second, your $40 offer produced almost 22 percent more customers. And those names are valuable for your own use in mailing similar or related offers in the future and renting to other people in Direct Response Business. In fact, there are many firms in this business who get the major portion of their income from renting their customer lists to firms with noncompetitive offers.

I said the names were valuable, and I'll prove it. We have one highly specialized list of about 330,000. I wouldn't take an offer of $2.50 per name on an outright sale! Why? Because I expect to make more than that this year alone, just "renting" the names — and I'll still own them.

3-TO-1 MARKUP

Back to Pricing. What do you do if you can't get a minimum of three times your actual cost? I can tell you the answer in two words: Forget it. And go on to something else.

Now the 3-to-1 markup doesn't assure you of success. It just gives you a fighting chance. I'm simply stating, flatly, that you have little, if any, possibility of succeeding without it.

Are there any exceptions? Yes — one: When you're handling a high-priced item and the number of dollars of profit generated by each sale is sufficient. What do I mean by "sufficient"? Let's say that you're selling a computer by mail for $1000 (assuming that that's a bargain price). Furthermore, let's assume that the manufacturers will absorb all of the delivery, installation, service and warranty costs. In that case, your only "product" costs are your overhead (including rent, phone, utilities, insurance, etc.) and salaries for people to write up and process the orders. And let's say that all that comes to $2500 a month.

If the manufacturer is paying you $100 for each sale, you'd have to sell at least 75 computers a month for a gross profit of $7500 before you could hope to make a decent profit.

So the exception isn't really an exception at all. You still have to have at least that bare-bones minimum markup of 3-to-1 ($7500 income for $2500 of overhead cost!). And if you have to stock any of the computers or perform any of the services that the Theoretical Manufacturing Company was absorbing in our example, those added costs have become part of your "product" cost — and you have to get that same 3-to-1 markup on those added costs as well.

Incidentally, if you thought that the idea of selling computers by mail was outlandish, keep in mind that thousands of Dell Computers have been sold by Direct Response. And Sears, Montgomery Ward, Spiegel, and the

A 3-to-1 markup doesn't assure you of success; it just gives you a fighting chance.

*If you think that a 3-to-1 markup
is exorbitant, consider this:
There's a brand name vitamin
that you take once a day which
sells for about $3.95 per 100. I
can buy (in large quantities) the
very same product for about
$.39 cents per hundred.*

hundreds of discount catalog operations sold quite a few more.

If you think that a 3-to-1 markup is exorbitant, let me point out a few facts:

The average manufacturer figures the retail price will have to be at least five times his manufacturing cost. If he doesn't, he'll go bankrupt just as sure as accountants use red ink.

The Brand Name vitamins that the manufacturer recommends you take once a day sell for about $3.95 for a bottle of 100. I can buy the identical product (in large quantities of course) for about 39 cents a hundred — and the man I buy them from makes a profit.

The finest lipstick that money can buy costs the manufacturer just pennies. The case costs anywhere from a few cents to over a dime, if it's really fancy. Check the retail prices of lipstick at the discount stores and the hoity-toity department stores.

In fact, almost every pharmaceutical or cosmetic manufacturer knows his product has to sell for 10 times — or as much as 20 times — his cost. Does that mean that all the pharmaceutical and cosmetic manufacturers who do provide for the price structure get rich? No, just a few of them. The others quit or go broke because they fail to take into account the enormous cost of doing business in America today.

If you have a Widget that retails for ten dollars and you want to sell it to a chain of Auto Supply Stores or Discount Drug Stores, here's what you'll have to face (if they agree to buy your Widget at all): They'll pay you three dollars if you agree to pay the shipping costs, pay for the advertising, agree to take back any Widgets that the customers return, and sell your Widgets on what they call "On Consignment" or "Pay on Reorder." That means that they'll pay you when and if they sell the Widgets and will return the ones that are unsold.

Some time ago I read that Eastman Kodak gets a 6-to-

1 markup on its film. And do you have any idea of the actual product cost of toothpaste, mouthwash, cigarettes, cereal, or laundry products? It's pennies.

The only time that a major store will operate on less than a 3-to-1 markup is when the merchandise is so highly advertised that they feel they have to stock it. Or it's a high-priced or "Big Ticket" item with enough profit-dollars to make it worthwhile. Or they want to use if for a "loss leader." And with all this apparent profit-gouging, most of the successful businessmen in this country end up with a net profit of a little more than five percent!

Now do you feel better? Do you see why that minimum 3-to-1 markup is not only "in line" — but necessary?

Unfortunately, it's not really enough. It's only a minimum, only the rock-bottom kind of markup you have to have before you decide to try selling something.

PUSH IT TO 5-TO-1 — IF YOU CAN

Personally, I feel much more comfortable with 5-to-1. And with 10-to-1, I haven't got a sure thing, but the odds are sure on my side!

Why do you — and I — need as much markup as we can reasonably get?

First, so we can afford to make mistakes. Show me a man that doesn't make a mistake, and I'll show you a man who isn't doing anything. In this business, as in any business, you have to keep trying: new products, new approaches, new media. And you can't do that unless you can afford to be wrong. The richest rewards go to the people who aren't afraid to take a chance. Even the turtle knows that he can't get ahead unless he sticks his neck out.

The second reason that we need the 10-to-1 markup, if the product merits it, is so that we can afford to spend a lot of money on advertising. So we can sell more product.

Did you realize that the actual product cost of many of the popular toothpaste, mouthwash, cigarettes, cereal, and laundry products you buy is just pennies on the dollar?

A minimum 3-to-1 markup is not only "in line" — it's necessary.

Personally, I prefer a 5-to-1 to 10-to-1 markup on most of the items that I sell.

Right off the top, you've got to be prepared to allocate 50% — 50 cents out of each dollar that comes in — to advertising.

So we can make more money. But if you lowered the price, wouldn't you sell more? Not necessarily. Sometimes the public equates quality with price. They feel that if it's too cheap it can't be any good. Want to find out? Test your prices in the way I outlined at the beginning of the chapter. The public will tell you how much — or how little — they're willing to pay. All you have to do is ask them. And when they tell you what your product's worth, you'd better pay attention.

How much do I budget for advertising? I go into a deal prepared to spend 50 percent on advertising — 50 cents out of every dollar that comes in. Now my actual advertising may cost me a lot less. I've spent as little as 3 percent — and as much as 300 percent. In other words, I've had some cases where a $30 order cost me 90 cents in advertising cost, and I've had other cases where every $30 order cost me $90. One offsets the other (hopefully), and the average is about 50 percent. The advertising cost to get a $30 order is $15.

That's not just my advertising cost. Give or take a few percentage points, that's the advertising cost paid by every successful company I know in this business. You'd better count on it and plan on it. If you can advertise for less, good! You can put the profits aside and use them the next time you try something and it bombs. But be prepared to spend 50 percent.

RUNNING A SMART BUSINESS

CHAPTER 6 OF BOOK TWO

A lawyer friend of mine told me why he thinks that the big companies survive and the little companies go under. It's not because the presidents of the big corporations are so smart. (I worked for a big corporation for nine months once. I couldn't believe that that many scared, stupid people could be gathered under one roof.) The secret of success for large companies, my friend said, was that they could afford to do inefficient, dumb things. They're rich enough to survive their mistakes.

I might add that that's not how they got big. It's just how they stay alive. Herman Wouk, who wrote *The Caine Mutiny*, described the operation of the Navy to this effect: "A master plan, conceived by geniuses and executed by idiots." The Navy doesn't want their plans executed by idiots. But they have to allow for the possibility.

The secret of success for many large companies is they're rich enough to survive their mistakes.

50% ADVERTISING COSTS

And you have to be financially prepared for the fact that you or someone who works for you will, from time to time, do something idiotic. Realistic planning helps — and 50 percent for advertising is realistic. Just how realistic it is can be emphasized by this bit of information: There are many, very successful advertisers in the Direct Response Business who are willing, even eager, to pay advertising costs of 100 percent — or more — for an order!

Why? Because they know that the customer — and what he'll buy in the future — is worth a lot of money! Video Clubs, Record/ Tape/CD Clubs, and Book Clubs (and similar promotions) are just three examples of Direct Response advertisers who lose a lot of money on the initial sale — but profit very handsomely in the long run.

But I'm not suggesting, at this point, that you go in the hole on your initial sale. I don't think you should

Fifty percent for advertising may seem like a lot, but there are many, very successful direct response businesses who are more than willing to pay advertising costs of 100% or more for an order. (But only the first order.)

Even with 50% for advertising, direct response merchandising is still one of the most efficient methods of distribution.

because it requires tremendous capital.

Now, let me tell you a couple of other things that should put your mind at ease about that 50 percent advertising cost.

First, it's just about your total "distribution" cost. It's the force that moves a product from you to the customer and there's no middleman in between taking his cut. You can allocate that 50 percent, and the product can still cost the consumer less than he would have to pay for something comparable in a retail store. That's because the retail item has to go through so many hands (and each hand has to reach into the customer's pocket and extract both costs and profits). In retail sales there are most or all of these middlemen taking their pound of flesh between the manufacturer and the eventual buyer: Wholesalers, Distributors, Brokers, Jobbers, and finally, the Retail Outlet. The retail product is sold again and again and again in ever-decreasing quantities until the customer finally completes the chain — and pays all of the expenses and the profits of the purchasers who preceded him. The retailer takes the biggest chunk. He has to, to recover his costs: advertising, display in an expensive location, "free" parking, breakage, shoplifting, clerks, and what have you.

That's why Direct Response merchandising is the most efficient, most direct method of distribution. It gets the greatest number of products to the most people at the lowest possible cost.

So let's take a final look at markup. If the actual cost of a product is ten dollars, here's how the various prices you might charge break down:

Sale Price	Product Cost	Advertising Cost	Gross Profit
$30.00	$10.00	$15.00	$5.00
$40.00	$10.00	$20.00	$10.00
$50.00	$10.00	$25.00	$15.00

You can see that the profit margin on a 3-to-1 markup

is painfully slim; because, out of that $5.00, you're going to have to pay your own overhead costs and have something left over for yourself. If you're selling Widgets, you'd better sell them by the carload.

But, as soon as you raise the price to $40, your advertising cost goes up only by one-third, but your profit margin doubles. Ahhh, that's better.

And if you can get $50 for your product, your advertising cost goes up by two-thirds — and your profit triples! The net effect is that you'll make more money selling half as many Widgets at $50 than you would if you sold them at $30! Let's see how that works out:

The profit margin on a 3-to-1 markup is actually quite slim.

1,000 Widgets at $30 each — Gross profit: $5000

500 Widgets at $50 each — Gross profit: $7500

So you can do half the work and have half the trouble — and make 50 percent more profit! Now the only thing that could offset your apparent windfall of profit is this consideration: Your prospect for "add-on" or "bounce-back" sales . . . additional sales to the same customer.

Will people be so pleased with your Widget that they'll want to order more for themselves and their friends? Did they buy an "Economy" Widget and do you have a "Super-Duper" Widget that they'll find irresistible when you describe it in the brochure you include in their package?

Is your Widget something they'll use up and buy again next month — and every month? Will they buy lots of attachments for your Widget to increase its usefulness? Will other Direct Response Businessmen want to rent your list of Widget buyers?

If any or a number of these things are true, and the quantity of "add-on" or "bounce-back" orders is sufficient, then 1,000 customers at a smaller profit could be more profitable in the long run than 500 customers at a higher profit.

If the quantity of "bounce-back" sales is sufficient, then 1000 customers at a small profit can be more profitable, in the long run, than 500 customers at a higher profit.

BUYER RESISTANCE

Here's why: Because you have little or no advertising cost for a reorder; you're making a $20 profit on each $30 sale and a $40 profit on each $50 sale.

Now, let's assume that 50 percent of your $30 customers reorder. That's 500 reorders and you make $20 apiece. That's a total of $10,000.

Now if 50 percent of your $50 buyers reorder, that's 250 sales times your $40 profit — or the same $10,000. But the fact is that if 50 percent of your $30 buyers reorder, it's likely that a smaller percentage of your $50 purchasers will! If your $50 reorders drop to only 30 percent, the profit picture changes drastically. Now your profit on your $50 reorder drops to 150 sales times $40 for a total of $6000.

That means that your total profit from your $30 customer (the original order plus the reorder) is $15,000. Your total profit from your $50 customer is only $13,500.

Why is it likely that you'll get a lower percentage of reorders on your $50 sale? Because, usually, the greater the amount of money involved, the harder it is to get the customer to part with it.

That's why you have to figure that it'll only cost you $15.00 to talk your prospect out of that first $30, but you'll need $25.00 in advertising cost to get him to part with a $50 bill.

The same kind of buyer resistance comes into play when it comes to reordering. After all, your customer has only a limited amount of money, and he has to decide who's going to get how much of it. And now that he's gotten the original order, the honeymoon is over. All the promises, all the mystery, all the anticipation have been replaced by reality. He has the product. Whether he reorders or not depends on two things.

The **first** is how well your product kept your promises and fulfilled his expectations. He'll probably forgive your

Once the customer receives your product, the honeymoon is over. He may forgive you if you were a little overenthusiastic. But he won't forgive you if you're a liar and a cheat.

having been a little overenthusiastic. (He probably discounted some of your superlatives beforehand.) But he won't forgive you — and he shouldn't — if you're a liar and a cheat.

Supposedly, a few shysters have gotten away with advertising a "Sure-fire Roach Killer" and sending two blocks of wood, with instructions to place the roach on one block and crush it with the other. Or advertising a "Breast Developer" and sending a picture of a man's hand. And the story keeps cropping up about the man who got rich by placing an ad that said "Last chance to send in your dollar!" But I don't believe it.

I did talk to one man who said he made a lot of money selling weeds that were supposed to produce a miraculous blossom on a "money-back guarantee." He operated on the theory that many of the purchasers wouldn't get around to planting the seeds. Of those who actually went to the trouble of planting the seeds — and were rewarded for their labor with nothing at all or a few scraggly plants — most would figure that the fault was theirs or the result of bad weather. As to the rest, by the time the plant had matured — many months after they had sent for it and planted it — they would have misplaced his address. Which was just as well because he'd moved anyway. And, needless to say, without leaving a forwarding address.

To me, the interesting thing is that the "entrepreneur" who was telling of his petty triumph was obviously down-at-the-heels. If he had indeed made a lot of money at his sorry little con game, he'd obviously blown it. As I listened to him, I couldn't help think of an old world curse: "May you make a lot of money and spend it ALL on doctor bills."

There was a time when the Sears catalog could unblushingly promise elixirs guaranteed to cure cancer, tuberculosis, and rheumatism. But today's consumer is pretty smart. And why not? Advertisers have spent billions educating him. He's learned at a very tender age

The consumer today is more skeptical than ever. And is it any wonder?

that most of the toys that seemed so miraculous on TV are pretty shoddy in real life (and that he'll have to wait till the day after Christmas to play with them, because Mother forgot that the "batteries are not included"). He's found that he can eat a whole loaf of Wonder Bread, and he still won't be tall enough and strong enough to lick the big brother or sister who's been tormenting him. He's learned that he can brush his teeth after every meal with Ultra-Brite and still not be irresistible to members of the opposite sex.

All in all, with the help of consumer advocates like David Horowitz and Ralph Nader, he's become a little skeptical. And it's a good thing. It doesn't mean, as they say in the childhood chant, that "Cheaters never prosper." It does mean that the Cheater finds it very hard to prosper and, I hope, spends it all on doctor bills. It means that you'd better have a unique product that provides a real benefit. That doesn't mean that you shouldn't make a handsome profit. In fact, you should be rewarded. But remember that no man can get rich unless he enriches others. And that enrichment can and does consist of making another's life easier, or simpler, or more fulfilling.

The **second** reason that getting that reorder is a challenge is this: There are only four basic Human Motivations — what I call the 4 R's. They are: Reincarnation, Recognition, Romance, and Reward.

REINCARNATION All of us hope for Immortality or Life after Death . . . and a few of us really believe in it. Most of us hedge our bets by creating works, or children, or monuments that will survive our physical being, so that at least some part of us will live "forever."

RECOGNITION We want the respect and admiration of others. Even if we have to inspire these reactions through fear.

ROMANCE Sex is the driving force, but even after the fires have been banked, most human beings have a continuing

No man can get rich unless he enriches others.

There are only four basic human motivations: Reincarnation, recognition, romance, and reward.

need for comfort, companionship, and tenderness.

REWARD This can take many forms: a nameplate on the door of an office; an office with a view instead of four blank walls; the services of a private secretary. But the most common, and most eagerly sought after, reward is Money. In this country at least, it's the coat-of-arms of the Aristocracy — the irrefutable answer to the question, "If you're so smart, why ain't you rich?"

PROMOTIONAL BOMBARDMENT

There are only these 4 R's — and they are being assaulted by 1500 advertising impressions each day! There are billboards, newspapers, circulars, letters, radio, and they're all appealing to any or all of these motivations, vying for the same spendable dollar. And the more they ask for — the bigger the size of the purchase — the harder it is to get. The ease of making a sale is in inverse proportion to the money it takes to complete it. Putting it another way, the farther it gets away from what the prospect will spend "on impulse" — without carefully considering the amount of money involved — the more difficult it becomes to convince a buyer to opt for your solution to his problem instead of your competitor's. Or to decide to attempt the solution of some other, apparently more urgent problem.

That is why it's harder to get someone to spend $50 instead of $30 for his original order. And that's the obstacle you have to overcome when you determine your sales price and go after that profitable reorder.

How do you set this optimum price? You don't. You let the public decide. You test in the way I've already outlined. You keep records and you take the course they dictate.

Incidentally, there are other methods to test components in your advertising. Many newspapers have what they call "split runs." Because they're mechanically set up to print two identical pages at the same time, you

The ease of making a sale is in inverse proportion to the money it takes to complete it.

So, how do you set the optimum selling price? You don't! You let the public decide.

can make what is called a "True A/B Split." Half of the subscribers will get the "A" Copy and half will get the "B" Copy. In theory, if there are two subscribers in the same block, one will get a publication with your "A" advertising copy, and the other subscriber will have a chance to react to the "B" copy. By keeping track of your results, you can decide which is the most effective.

"Regional" or "Zone" editions of magazines or newspapers are not meaningful in copy testing. Even if you adjusted mathematically for the difference in the number of copies of the publication sold in each area, there may be geographical, ethnic, educational, or economic differences that could affect results.

In this discussion of pricing, here are some experiences I've had that might be helpful:

THE 3-5-7 STRATEGY

In two of my businesses, I've used what I call the "3-5-7 Strategy." This is a strategy we have used for almost thirty years and is as valid in the 1990s as it was in the 1960s. Let's say my basic sale is $30. But I offer the prospect a substantial saving if they order double the quantity for $50 or triple the quantity for $70. I can do this because the clerical cost is the same for all three orders (it takes the same time to slit the envelope, type up the order, and keep the accounting records, no matter what the size of the order).

The difference in packaging (materials and labor) is increased very little for a large order. In one business, we use the same size "jiffy bag" — a mailing package — for all three sizes of orders. In the other business, we designed a package that will accommodate a single or double order. When we get a triple order, we send one double and one single. (In both businesses, our "standardized" packaging means that we can order in larger quantities and save money.)

The 3-5-7 strategy: If the basic sale is for $30, for $50 you can get a double order and for $70 you can get a triple order.

The differential in postage does not increase proportionately. Only the weight of the product has gone up. The packaging is the same and one set of instructions and literature to resell the value is all you need. (Reselling is important. They might have forgotten "why" they ordered and what your product will do for them.)

The net result is that I'm working on a somewhat slimmer profit, but I've increased the size of my "average" order — generally, to about $48.40. I've also gotten the people who might not have ordered at $50 but would spend $30 to place an order, and I've picked up some who were willing to invest $70.

The approximate percentages break down this way: 45 percent order the $30 package; 38 percent order the $50 package; and 17 percent order the $70 package. A thousand orders typically produce an income of $44,000 or $44.40 per order. But that's only $44.40, and I said earlier that my average order was $48.40. Where does the other $4.00 come from? I ask the buyer to "Please enclose an extra $3.50 for postage and handling." About 80 percent of them do. Even if they don't, we send the package anyway.

Why don't we return the order and ask for the amount due? Or at least enclose a bill? Because, in the first case, I believe that the extra handling would cost as much or more than it would produce in "collections." Besides, the delay in shipping might antagonize the customer and cause him to say "Forget the whole thing." In trying to collect $3.50, I would risk losing the $44.40.

In the second case (enclosing a bill), I've told the customer that I've caught him trying to cheat me. Or, at the very least, I've proved that he's careless or semi-illiterate since he obviously didn't follow the instructions in the coupon. Either way, I've embarrassed him or made him angry. If that's true, he might decide to "get even" by returning the package — and I've lost a friend and a customer.

With the 3-5-7 strategy I'm working on a somewhat slimmer profit, but my "average" order size has gone from $30 to about $48.40.

The "Strategy" allows you to both offer your product at a price that meets the lowest point of buyer resistance as well as capitalize on those who are willing to spend more.

The "3-5-7 Strategy," where it's applicable, does more than allow you to offer the price that meets the lowest point of "buyer resistance" (in this instance, those who are willing to spend $30). It also enables you to capitalize on those who are willing to spend more. Furthermore, and perhaps more important, it gives people a chance to "sample" your product. If they like it, they'll buy more. In our case, our average reorder was getting closer to $66.00.

The only time you can use the "3-5-7 Strategy" is when the choice lies between quantities or sizes. Not when the customer has to choose between products. Supposedly, you've offered the best solution to his problem. His only decision should be "how much" he wants to buy, not "which." If you're selling luggage, it's O.K. to offer small, medium, or large. You can also offer "regular" or "deluxe." But don't offer a choice between a briefcase and a two-suiter or a cardboard box. It confuses the customer. And if he can't make up his mind, he will make up his mind to buy nothing.

Be careful about the choices you offer the customer. If you confuse him and he can't make up his mind, he will, and buy nothing.

HOW TO SHIP

Should you ship C.O.D.? Not without a deposit that at least covers your shipping cost. Your cost will be the regular postage, plus a special C.O.D. charge that the post office imposes, and the cost of return postage if the package is unclaimed. (Even after making a deposit, about 12 percent of your customers aren't home when the postman comes, or don't have the money, and never get around to redeeming the package at the post office.) There's also a considerable amount of paper work in preparing C.O.D. packages — but at least you get your product back.

Because of the extra costs and paperwork they involve, I don't recommend shipping C.O.D. or insuring your packages.

All of these are extra costs that the customer has to pay, over and above the cost of the merchandise. For example, on a $30 order, the extra charges could be as much as $8.00. That means that if the customer sends you an eight-dollar deposit, the postman will still have to collect $30 (or even more, including a money order fee) for you to break even. And the customer won't be happy. For the beginner, I recommend a line in the ad that says "Sorry — no C.O.D.'s."

Should you insure packages? I don't recommend it. The costs of paper work and the insurance itself would be horrendous. If one of my customers says he never got his order (and a reasonable time has elapsed), I take his word for it and send him a replacement immediately. My records might show that we sent it, but that doesn't prove he received it. Some time ago a post office official publicly admitted that nine billion pieces of mail are either delayed, lost, or stolen each year — that's about 10 percent of the total! The figure doesn't surprise me. Not when I see how many little pieces of paper can get lost or misplaced in an area no larger than the top of my desk. And when I think of how many hands it has to go through and the distances traveled, I'm amazed that any mail gets delivered at all. An exception to the rule might be if you were selling a high-priced item such as a computer. In this case the extra cost of the paper work and insurance might be warranted.

ACCOUNTABILITY

To establish some control of those thousands of itty-bitty coupons we get every day, we've set up the following procedures. They serve three purposes: (1) Show us which ads are producing what income. (2) Provide an accounting method so we can reasonably expect to catch anyone who might be tempted to steal a cash payment included with an order. (Yes, some people still send cash through the mail.) (3) Make sure that an order is typed and shipped.

Here's what we do: When the mail is picked up or delivered, it's sorted by "department number." That number, which appears in the coupon as part of the address, tells us which ad the customer is responding to.

Without some sort of accountability I'd be operating blindly.

By setting up specific step-by-step procedures, you'll have control over your cash, and have immediate access to important media information.

(I'll go into greater detail on how to "key" or "code" an ad later on.) Any mail that doesn't bear a department number is opened. If the "code" does appear on the coupon (but the customer forgot to put it on the envelope) — or it can otherwise be identified (say, for example, that the coupon is on newsprint and the envelope or coupon bears a St. Louis address, you know that you ran an ad in the *St. Louis Globe* so you can reasonably assume that this order is a result of that ad) and if the payment is enclosed you put the now-identified letter in the appropriate stack. If no money is enclosed, or if it's a request for information, or a complaint, it goes in a "No Money" stack.

When the sorting has been completed, a report of mail received for that day is made up. It lists the department numbers in numerical order, followed by the number of pieces of mail received for each department, as well as the total of the number of pieces received by all "departments." Remember that, at this point, none of the mail with the "department" number on the envelope has been opened.

ACCOUNTING FORM

Then, an Accounting Form is made up for each "department." It includes the department number, the total quantity of orders included as well as a space for each of the orders expected. (For example, if you're using the "3-5-7 Strategy," you'd have 7 spaces. One for $30, another for $33.50 and so on. The last space would be for an occasional "Other" — or people who order combinations or multiples of the prices offered.) There's also a space for "extending" or totaling the amount of money that a particular order represents. (For example, in the space that says "$30," there's room to write the number 40 if that's what the mail produced, and another space to show that this comes to $1200. Now there's another space to show the total number of orders accounted for, and still another to show the total number of dollars those orders

NIXON • KARBO ACCOUNTING FORM

Date: _____   Number of Pieces _____   Dept. _____

Product: _____   1st Count _____ OK_____ Date _____

CASH, CHECK, MONEY ORDER AND
CHARGE CARD SUMMARY

ORDERS			
_____ @ $30.00 totalling	$ _____		
_____ @ $33.50 totalling	$ _____		
_____ @ $50.00 totalling	$ _____		
_____ @ $53.50 totalling	$ _____		
_____ @ $70.00 totalling	$ _____		
_____ @ $73.50 totalling	$ _____		
_____ OTHERS	$ _____		
_____			
_____ TOTAL ORDERS	$ _____		

CASH

_____	$50 BILLS	$ _____
_____	$20 BILLS	$ _____
_____	$10 BILLS	$ _____
_____	$5 BILLS	$ _____
_____	$1 BILLS	$ _____
_____	$.50 COIN	$ _____
_____	$.25 COIN	$ _____
_____	$.10 COIN	$ _____
_____	$.05 COIN	$ _____
_____	$.01 COIN	$ _____
	TOTAL:	$ _____

OTHER MAIL

_____ No $ enclosed

_____ Not enough $ enclosed

_____ MAIL TOTAL

COMMENTS:

CHECK / MONEY ORDERS

_____	$73.50	$ _____
_____	$70.00	$ _____
_____	$53.50	$ _____
_____	$50.00	$ _____
_____	$33.50	$ _____
_____	$30.00	$ _____
	TOTAL	$ _____

CHARGE CARDS

_____	$73.50	$ _____
_____	$70.00	$ _____
_____	$53.50	$ _____
_____	$50.00	$ _____
_____	$33.50	$ _____
_____	$30.00	$ _____
	TOTAL	$ _____

(This form assumes items are selling for $30, $50 and $70 with a $3.50 postage and handling fee.)

GRAND TOTAL $ _____

REVISED 7/93

should produce.) Finally, there's a space for reporting the number of pieces of "No Money" mail and still another for "Not Enough Money."

The Accounting Form, together with the appropriate mail, is given to one of the people who opens the mail. This person re-counts the pieces. If it's correct, he puts his initials on the Form to indicate that he's received it and accepts responsibility for it. If there's a difference in the count, he adjusts it (with the approval of the supervisor who made the original count) before initialing the Form. (If the response to a particular ad is very heavy, the "department" is divided into bundles of 100 or fewer letters to reduce the possibility of error and make rechecking easier.) Then the person opens the mail and they first verify that the name and address on the coupon are legible. If not, he checks the address on the envelope or the check or money order, with the hope that one of them can be translated. (I'd like to have a nickel for every order we haven't been able to process because we couldn't read the name and address. And then we get a nasty letter, threatening to report us to the post office, the district attorney, and the Better Business Bureau if we don't ship the order immediately — and we can't read the name or address on that letter either.)

Assuming that he does solve the puzzle when necessary, he prints the corrected address on the coupon. If the payment is by check (and the address is imprinted), and it differs from the address on the coupon, he prints the coupon address on the check (so that if the check bounces, or the account is closed, we have some idea of where to look for our delinquent purchaser.

Another technique we use when we can't decipher a name and address is this: If the payment was by an unprinted check (such as a new account, counter check or temporary check), we write to the bank giving the account number and explaining our problem.

By following these triple-check procedures you'll keep the post office, district attorney, and the Better Business Bureau off your back.

If the customer is paying by credit card, we fill out a credit card slip. (These slips are available from your bank if you are fortunate enough to get a credit card merchant account. I say this because it has become increasingly difficult for "mail order" companies to obtain a merchant account. If you are able to get one, often times the bank will require that you have a "large" amount of money on deposit to offset any potential "charge backs"— where a customer rejects or disputes the charge. Banks are often wary of "mail order" companies as they tend to have a higher percentage of returns than "normal" businesses because of their customer-friendly return policies.) All I can say is, this is something you will have to take up with your banker.

Next, the Opener verifies that the merchandise ordered coincides with the payment enclosed. If it's too much, even by a penny or two, he notes the overpayment on his Accounting Form. Later a Credit Memo or refund check will be issued. If it's too little, but the unpaid amount is less than 10 percent of the purchase price, he notes the underpayment on his Accounting Form. (The order will still be shipped for the reasons I outlined before.) However, if the underpayment exceeds 10 percent, he notes that fact on his Accounting Form in the "Not Enough Money" space. (The order will not be shipped, and the matter will be handled as I'll tell you in a few moments.) If there's no money enclosed, or if it's a request for C.O.D. without an appropriate deposit, or a request for information, or a complaint, he leaves the contents intact and stamps the envelope with an appropriate rubber stamp. And all the while that he's been performing these tasks, he's been separating the orders into the necessary stacks — one for each category. When he's finished, he uses a numbering machine (they range in cost from $30 to $60) to imprint the identical number on the coupon, check, money order or credit card slip that accompanies it. If an order is

Credit card merchant accounts — if you're lucky enough to get one — and you want to keep it — be especially accommodating to your credit card customers.

paid for with cash, the name and address and the amount are written on a piece of paper and numbered in the same way as the checks, money orders, or credit card slips. (You can buy numbering machines that repeat the same number in a series of three. In other words, it'll print the number "1" three times before it goes on to "2," etc.) So now he's separated his orders by amount and numbered them in sequence. Then he puts a rubber band around each stack — one around the coupons; another around the checks, money orders, credit card slips or cash; and still another around the "No Money" or "Not Enough Money" mail. (Which we'll now call "Miscellaneous Mail.") The coupons, the payments, and the Miscellaneous Mail all are wrapped in the Accounting Form and given to the Accounting Department.

The Accounting Department checks to see if the actual amount of money turned in "balances" with the orders reported. They do all of the "extensions" or final totals. The Opener does none of these figures, so he has no idea of how much money "should" be there.

If there's a shortage or overage, the coupons are rechecked to see if one or more was placed in the wrong stack. (This is usually the case when there's a discrepancy, and the error is corrected.)

If everything is O.K., the coupons are given to the Data Entry Clerk. Since the data entry demands painstaking accuracy and is deadly dull, the sequential numbering system gives the Data Entry Clerk a safeguard against "skipping" a coupon or having one blown off his desk by a puff of wind. If, as the Clerk types the number in each record, he finds one missing, he is immediately alerted. He knows that two coupons have stuck together, or one has fallen to the floor, or he's been daydreaming. In any case, he can start his search for the cause. If he can't find the coupon, he can look up the corresponding missing number on the check, money order, or credit card slip. The amount of the payment should provide the information he needs to replace the coupon. If payment was in cash, hopefully he can match the missing number with the piece of paper included with the checks, money orders, or credit card slips, and the size of the order can be deduced.

Let's say that the clerk didn't notice that a number was missing. For that possibility, he checks the number of records he's entered and sees if it balances with the number of coupons he received. If he has fewer records than the numbering system indicates, he can start a search.

ACCOUNTING FOR YOUR PEOPLE

Now let's retrace our steps for a moment. What if an Opener's Accounting Form is frequently "out of balance." Then we have to conclude that he is either unsuited to this kind of work or may be stealing. Either way, we can't afford to have that person around.

How would we know if someone took cash out of an envelope and then put it in the "No Money" stack? When we send out a form letter requesting payment, we enclose a return envelope that's coded with the "number" of the Opener. If we get back a few indignant letters protesting that the sender had enclosed cash — and we trace them to the same Opener — we advise him that his services are no longer required. He may be innocent, but we can't afford to take chances.

We take one additional step to save employees from temptation. No one opens mail or handles money in the Accounting Department when he's alone. At least two people must be present, and their desks must be facing each other. When they go to the restroom, or on a coffee break, or out to lunch, they leave at the same time. They do not leave the room until the Accounting Form they're working with has been completed and locked up for

Do these procedures make it impossible to steal? No. But they will discourage amateurs.

safekeeping.

Do I think that these procedures make it impossible to steal? No. A dedicated thief can always find a way to beat the system. But it does discourage amateurs. And I think that a more complex system for security would probably cost more than it would save.

The faster you ship, the sooner they'll receive, the happier your customer will be. And a happy customer will order again and again and again.

TIME FOR SHIPPING

Now, on with our story. After the orders have been entered, the labels are run off and given to the Shipping Department. In the Shipping Department, there's one final check to make sure that no order has been missed. The labels are counted, and the total compared with the number that the sequential numbering system indicates there should be. If there's a shortage, back to the Data Entry Room they go. If the numbers are O.K., the labels are put on the packages.

Assuming that the errors or omissions have all been corrected, and the package has been consigned to the tender mercies of the Post Office, back to the Accounting Department. The total amount of payment received on each Accounting Form is added up. That's how much the deposit prepared for the bank should be. If the totals, taken from the Accounting Forms, and the actual deposit are "in balance," that winds up the day. If not, it's back to the calculator and re-counting the checks, money orders, credit card slips, and cash until the error is discovered.

At this stage, if you are using a "hold the check for 30 days" guarantee, the checks are placed in the safe, in numerical order (that's the reason for the numbering machine), where they are held for a full 30 days. At the end of 30 days they are deposited in the bank.

POST THE RESULTS

The final activity of the Accounting Department is posting the results. What they now produce is your most important record. For this purpose you make up a sheet of paper that can go into a binder, with these headings listed at the top:

Source of Order— The name of the publication, call letters of the radio or TV station, mailing list used, etc.

Unit— The size of the ad or the length of commercial, number of pieces mailed, etc.

Key— The identifying code you used.

Day /Date Ran— For obvious reasons.

Cost— The total cost of the advertising medium, including "production" charges (to have an ad set by printer, artwork, a film or tape made, etc. — this is not applicable for direct mailing).

Product— Useful if you own a company selling more than one.

Comments— Here you write anything that could have influenced results: weather, a strike, a holiday, good or bad positioning of an ad, bad reproduction, etc.

Under the above information, set up columns using these subheadings, so the pertinent information can be entered:

Date   Day's Orders   Cumulative Orders   Day's Receipts   Cumulative Receipts

This gives you a day-by-day picture of how your advertising is doing. It shows you what your "average" order is (divide the Cumulative Receipts by the Cumulative Orders). It gives you the pattern of results.

For example, most morning newspapers will produce

The single most important record in the direct response business is the daily posting sheet. It should give you a breakdown of the exact number of orders received from each and every ad, commercial, or direct mailer used.

These daily posting sheets tell you instantly — and daily — at a glance exactly how your business is doing.

double the first three days' orders; most magazines will end up pulling twice as many orders as you get in the first 25 days; most first class mailings will reach their "halfway" point in 10 to 11 days and most third class bulk rate mailings will reach their halfway point in about 25 days. But they differ, and you have to know what each particular medium will generate in orders. The only way to find out is to keep records. And as you accumulate these records, you'll be able to look at what you've done in the past and be able to forecast the success or failure of a new ad in that medium. The speed of your reaction to that forecast — whether it's to expand your advertising, repeat the ad, or even cancel advertising you've already placed when that's possible — can be the difference between making or losing a lot of money.

These "Posting Sheets" can tell you "how you're doing" at a glance when you're getting started. Later, they'll tell you what you should do. I can't overemphasize the importance of keeping and using them.

I'm still getting $100 worth of orders every week for ads I stopped running many years ago.

For practical purposes, I keep Posting Sheets "active" for 30 days after a newspaper ad has run, for 6 months after running a magazine ad, for 45 days after a first class mailing has gone out and for two to three months after a bulk rate mailing has been mailed. Results will still trickle in after that time. (I'm still getting about $100 worth of orders every week for ads that I stopped running many years ago!) It's delicious revenue since there's no advertising cost; but statistically, it's insignificant.

THE DRAG FACTOR

Incidentally, I heard about one large Direct Response firm that sold out to a large corporation for several million dollars. The large corporation acquired the business because it showed such fantastic profits, particularly in the year or so preceding the acquisition. What they didn't discover until later was the reason for the sudden jump in profits. The Direct Response firm had simply stopped advertising. So they had a large income and very little outgo!

In this business, these extra orders are called "drag." And when and if I ever retire, I expect the drag to provide my wife and myself with a very fat "pension!"

Meanwhile, back at the Accounting Department . . . What happens to requests for information and complaints? Answer them — preferably on the day they're received. Certainly as quickly as possible. Even if a complaint's unreasonable — even if the merchandise couldn't possibly have been delivered in the time that's passed since you received the order — even if you're "sure" that the customer probably received his order a day or two after he wrote — ANSWER HIM.

Let him know, in writing and immediately, that his order and his money haven't disappeared — that all those terrible things he's heard about Direct Response companies aren't true in your case. It'll pay off and, someday, make you rich.

Don't do what I saw one man do, with my own eyes. I visited this character, who was running a one-man business, and watched him opening envelopes. As he slit them, he peeked inside. Some, he stacked on his desk; others he threw into the wastebasket. I asked him what he was doing. He said that he was throwing away the envelopes that didn't contain any money. He "explained" that the envelopes without money either wanted more information or were complaints. His experience, he went on to say, was that he couldn't sell the former and couldn't satisfy the latter. So he just threw them away.

Well, I'll tell you something. I could have made money out of his trash basket! Because people asking for information are begging to be sold. And if you take care of a complaint, you make a friend — a friend who buys.

I know another man, who's probably the best salesman I ever met. When he worked for a Real Estate

If you get a customer complaint, even if the complaint is unreasonable, answer it.

Requests for additional information — answer them, they are potential customers just begging to be sold.

firm, he asked to be put in charge of the "Complaint Desk." His philosophy was that once he'd solved the customer's problem — and most problems can be solved — the customer was pleased and grateful — and ready to buy again from someone he trusted. It worked. He sold more property than anyone else in the firm.

A long time ago, when I was in the wholesale paper business (remember, it all started with those surplus cartons), I learned a valuable lesson. At first, if an order had been goofed up, I'd tell my secretary to say I was out if the customer phoned. When I finally had to face up to him, he was mad. Frequently, the outcome would cost me money and the customer.

Then I decided to try another approach. If anything had gone wrong, I'd call him. Preferably before he even knew about the mistake. I'd explain, apologize, and ask him what I could do to make it right. Nine times out of ten, he was so pleased at my interest that he'd tell me to forget it, or offer a settlement that was a lot less than I was prepared to give. As for the tenth man, I simply tried to settle as gracefully as possible and keep his business.

I've shown you that your BIG profit comes from reorders. Only satisfied customers reorder.

Your BIG profit comes from re-orders. Only satisfied customers reorder.

EIGHT TIPS TO SAVE YOU MONEY

CHAPTER 7 OF BOOK TWO

Here are some tips to keep your costs down and improve your results. These are facts that I found out the hard way — after wasting enough money to put each of my kids through college. And I have a lot of kids.

TIP #1

Watch the weight of your package very closely.

Any advertising that you insert has to pay its own way. First, from the standpoint of what it costs to produce (including printing and amortized art and typesetting costs). Second, what does it add to your postage costs? Sometimes, you can use a lighter weight paper stock and keep the postage scale from moving up an extra notch. Then you can mail it free!

If it's at all possible, keep the total weight under a pound. Even if you have to, ship the order in two or more packages (assuming that's feasible). Because, unless you do, you can't get the savings made possible by shipping "Bulk rate" (more about that later).

Watch the weight of your package very closely. The difference of just one ounce can end up saving — or costing — you thousands in the long run.

And as soon as you go over a pound, even if you're using ordinary Parcel Post rather than "Bulk rate," the postage costs skyrocket. For example, if the package weighs less than a pound, you pay so much per ounce, no matter where you ship it in the United States. But as soon as you go over a pound, the postage is based on the "zone" it's going to. To illustrate (at the rates in effect as this is written): you can mail a package anywhere in the United States for $2.43 or less if it weighs under 16 ounces. But if it weighs more than one pound, and less than two, it'll cost you $2.63 for local delivery and $2.95 for shipment to the furthest zone. All you can do is figure out what's best in your case — but don't forget the clerical and handling costs involved in computing the varying postage.

Avoid any product that's packed in glass. The increased costs in protective packaging — to say nothing of the weight of the glass — make it tough to market. Attractive plastic containers are cheap, lightweight, and virtually unbreakable. In my vitamin business, we use what's called "strip" packaging. Each pill is encased in an individual cellophane cell, and there are 30 cells in a "strip." This protects freshness; makes it easy to carry a day's supply in your pocket or purse. From our viewpoint, the feather-light flat strips can be slipped into a "Jiffy Utility Bag" (one without padding) and cushioned against breakage by putting our literature on each side.

Economies like this have made it possible for us to hold our prices in this business at the same level for as long as 15 years before we have had to revise them — in spite of advertising costs that have tripled and postage costs that have soared and are continuing to rise. (Remember the penny postcard and the four-cent first-class stamp?) We do it by constantly playing the game of "What Would Happen If . . . " And, of course, buying pills by the millions helps.

TIP #2

By using the lowest possible postage rate, you can save as much as 65% in postage costs.

Use the lowest possible postage rate!

If you don't have enough volume (200 or more identical packages or the number of identical packages it takes to make up 50 pounds) to ship "Bulk rate," use "Third Class." Shipping a product by "Bulk rate" as opposed to "Third Class" has saved us as much as 65 percent in postage costs.

You've heard some horror stories about the slowness of Third Class mailing, and some of them are true. But First Class mail can get snarled up too . . . and First Class rates will kill you.

We've done test-mailings around the country, mailing

three identical packages, on the same day, to the same destination. We sent one First Class, another Third Class, and the last as part of a Bulk rate shipment. In almost every case, they all either arrived at the same time or, at most, delivery was delayed by a couple of days! Although "Bulk rate" enjoys the lowest cost, delivery is usually satisfactory because you're doing most of the Post Office's work for them in terms of sorting and bundling.

Sure, you'll have an occasional Third Class or Bulk rate package go astray. When you do, replace it promptly. It's still a lot cheaper than sending everything first class.

The only exceptions I make are these: (1) Merchandise replacements are sent First Class. If I can believe my tests, they won't arrive much sooner, but I think the psychological impact on the customer is worth the added expense. That extra postage is meant to say "I'm sorry — and I value your business." (2) Sometimes, customers are in a dreadful hurry to get the product (for example, with Larry Voegele's book on how to beat the horses). So I've offered, in the coupon, to send the book by first class if they'll pay the extra cost; and if they do, I do.

The Post Office has some bargain rates for certain kinds of merchandise. Books, records and tapes (both audio and video) for example. Books can be sent out at a special rate. It's a bit higher in cost than "Bulk rate" — but you don't have the added expense of sorting and bundling or the necessity of identical packages and minimum shipments. All you have to do is write or rubber stamp the words, "Special Fourth Class Book Rate," on the package. One Caution: You can't enclose any advertising literature.

Other materials such as certain films, test materials, sound recordings, and the like also enjoy the "Special Fourth Class Rate." All you must do to take advantage of it is to write or stamp the magic words, "Special Fourth Class Rate."

I think it's accurate to state that no one in the post office will volunteer information on how you can save money on postage rates — or tell you that you're paying more than is necessary. But with these guidelines, persistence, and a thick skin, you can wheedle out the information you need. Always go to the Head Man; he's most likely to be well informed or know whom to ask.

SAME DAY FULFILLMENT The one factor that's indispensable in making lowest-cost postage work is this: Fill your orders the same day they arrive. Or, at the very latest, the next day. If you're out of stock, or there's some other problem, send an explanatory card or a letter to the customer immediately. Don't forget: he's sent money to someone he doesn't know for something he hasn't seen — and he's nervous. He's eager to get the merchandise, or he wouldn't have ordered it in the first place. Reassure him, before he complains.

TIP #3

Keep on top of your state's Sales Tax!

I don't know about the laws in other states, but I can tell what I think I know about California. (We've been "audited" three times in the past 16 years and have gotten clobbered each time. I have the uneasy feeling that every time the Governor needs money for a new State project he sends a guy around from the State Board of Equalization to pick up the down payment from me.)

Watch — stay on top of — your state sales tax. Here in California with the rates going up and down (mostly up), and the tax laws keep coming and going (mostly coming), I find it difficult to keep on top of it all. Three times I've been audited and three times I've been clobbered.

The only hopeful note is that the "assessment" has been for a lesser amount each time. What's discouraging is that each new auditor tells us that the instructions given by his predecessor are wrong — and this is the way we should keep our records. I can hardly wait 'til the next time. Maybe they'll discover we've overpaid. And maybe the moon really is made out of cheese.

O.K., back to business. You'll need a resale permit number. There'll be a fee, and you may have to post a cash deposit (or a bond), consistent with the tax you'll owe, based on the volume of business you expect to do. There's even some way that you can put the money in a bank and earn interest, even though the principal is pledged to the state board (ask your accountant).

The resale permit number allows you to buy all the supplies that you resell, without paying tax. For example, you don't have to pay sales tax on your Widgets or the instruction booklet that goes with them. You do have to pay tax on the advertising literature you put in the package. There are all sorts of fascinating, trifling differentials like that, and your accountant is, again, your best source of advice.

One sidelight: My wife uses our resale permit number to get into wholesale showrooms, which do business only with "dealers." She has to pay the tax as she is not buying for resale, but she saves a lot of money. Or so she tells me.

Now, how much tax do you have to collect and remit? Well, on all sales made to customers living in the city (if there's a city sales tax) or the state where you do business, you have to pay the tax. On out-of-state sales, you do not have to either collect or pay. (This is a fact that was reaffirmed by a Supreme Court ruling on May 26, 1992. Basically, they upheld part of the "Bella Hess" decision that stated that, "a business is not liable for sales or use tax in a state in which it has no physical presence.")

Now, if you're doing a big volume and a substantial number of your sales are out-of-state, how do you know how much is taxable — without getting buried under piles of records that you're required to keep for three years? One answer, of course, is to go on computer. If you're not quite ready for that, there's an alternative. I can't say that this method will be accepted on the next "audit," but it was the last time. Here's what we did: We selected a representative day of the week and saved all the envelopes that came in that day, every week. Once a month, we checked

There is one positive side of the sales tax picture for mail order businesses. At least it's true for now. It's this: you are not required to collect — or pay — a sales tax on any sales that are in a state which you have no physical presence.

◀ *Note: This can change at any time. Be sure to check with your accountant and stay on top of it.*

the postmarks on those envelopes and determined which were in the city and which were in the state. Then we took those totals and divided them by the total number of envelopes to get our percentage of taxable sales.

At the end of three months, before submitting our "quarterly return," we averaged the percentages. Then we applied those percentage figures to our total sales for the quarter and sent off a check. When we were audited, we had the envelopes to support our figures. (They accepted our proof; the "error" was in another area.)

Incidentally, if you are assessed, you don't have to accept their figure. You can arbitrate or appeal; and if you're in the right, I recommend that you do. We've had assessments reduced by two-thirds.

Finally, should you collect sales tax at all or simply absorb it in your price? The latter course will certainly simplify bookkeeping and require less time for making up bank deposits. It's really up to you. If you decide to collect the sales tax, don't put a line in your coupon that says something like "California Residents, please add 8.25% sales tax." That's too much of a strain on the customer. He's a buyer, not a mathematician. Prefigure it for him and ask him to enclose so many cents for sales tax. (As a rule of thumb, I normally do not charge additional sales tax on my first offer to a customer. On my second and subsequent offers, I often do request the additional tax.)

TIP #4

Don't hold orders, waiting for checks to clear!

In the first place, it can take days or weeks — and how will you know which checks have cleared and which have not? Even more important, why should you punish all of your customers for transgressions of a few? Trust them. Most of them will justify that trust. After all, they trusted you.

Our bank has instructions to put any check that

Ship orders promptly — don't wait for the customer's check to clear. The sooner the customer gets his product, the happier he'll be. And a happy customer is the kind that will order again bounces through a second time before returning it to us. When a check is returned, we write to the customer, asking him to make good and reimburse us for the fee the bank charged. Most do. From time to time, we gather up a batch of checks we have not been able to collect on, and turn them over to a collection agency or our attorney. For a percentage, they try again, and we get some more of our money in. If your experience is like mine, the remaining uncollectibles are a stiff figure at the end of the year, but only a tiny fraction of your sales volume.

TIP #5

Shop around for a bank! Banks differ widely in their policies and those differences can add up to a lot of money for you. I've found that an independent bank, or one that's part of a small "chain," usually offers the most advantages.

Here's what you want to compare: (1) Will there be a service charge if you maintain a minimum balance — and what's the minimum? (2) Will they charge you for each check you deposit? (Most large banks will make a charge for each check you deposit, if you deposit a large volume of checks of small denominations. Depending on the volume, this can be anywhere from three to five cents — or even more — per check.) This seemingly insignificant amount can run into BIG money. Before I switched banks, I was being charged about $14,000 a year for this "activity" — and this was the net figure after I'd been given "credit" for the "average balance" in the account! Based on my present volume, that figure would have been multiplied again and again. (3) Will they allow you to deposit checks and money orders without listing the bank numbers and itemizing the checks? (There's a procedure for doing this, attaching only an adding machine tape after the checks have been separated. A cooperative bank will show you how.) Eliminating the bank number listings and listing each check will save you hundreds of manhours. (4) Can you bank by mail, and will the bank pay the postage? If you have a wad of checks, the postage can be two or three dollars a day. That's over $1,000 a year — and they can afford it better than you can. Actually, I don't recommend this today. In the first place you'll lose two to three days float and besides, when your deposits are sufficient enough, your bank will pick them up on a regular basis. (5) If you're able to get a credit card merchant account, what is the service fee that a bank will charge you? The range of fees is from 1.75% to as high as 8% with an average more in the range of 3% to 5%. The rate is negotiable so it pays to shop around.

After you've shopped for your best deal and weighed the other obvious considerations — like convenience of location and availability of credit for your operation — pick the one that has the most to offer. But think in terms of your future, as well as your present needs. Incidentally, your bank can also help you file a "Certificate of Fictitious Firm Name" if one is necessary.

TIP #6

Make refunds promptly.

Next to shipping orders on a timely basis, the single area that will get you in hot water quicker than anything else, is failing to issue a prompt — if not cheerful — refund.

The only thing that I can add to that is "cheerfully." We've made some so fast that we discovered that the customer's check had "bounced" after we'd already sent him a refund. But that's more than offset by the people who are so pleased at the speed of the refund that they ordered again. (And we got our money back in most of the other cases.) One other thing while I'm at it. Even if you never received the returned product back, yet the customer claims to have returned it, take their word for it and issue a refund. Don't ever, and I mean ever, argue with a customer over this point.

I know of one competitor of mine who once told me with great pride how he would never allow any of his customers to take advantage of him. No way. In fact, there was even the time when he boasted that he'd responded to the same customer on ten separate occasions, refusing to issue the customer a refund because no product had ever been returned.

What a waste. My competitor probably spent two hundred dollars in time, energy, and effort, yet saved himself from having to issue a $30 refund. How stupid! (By the way, this competitor of mine is no longer in business. I wonder why.)

Your customers are your best friends and should be treated as such. I can't tell you how many customers have continued to do business with us after we cheerfully issued them a refund. At our seminars, these people come up to us and thank us for the way we handled their problem. I love that! Now I have a satisfied customer and a friend. It's the old "Golden Rule" and you can't run your life or your business without it.

Ideas. They are the lifeblood of this business. They are, as Frank Lloyd Wright best put it, " . . . salvation by imagination."

TIP #7

Read D*irect Marketing Magazine* and *Direct Marketing News!*

You can probably pick them up at your local library. I recommend looking over as many back issues as they have, or you can subscribe. If you want a subscription you can write to them at:

Direct Marketing Magazine
224 Seventh Street
Garden City, N.Y. 11530
(516) 746-6700

Direct Marketing News
19 W. 21st Street 8th Fl.
New York, N.Y. 10010
(212) 741-2095

No, I don't make a commission (although I have to admit that the thought crossed my mind).

But I want you to read them, because I think you'll find them chock-full of information and help you'll want

Ralph Waldo Emerson said "Books are for nothing but to inspire."

and need. Each month, they describe dozens of brand new products you might want to take on — or that trigger ideas of your own. There are great articles by some of the best pros in the business, examining every phase in great detail. There are directories, itemizing the names and addresses of the people who provide the services and the products you'll need. And Ideas, Ideas, and more Ideas! They're invaluable — and if you're serious about taking a crack at the Direct Response Business, you can deduct your subscriptions as a business expense.

TIP #8

Read these books. They are all very informative and will give you many additional — and valuable — pointers on starting and operating a successful direct response mail order business. They are:

How I Made $1,000,000 in Mail Order — And You Can Too by E. Joseph Cossman

Dollars in Your Mailbox:
(The Beginner's Guide to Selling Information by Mail) by Ernest P. Weckesser, Ph.D.

Successful Direct Marketing Methods by Bob Stone

Profitable Direct Marketing by Jim Kobs

Building a Mail Order Business by Dr. William A. Cohen

How to Make Big Money in the Next 30 Days by David Carter

Some of these books should be available at your local library or, if you wish to buy them, check with your neighborhood bookstore. If you can't find them you can order them from our catalogue.

Well, I've covered almost everything you need to know about Pricing and Business Practices. Plenty to get you started, keep you going, and help you get big and stay big.

None of it will guarantee success. That depends on you and what you do about your ISI! But it'll sure keep you from making the dumb mistakes I made when I was starting out.

Here are a few questions you might have at this point.

Q. Is there any simple way to make up my shipping labels?

A. For the beginner, I recommend using "Duplistickers." There are 33 perforated labels to an 8½ x 11 sheet — and you can buy them with the carbon interfolded, so that a single typing produces two or three copies. You can use one duplicate for a follow-up mailing and put the other on a 3 x 5 file card. (I recommend you file these cards in zip code order. I've found it to be the most efficient way of keeping track of customers.) When you are ready to take the next step, you can get a computer with one of the many "mail order" programs that are available.

Q. How do I keep my list current?

A. By "cleaning" it. You do this, after a follow up mailing, by removing the names that are returned to you by the Post Office as undeliverable or giving a change of address. You can also ask people who "rent" your list to return the "nixies" — those that can't be delivered.

Q. What's a good way to "key" my response?

A. We assign numbers to every publication we use. The first ad we place gives that number as the "Department," followed by the letter "A."

The next one is "B" and so on. We "skip" sequential letters that look too much alike and will slow down

None of this will guarantee your success. But it will (hopefully) keep you from making some of the dumb mistakes I made when I was starting out.

Keep your mailing list "cleaned." In this business it's your most important asset.

For every ad, every piece of mail you send out, make certain it is keyed. Without doing so you are lost.

the sorting. To illustrate, our "alphabet" is A B C D F G H J K L M O P Q R S T V X Y Z. For radio or TV, we use a Department number, or if we're using a post office box address, we add a letter. For example, "Box 345-A."

For a direct mailing, I have found that using a three-letter key (the first two letters for the mailing list used, the third for the product — offer — being mailed), followed by a number. For example, if I were to mail an offer for my book by Larry Voegele (*Professional Method of Winner Selection*) to my *The Lazy Man's Way to Riches* list, and it was my first ever mailing, I might "key" the mailing "LMV-1." "LM" for "Lazy Man's" list, "V" for "Voegele" offer, "1" because it was my first mailing. My next mailing would then be keyed "LMV-2," the third "LMV-3," and so on. (By the way, this key code is usually placed on the mailing label. The mailing label is then attached to the back of the reply envelope or the coupon the customer would be using for his/her reply.)

I can tell you how to write an ad in one word:
Don't.
Most people who try to write "ads" immediately adopt a stilted style, or try to be terribly clever, or use words that they — and the rest of us — have to look up in the dictionary. The result is a special language and form that I call "Advertise-ese" — there's only one problem with it: it doesn't communicate. It's not personal. It's all skin and no flesh. And certainly no guts.

When you've found something you want to sell, here's all you have to do to create a successful ad. And I promise you that it'll work.

WHAT WILL YOUR PRODUCT DO FOR PEOPLE?

First think of all the things your product will do for people. Then pick out the one, most important, specific thing it will do. Not just "Makes Long Life a Reality" but "Guaranteed to Make You Live to 100!" Not just "You Can Be Important!" but "How to Get a Promotion and a Raise in 5 Minutes!" Not just "You Can Be Beautiful" but "7 Ways You Can Make Him Ask for a Date!" Not just "It's Easy to Make Money" but (will you forgive me?) "*The Lazy Man's Way to Riches!*"

Every one of those "headlines" appealed to one or more of the 4 R's. (Remember? Reincarnation [immortality], Recognition, Romance, Reward.) And the strength — the drama — of your appeal to these four Basic Human Motivations will determine how successful you will be in getting the attention of your reader, listener, or viewer.

There's no mystery to it. (Although a lot of ad agency copy chiefs who are pulling down $200,000 a year would like you to think so.) I'm showing how they do it, step by step, and you can do it, too! So let's continue.

Successful ads communicate on a personal level.

It has been said that an advertising agency is eighty-five percent confusion and fifteen percent commission.

Keep a pad and pencil within easy reach. If you don't capture your inspiration and make it a prisoner, it'll escape and be lost forever.

People buy things or hire people, but what they are after is results.

Think about what you'd like the product to offer you. What problem you'd like it to solve. (You're really not that much different from anyone else.)

Write down all the ideas that come to you. Even if they seem silly or wild. Don't try to judge them — not yet; just write them down. Keep a pad and pencil in your pocket or within easy reach. If you don't capture your inspiration and make it a prisoner, it'll escape and be lost forever.

All of my best ideas were generated when I was driving my car, or riding my bike, or reading a book, just falling asleep, or just waking up.

Do you notice what each of these activities had in common? Nothing. That's right, I was doing absolutely nothing about solving my problem — how to sell a particular product — and then the right idea suddenly popped up. Not out of nowhere — out of my Subconscious Mind.

What had I done to feed the subconscious mind the information it needed, so it could spit out the answer? I'd simply thought about the product. Not so much what it is, but what it does. My wife bought a vacuum cleaner and hired a housekeeper. But what she really wanted was an easy way to clean the house. Do you see the difference? People buy things or hire people, but what they're after is the *result*. If she could press a button and, through some miracle of electronics or ultrasonic sound waves, the house would be cleaned spotlessly — and the cost was within reason — she'd junk the vacuum cleaner and fire the housekeeper. (At least when I asked her she said she would.)

So think about what the product will do. Better, or cheaper, or faster than anything else you know about.

REASONS FOR BUYING

Think about all the reasons you would buy it. Think about all the reasons you wouldn't buy it. (How many of those objections can you overcome?) Write it all down. Read magazines and newspapers. Notice how articles about the problem leap right off the page and hit you in the eye (remember, Selective Perception). If you must, talk about the product with people who are as enthusiastic as you are. But even if you try to avoid the Wet Blankets, there's a danger. You might, literally, talk it out and release the energy you've been building up.

Because that's exactly what you've been doing; fueling the subconscious. Warming it up. So it can produce that spark you're looking for.

When you feel you're saturated with facts and insight — when you've racked your brain, simply forget about the problem. The next step is to do *nothing*. Go on with the other things that make up your life. What could be easier? But, at that point, the problem is as good as solved. In an hour, or a day, or a week, you'll get the idea. The one, perfect way to express exactly what your product will do. It'll come when you're not "thinking" about it at all. Write it down! And keep writing. Because the "headline" or the attention-getting idea is just the valve — and it's been blown off by the pressure of the whole idea that's boiling underneath. It'll all come out now. Just keep writing. Keep writing 'til you run out of steam. Chances are that you won't until you're finished. But if you do, don't worry about it. Forget it again. When it's ready, the subconscious will let you know that it's raring to go back to work.

What about all those notes you made? Don't look at them or think about them until you're finished. That's because you want to give your Subconscious Mind a chance to "edit" them — to polish up the good ones, combine some to produce a new idea, discard the ones that are unworkable or simply don't fit into your new concept.

After you're all through writing, look at your notes. There might be a phrase or two that you'll want to include.

Fill your head with as many facts and insights as you think you can handle, then let your subconscious go to work!

Once the idea "hits" you, start writing. And don't stop writing 'til you've run out of steam.

But it's not likely. You'll be amazed at how your subconscious has sorted out your input — keeping the good stuff and rejecting the junk.

At this point, put what you've written away for a couple of days before you look at it again. Make minor corrections. Read it aloud and listen to whether it sounds like you talking. That's important. It should use the same words you'd ordinarily use in talking to another human being. If you've included something terribly clever or coined a great little slogan — kill it. Or it'll kill you. As soon as people become aware of your "style," you've lost them. They may be entertained. They may be amused. But they won't buy.

GO FOR FEEDBACK FROM PEOPLE

The next step is the hardest. Have other people read what you've written. But you're not to listen to their opinion. Not 'til you've had a lot more experience and know which opinions to accept and which to reject. And that takes years. At this point, the only thing you want to know is whether your ad is clear. Not whether they like it or dislike it — only whether they understand it. If you find yourself explaining or, worse yet, defending the ad, you know it isn't clear. If they don't know what you mean, clarify it. If they have to reread a phrase before they understand it (watch their eye movements!), change it. But don't change your approach or change a single word because they suggest one that's "more refined" or "sounds better." After reading your ad, if they know what your product will do for them, what its advantages and disadvantages are, if they know how much it costs and where to buy it — that's all that's necessary. Why do you tell them about the disadvantages, the small weak points? So they'll believe you. And if you've been completely honest, they'll have to believe you. Because it's the truth. The truth, told as attractively as possible, perhaps. But still the truth.

If after reading your ad, they know what your product will do for them, they know its advantages and disadvantages, they know how much it costs and where to buy it — that's all that is necessary.

Do you still think it is hard to write a good ad? Let me show you how easy it is.

Dear Betty,

I love you very much.

I want to take care of you and our kids for the rest of your lives. There'll be good times and bad. But I'll try to do my best with what I've got.

From time to time, I'll probably exasperate or annoy you. But I promise that you'll never be bored.

I read somewhere that the contract for marriage is the only one that doesn't have a definite term — a point at which it ends or can be renewed. It just says ". . . 'til Death do us part." Well, I want you to know that, in our case, I'm satisfied with that arrangement. But, to be perfectly honest, I sometimes wish that we weren't married — so we'd both know, every day, that we were sharing our lives because we wanted to — not because we had to.

All my love,

Joe

You're saying, "That's no ad. That's a love letter!" Well, every ad should be a love letter, a personal communication. And let's see if this one contains the basic elements.

You may not like the headline "Dear Betty" — but my wife will be crazy about it. It has her name in it, it's directed to her. And that's the secret of a good headline. The person reading it, the one you're trying to reach, should say, "Hey — he's talking to *me*."

The subhead, "I love you very much," isn't bad either. I've told her that she's a very important person, a great human being, and that I care about her.

Next, at the start of the body copy, I've made my promise — to take care of her and our kids for an unlimited

Every ad should be a love letter, a personal communication.

I once read somewhere that advertising is simply salesmanship in print.

time. Then I've gone on to enumerate the advantages and disadvantages of such an arrangement. (If she wasn't already so familiar with them, I'd probably have gone into greater detail and been more exact. But, after all, I made my sale some years back and am now looking for a reorder.)

The rest of the copy is simply reassuring; it repeats the promise, and identifies the seller. Although there hasn't been a specific call for action, it's certainly implied. She knows what I want, which is why I married her in the first place. As you can see, you don't have to be a literary genius to write a good ad. Not a great ad, perhaps, but enough to get the job done.

Let me give you another example. Let's say that you found the following note from a friend in your mailbox:

> *I have a new Caddilac that I got to sell because I'm leaving for the Service next week. It cost me $34,000 and only has 732 miles on it. Rather than sell it to some thief of a car dealer or going to the trouble of advertising, I'll let you have it for $24,000.*
>
> *If you don't have the cash, don't worry about it because I only owe the $24,000 and you can take over my payments which are about $397 a month.*
>
> *You know I drive careful, but I'd feel better if you'd have your mechanic check it out before you buy. In fact, if you'd like to drive it for a couple of days, I'll be glad to deliver it to you with a full tank of gas. And if you don't like the car, I'll take it back and you've had a free ride. No obligation.*
>
> *One thing — it's an awful green color (but you could have it painted).*
>
> *If you're interested, call me at (714) 555-1212 between 7 and 9 tonight.*
>
> *Your friend,*
>
> *John Doe*

Now, that's a good ad! It doesn't matter that your friend doesn't know how to spell "Cadillac" or that his grammar is atrocious. He's told you what he's selling, why it's cheap, how you can easily afford it, revealed its one shortcoming (correctable), offered a free trial, and told you just what to do if you want to buy.

There are still a number of reasons that you might not want to buy it — you might hate Cadillacs or not be able to afford $397 a month — but you'll have to admit that it's an almost irresistible offer. Even if you only bought it for resale.

The whole point is that a good product will almost sell itself — if you don't garbage it up with a lot of things that people think are "advertising."

The best ad is a good product — as long as you don't garbage it up.

SIZE OF AD

Maybe you've noticed that I haven't said anything about how big or how long your ad should be. The answer to that is: as big or as long as it needs to be. It takes less space or time to sell a Cadillac at half-price than it does to sell a Widget. That's because the Cadillac has been pre-sold by General Motors, and all you have to sell is the bargain price and the terms — and make it believable. With your Widget, you're starting from scratch. I never start out to write a certain size ad. I simply write the best, most simple ad I can. I try to describe every sales feature, anticipate and overcome every objection.

Not 'til I'm finished and am satisfied that I've done a good selling job do I decide what media I'm going to use. A very long ad can go into a letter — or be used in newspapers or magazines if you can afford the greater risk. A short one can be used in all of those and might work even better on radio or TV. Because a small ad might be "lost" in a magazine or newspaper, but every radio or TV commercial is the equivalent of a full page. Your radio or TV commercial is just as important and can be just as

Be careful about cutting down the size of your ad, simply for the sake of size. After all, what's the point of knocking on the door if the salesman disappears when it's opened?

effective as the one produced by the biggest, richest advertisers in the country.

But I won't cut my copy down to "size" — not yet. (After all, what's the point of knocking on the door if the salesman disappears when it's opened?) So, first, I'll test the ad just as I've written it. If it works, then I'll cut it — and test it again. If the second ad is more profitable than the first, I'll cut it again and test again and make my next decision, based on results. Writing advertising copy is partially art, but mostly science. You can measure the effect of what you do.

What do I cut? What seem to be the lesser points, the apparent repetitions. I'll see if something can be said more economically — but without lousing up the ad's "conversational" quality or flow. In cutting, I use what I call the "RCA principle." First, I build the best product I know how. Then I see how many parts I can remove before it stops working.

If I cut too much, the ad won't pull as well and I'll go back to the original.

You say, "No one will read long copy." And they won't. Not unless they're interested — unless it's got their name on it.

But, you say, no one will read long copy. And you're right, no one will unless he's interested — unless it has his name on it. Then he'll read every word. And that's the only guy you want to read your copy.

DON'T LET YOUR AD LOOK LIKE AN AD

Do I turn my copy over to an artist so that I can get a "professional" layout? No. The last thing I want is for my copy to look like an "ad." People buy newspapers or magazines to read the news. "Ads" are a necessary but unwelcome intrusion, and the reader's experience is that many of them are overblown or untrue. So I want my copy to look like a news story (which is what it should be), matching their editorial layout and typestyle as closely as the publication will let me.

So, if I want to save money, I send my copy to the

newspaper or magazine, with those instructions. They'll "pub-set" it — do the job free. Or, if I'm flush, I'll take my copy to a printer or typographer and ask him to make it look like an article, not an ad. And now, with the sophistication of Desktop Publishing, you can stylize your ad to each specific publication. Ideally, the only way that the casual reader will be able to distinguish the difference between my "ad" and the editorial content will be the small "Advertisement" line the publication may put at the top. I want the printer to do everything he can to achieve that effect.

Don't use small type or a type-face that's difficult to read (again, "imitating" the editorial content is your best guide). Anything that's worth saying is worth saying aloud. And small type is associated with something you're trying to hide.

For newspapers, assuming you can't afford the expense of a full page ad, the "ideal layout" is usually three columns (about 5½ inches) wide and about eight or more inches deep. This size is harder for the make-up man to bury. It's likely to go on top of a larger ad. Or, if it does wind up at the bottom of the page, generally only one or two much smaller ads will be stacked on top of it. (Later, we'll go into what your position request should be.) A bottle of booze and some conversation with the make-up man are a good investment. He can tell you if there's some "shape" that's easier for him to work with, to give you the "position" you need.

I've already told you to stick with a "news" format. It's cheaper to produce and, most important, more effective. You won't win any art awards or get the admiring comments of your friends. But, with the money you'll make, you'll be able to buy your own trophies and be able to afford to move into a better neighborhood.

To emphasize my point about ads that look like ads — and are therefore suspect — here are some DONT'S:

The best layout for an ad is one that matches, as closely as possible, the editorial layout and typestyle of the medium being used.

For newspapers, I like to stick with a "news" format. It's cheaper and more effective.

The most effective ads are those that don't look like ads.

1. Don't use "reverse" printing (white type on a black background). It may "stand out," but you've pleaded guilty to running an ad and it's also hard to read.

2. Don't use "Ben Day" backgrounds (a grey "screen" that artists seem to love). For the same reasons you shouldn't use reverse printing.

3. Don't use illustrations, unless they show the product in dramatic use — what it does, and words can't paint the picture. You're usually better off letting the prospect's imagination take over. (If I say the word "house" to you, what do you see? But if I show you a picture of a house, you may not like it — and I've stopped you cold.) What's more, the prospect may not be able to "identify" with the illustration — and you've lost him.

4. Don't get talked into a need for "white space" for aesthetic effect. The publication is charging you for both paper *and* ink. Make them use the ink. It'll imprint words that will sell for you.

Here are some other points to remember:

RESTATE YOUR OFFER IN THE ORDER FORM The customer is signing a contract —and he knows it. And you can use the space (I summarize the deal) and "sell" him again. Incidentally, don't make it "sound" like a contract. In conversational language — what Rudy Flesch used to call "shirt sleeve" English — tell the prospect what he's getting, what it'll do for him, and what your guarantee is. Be sure it's clear, easy to complete, and there's enough room to write the mailing information you need.

DON'T USE A POST OFFICE BOX AS YOUR ADDRESS It looks like you're trying to hide. Besides, giving your street address can produce an impressive number of walk-in sales. We do more than enough each year to pay the rent.

READ THE LARGE-SPACE MAIL ORDER ADVERTISING YOU SEE REPEATED TIME AFTER TIME IN MAGAZINES AND NEWSPAPER (That would indicate that the ads are successful.) See how well they've followed the "rules." If they've "broken" one, it may be an act of daring innovation that they've found improves results. Or the ad may be working in spite of the "mistake" — and the results would be improved if it were corrected. Direct Response ads have to work for a living. Every ad has to stand on its own two feet. Learn what you can from them, every chance you get.

MUCH "NATIONAL" AND A LOT OF "RETAIL" ADVERTISING IS WASTEFUL It publicizes the "name" and does very little else. It doesn't motivate people to buy; instead, it relies on the hope that when, and if, they buy a product in that particular category, they'll remember a certain brand.

Most advertising agencies would be terrified at the thought of putting a coupon in the ad of a major advertiser; not because, as they'd like you to believe, it would "cheapen" the product, but because it would accurately measure results — and that's the last thing they want.

In some ways, it's not the agencies' fault. They have to sell every ad twice. Once to the company that's paying the bill; and after it's been watered down, prettied up, and approved by the client's wife and 13-year-old son, they have to sell what's left to the public.

A case in point is the cigarette companies. After they were "forced" off radio and TV and saved millions and millions of dollars in advertising costs, their sales went up, which only goes to prove that if people really want to get cancer badly enough they'll find a way. Or perhaps what the cigarette companies thought was "soft-sell" was really "no sell."

We've gone quite thoroughly into the physical production of newspaper ads. (You'll see why when you read the next chapter.)

Now, here are some tips for preparing your copy for other media.

Look for and study ads that you see repeated time after time and in several different publications. It's an indication that they are successful. Learn what you can from them.

Make your letters friendly and personal. People like to get letters; they hate to get ads.

LETTERS

TIP #1 Send a friendly, personal letter — not an advertising circular. People like to get letters; they hate to get advertising.

TIP #2 Avoid salutations like "Dear Sir," "Gentlemen," "Fellow Fisherman," or "Dear Friend." It's a "form" letter, sure, but why rub the customer's nose in it? Don't type in his name (and/or address) either. In the first place, it's expensive; in the second place, the type probably won't match the rest of the letter and he'll feel that you're trying to put something over on him.

So, unless you can afford to go to the expense of a "computer" letter, what kind of salutation do you use? None. Just start right out with a headline — in this case, your first sentence — telling him, specifically, what problem your product will solve. If it's his problem, and your solution sounds good, he'll know that the letter is addressed to him.

Keep your sentences and paragraphs short, simple, and easy to read.

TIP #3 Keep your sentences short and simple. Probably no more than 10 to 12 words, with paragraphs short, and no more than five sentences.

You can send a four, six, or even an eight-page letter — and you should — if the selling job requires it, but it'll look easy to read if you follow Tips #2 and #3.

Stand back and just look at your letter. It should look inviting — easy to read.

TIP #4 It'll also make the letter look easy to read — and add visual interest — if you do these things: (a) Indent some of your key paragraphs. (b) Add what appear to be handwritten notations. (c) Underline some of the important words, capitalize others. But don't overdo it. Don't, for example, put a whole sentence in capital letters. They're harder to read and seem a little pushy or "immature." (Overselling is just as bad as underselling. A guy has to wonder, "If this deal is so good, why is he trying so hard.") (d) If the letter is two or more pages long, never have a sentence end on the bottom of a page. "Carry" the reader to the next page. If possible make that last sentence a cliff-hanger. For example, the last partial sentence at the bottom of page one might say "Forty thousand people have found that their sex" with the balance of the sentence on the next page.

TIP #5 Use a word processor or computer with a laser or bubblejet printer or reproduce a typewritten letter, using the offset printing process. Do NOT have it typeset. Do NOT have it mimeographed or photocopied. The first looks like an "ad." The second, unless it's expertly done, looks shoddy.

Tip #6 Use two colors. For the beginner, the reproduction of the typewritten material should always be in black. But the letterhead should be in a contrasting color. You can either furnish your printer with stationery if you have it, or he can give you a two-color print job. The extra expense is worth it.

TIP #7 If possible, hand-sign the letters (if the quantity is small) or have the "signature" imprinted in blue ink. (Signing with a felt-tip pen gives an impression of strength.) You can take care of Tips #6 and #7 by having the letter done in black; the letterhead and signature in blue. You can also use the blue to simulate the "handwritten" notations, but don't go wild with it.

TIP #8 Use color for added attention and a "second chance." Your letter should always be printed on white paper. But if you're enclosing a brochure or some other supporting material, use colored paper stock. A different color for each piece. Chances are your prospect will look at each enclosure before he decides to throw it away. Make each enclosure a "selling" piece. If your letter didn't "grab" him, maybe something else will.

TIP #9 Include an order form and a return envelope. (These will be at least two opportunities to add colored paper stock.) You do not have to use a postage-paid envelope. It might improve results, but that wasn't the

Signatures in your letters should always be signed in blue.

experience of one large mailer who recently ran some tests. He reported that he got more orders when people had to buy their own stamps than when he enclosed a postage-paid envelope. He was surprised — and so am I.

TIP #10 Fold your letter so the printed side is out.

TIP #11 Time your mailings so they don't arrive on Monday or the day after a holiday. The mail piles up, and you have too much competition.

TIP #12 Avoid mailing during the summer months. Families go on vacation and really tear through the mail when they return.

TIP #13 Use First Class postage if you can. And if you do, rubber stamp a big "FIRST CLASS MAIL" on the envelope. The only time I can't use First Class postage is when the contents are so bulky that my cost would be doubled.

TIP #14 Test your mailings! I've known advertisers to put together a mailing they liked and mail out 100,000 — only to have it flop. They could have found out it was a dud with a 2,000 mailing test — for two percent of the cost.

Does Direct Mail pay off? You bet it does!

Let me give two examples from my personal experience. On one item, after testing, we mailed 25,000 letters. Our cost was $9,800. The mailing produced over $40,000 worth of orders! In another instance every batch of 1,000 letters we mailed (at a cost of $500) brought in $9,000 worth of business! Now, these are unusually good results from a specialized mailing list. But, as of now, you know everything it took me years to find out about making Direct Mail work.

It's interesting that the newspapers grumble about "Junk Mail." But they use it themselves to sell subscriptions.

Time your mailings so they arrive during the middle of the week (Tuesday, Wednesday, Thursday). There's less competition.

Just how profitable can Direct Mail advertising be? Well, how does a 1,800 percent return on your investment sound to you?

RADIO

Radio commercials can be produced in any one of three ways: (1) Live, (2) E.T.'s (electrical transcriptions or recordings), (3) Tape.

If the announcer understands some of the rudiments of selling and realizes, as few do, that his job depends on the sponsor's success — live presentation is best. Some of those who ad-lib, amplify, and personalize the copy can do an exceptional job. But most announcers think of themselves as entertainers and only tolerate commercials as a necessary evil. Many announcers like to demonstrate their prowess at "sight reading" . . . their skill in being able to go on the air with a piece of copy they've never seen before. The result of these attitudes is a sing-song style of delivery, where the announcer's tongue is in gear, but his mind is in neutral. This is known as "throwing the commercial away" — along with the money that was paid for its delivery.

In the Los Angeles market, with its dozens of radio stations and hundreds of announcers, I can think readily of only two announcers whom I consider "star salesmen." The rest range from indifferent to bad.

As of early 1995, there are no local announcers in Los Angeles who can deliver a commercial for a direct response product the way a national talk show host of the stature and effectiveness of Paul Harvey or Rush Limbaugh can.

When Paul Harvey delivers a commercial message, he *sells* it. You believe him, and that is that.

For the ultimate in "selling" on the radio today there is no one better than Rush Limbaugh. When he breaks into his own commercial with, "Stop the tape, stop the tape!" your attention is riveted to one of the finest examples of a radio commercial you will ever hear. You just *know* if Rush says it, he believes it, and so do you.

You want your radio commercial to be delivered with conviction, passion, and enthusiasm. And if you can't afford to hire Rush Limbaugh or Paul Harvey, I suggest you do them yourself. That's the only way you'll get the same kind of enthusiasm and believability.

If you don't think you can do a radio or television commercial, think again. Victor Kiam does it for his *Remington Shavers*, Lee Iacocca did it for *Chrysler*, Al Eisner for his blue toilet cleaner *2000 Flushes Blue*, Orville Redenbacher and his grandson for their popcorn, or — one of my favorites — Sam Winston for his *Winston Tires*.

Each of these people have the special quality of believability in the product they are selling.

The difficulty with radio as a medium for Direct Response advertising is the limited length of commercial time. It's difficult — and often impossible — to create desire and tell people how to order in 60 seconds. (And I wouldn't even attempt anything less.) Einstein's Theory of Relativity comes into play here — 60 seconds is a long time if you're listening and a short time if you're paying for it.

Here are some tips if you're preparing radio commercials:

TIP #1 Direct it to one person. Don't think of yourself as being in the Coliseum, addressing 100,000 people. Think of yourself as talking to a friend and saying, "Hey! I've got something I want to tell you" — and then telling him. Simply and directly.

TIP #2 Don't use music to introduce your commercial or as a background. Not unless you're selling records, tapes, and CD's. (And more records, tapes, and CD's are sold by mail than in any other way!) But, ordinarily, music as an introduction wastes precious seconds. As background, it's distracting.

TIP #3 Allow at least 20 seconds for ordering information — the amount and where to send it. Repeat the information at least twice. If possible, three times. This repetition is annoying to the person who's not

When it comes to the ordering information you need to repeat the information at least twice. Though this may be annoying to the person who's not interested, it's vital to the person who is.

interested and vital to the person who is.

TIP #4 Don't try to use your "3-5-7 Strategy" on radio spots. Too many numbers confuse the listener.

TIP #5 Use a very simple address. If possible, it's best that the mail be directed to the station. They announce their call letters frequently, and if the listener missed it the first time, he has another chance to pick it up. Ask the listener to "Send $30 to Widgets in care of KABC Los Angeles 4"; not "Widget Company International in care of KABC, 17242 West Hyacinth Avenue, Los Angeles 90004." Sending the mail to the station is also reassuring to the customer. He probably trusts them. He's not too sure about you.

If the radio station won't accept and forward the mail (and a few won't), it's better to use a post office box number than a complicated street address. Try to get a box with no more than three digits and, if possible, in sequence (like "3-4-5"). If the post office can't give you a decent box number, try one of the private mail services (like Mail Boxes Etc. USA). They should be able to give you the kind of number you'll need.

TIP #6 Keep your price in even dollars. "Thirty dollars" is less confusing — and takes less time to say — than "twenty-nine dollars and seventy-nine cents."

TIP #7 Do the commercials yourself. If you don't sound like an announcer, so much the better. The only caution is this: Don't try to sound like an announcer. If you stumble and stammer a bit, that's great. (Unless you're selling a course in diction.) It only adds to your believability. And people buy things from people they trust. It'll take a little practice, but you're better off ad-libbing from a "fact sheet" instead of a script. That's because you're not accustomed to reading material and making it sound as though it's coming off the top of your head. A "spontaneous" presentation is the best kind.

With radio it's important to keep everything — the options, the addresses, the price, etc. — simple.

When advertising on television, just as with radio, the three most important rules are: keep it simple; keep it simple; keep it simple.

TELEVISION

It's too bad, but there are very few stations that will allow you to do "live" commercials any more. Live commercials are more effective because they have a greater sense of immediacy and can be varied from one commercial to the next. They're especially good if a product is being demonstrated, because the customer can see whether it really works or not. They're hoping it won't, but they're impressed when it does.

However, most commercials are on tape, and a few are on film.

Here are some tips:

TIP #1 Reread all the tips on producing radio commercials. Almost all of them apply to TV.

TIP #2 Don't clutter your commercial with special effects. The technicians love to show off their electronic wizardry, but it just reminds the audience that what they're watching is staged. The impression you want to give is that you're in the viewer's living room and talking only to them.

TIP #3 Don't read your commercial. If you must, memorize it. If you can, ad-lib it. But don't ever read it from cue cards and try not to use a teleprompter either; in the first place, you'll sound like you're reading, in the second place, you'll lose direct eye contact with the viewer. And who'll buy from someone who won't look a person in the eye?

TIP #4 Don't use a "super" (printing that's imposed on a picture) unless it's absolutely necessary. It divides the prospect's attention. If you do use them, be sure that the talk matches the sign word for word. Otherwise, the prospect gets confused or suspicious because he's hearing one thing and seeing something else. What you're buying, the impact of sight and sound, is lost.

TIP #5 Ask the cameraman or director for a "medium"

shot. The picture of you (if you're doing the selling) should be from slightly above the waist. That matches the way people would see you if you were visiting them in their homes, and that's exactly what you're doing. A "close-up" makes you look pushy. A "long shot" gives the impression you're afraid to come close. You may be talking in a conversational tone (and you should) but his eyes will tell him that you've raised your voice in order to be heard. It's just plain not intimate, and TV is an intimate medium.

TIP #6 Keep it simple. Keep it simple; ten thousand times repeat, *keep it simple.*

MAGAZINES

Almost all magazines are produced on computers for letterpress or offset printing. In either case, your preparation is exactly the same. Most magazines will pub-set your ad (Remember? — do the typography free), but I prefer to send them a finished ad for reproduction. It saves time and the chance of error. If it's "offset" (a photographic process), that's all they need. If it's letterpress (which means that a "plate" must be made), I ask them to make the plate and charge me for it. It'll probably cost me less and will certainly save me the trouble and expense of carefully packaging a plate.

Don't ever send the magazine your "original" layout. The printer can "pull reproduction glossies" or use a photographic process to make as many "velox prints" as you'll need. In the latter case, save the negative so you can order more.

All magazine (and most newspaper) space is sold by the "line." There are 14 lines to the inch — and one inch is usually the minimum.

How big should your magazine ad be? As big as it needs to be. You can use a slightly smaller type-size in magazines because the paper stock they generally use reproduces more sharply than newsprint does. But don't use type so small that it discourages the reader. I've seen

TV is an intimate medium. Have the cameraman shoot you from slightly above the waist. This matches the way people would see you if you were to visit them in their homes — which is exactly what you are doing.

ads with type so small that it looked like the typographer's hobby was inscribing Bible verses on the head of a pin. I've "seen" them — but I haven't read them.

I usually run fairly large space in magazines. Two-thirds of a page or full pages. First, because I have a lot to say. Second, I think that, psychologically, it makes the offer look important and the company solvent (at least we had enough money to pay for a big ad).

More advertisers go broke by not spending enough to do the job than as a result of spending too much. Personally, I'd rather be chewed up by lions than tickled to death by ants.

I suggest that, when you're ready to try magazine advertising, you wait until you can afford to buy big space. More advertisers go broke by not spending enough to do the job than as a result of spending too much. Personally, I'd rather be chewed up by lions than tickled to death by ants.

In addition, big space gives you the muscle you need to get the *positioning* that can make the difference between failure and success. (More about that in the next chapter.)

WHEN TO GO FOR IT

Here's one tip that can save you a lot of money:

The best months for Direct Response results are generally January, February, March, April, and May. June is shaky, and July and August can be disastrous. In September, October, and November, business bounces back; and December is iffy.

The three best months for Direct Response advertising are January, February, and March.

So time your ads for those prime months, unless you have a seasonal product. For Christmas items, October is the month to advertise in magazines. And November issues are good if they're "on sale" before the 15th of the month.

Speaking of Christmas items, my experience in newspapers is to advertise after Halloween and before November 15. Period.

The thing to be careful of is that the months you're buying in are those that the magazine goes on sale. The "issue" on the cover of the magazine may be an entirely different matter.

It may be the "January issue," but if it goes on sale (copies are mailed or put on newsstands) about December 15, you could be in a lot of trouble.

So I buy the February issues that are on sale after January 1. Some small magazines postdate their issues by several months. For example, the "July issue" hits the newsstands in April. I presume that this is to give their product a longer life before it's outdated.

So now you know how to write an ad and the basics of preparing it for newspapers, direct mail, radio, TV, and magazines.

Q. Are there other books on advertising that you can recommend?

A. Yes! At a minimum, your library should consist of the following. (I want you to read, reread, and read each of them again. Do this and you will have as much expertise as — probably more than — 99.9 percent of the people working in most ad agencies. There are very few "professionals" who really know how to write good copy.) At any rate, I want you to start with these:

Tested Advertising Methods
   by John Caples

Confessions of an Advertising Man
   by David Ogilvy

The Robert Collier Letter Book
   by Robert Collier

How to Write, Speak and Think More Effectively
   by Rudolf Flesch

My Life in Advertising/Scientific Advertising
   by Claude Hopkins

Read these books! Do this and you will have just as much expertise as most so-called ad agency people.

Some of these books are no longer being published, so you won't be able to pick them up in your local bookstore. However, there is one place you can go (write or phone, actually) to get all of them. That is:

CARL GALLETTI
ONE PADDOCK DRIVE
LAWRENCEVILLE, NJ 08648
PHONE: (609) 896-0245
FAX: (609) 896-2653

Ask Carl to send you his catalog of "Hard-to-Get Books and Tapes on Advertising." As far as I know, he's the only source in the entire country (or world for that matter) where you can get your hands on some of these titles. He also carries many other books and tapes you might want to add to your library.

(By the way, even if you choose not to pick up any of these books, at the very least, send for Carl's catalog. It is exceptionally well written; and in the back of the catalog, you'll find "The Magic Story," Part 1, by John McDonald. I think you'll really get a kick out of it.)

I simply can't overemphasize the importance of these books. Get them. Read them. Study them. Use them.

Some time back, I said that I would tell you everything I know about the Direct Response Business. And I've tried to keep my promise. But now I'm getting into an area where I can't tell you "everything." Not because telling the truth would hurt me. But because it might embarrass and harm people I do business with and who have relied upon my discretion.

I know I promised to tell you "everything," but I'm afraid this is one area where I can't.

The "secret" I can't reveal is the names of the newspapers, magazines, and radio and television stations that will sell your product for you on a "commission" basis — the people you pay only for the orders they deliver. With this kind of arrangement, of course, you can't lose. Every order represents a small but sure profit.

TRY A PARTNERSHIP

You'd be surprised at some of the Big Name Media who are willing to be a partner in your business — provided (and this is important) they are convinced that you are reliable and honest.

It would probably surprise you at some of the Big Name Media who are willing to be your "partner."

This kind of a deal is called a "P.I." The letters stand for "Per Inquiry," because you pay the media a percentage of the sale price for each "inquiry" or order they generate.

Although many of them might go along with a lesser percentage, I pay them 50 percent of the retail price. In the first place, I've "budgeted" for this expenditure. In the second place, I want them to make money. Because, if it's profitable to them, they'll give my advertising the greatest possible exposure and increase my volume of sales — without increasing my overhead. And don't forget that, although my profit on the original order is limited, the profit margin skyrockets on the reorders I'll get — because I have virtually no advertising expense!

In "P.I." deals, the mail is generally directed to the

media. After they've verified the number of orders, they forward it to you.

In addition to the "P.I." deals that can be negotiated, there are two other ways to buy space or time that have almost the same effect.

The first relates to magazines and is called "H.I.N." or "Help If Necessary." This means that you agree to pay for the ad, but if the results aren't profitable, the publication will run the ad again without charge. And will run it as many times as they have to in order for you to at least break even.

Since the orders are being directed to you, how do they know how many orders you received — and whether you need "help?" They don't. They have to trust you. And, of course, they make this deal only with people they trust. In a sense, it's self-policing. Obviously, you will want to continue buying space in a magazine that produces profitable results. And it might be a little awkward if you asked for "help" — and then came back in a few months and said that you'd like to run in the same magazine again. Why would you want to do that if the first time was unprofitable? Naturally, the best reason for playing it straight is that that's the most rewarding business practice in the long run.

If you are a straight shooter and you've got a really "hot" offer, you may be able to let the media be your "partner" and pick up your ad costs.

The second way to reduce your risk, and this applies to radio and TV stations, is the "Guaranteed" deal. Some of the stations that won't "P.I." will go along with this one: You buy the time, and they run your "spots" (that's what broadcast commercials are called). However, if you don't get a prearranged number of orders, they'll keep running your commercials until that number is reached. Again, it doesn't pay for you to be greedy, or they won't make the same arrangement a second time.

Why are some of the media willing to be "commission salesmen?" Because they've made a commitment and are working against a deadline.

A publisher, for example, has to decide long in advance how many pages he's going to print. He allocates a certain amount of space to editorial, and the balance to the advertising he hopes he can sell. If, as the deadline approaches, he has unsold space, he can do one of three things: (1) Fill the unsold advertising space with editorial — which means he has not only lost the revenue he hoped for, but he'll have to pay someone to write it. (2) He can run "Public Service" ads — free. "Smokey the Bear" is nice, but what's really going up in smoke is advertising revenue. (3) He can make a "P.I." or "H.I.N." deal with some Direct Response advertiser.

Why a Direct Response advertiser? Because: (1) He's the only kind of advertiser who can make an immediate decision without checking his "budget" or submitting the proposal to a committee (and don't forget, time is running out). (2) He's the only kind of advertiser who keeps exact records of his results and is willing to pay accordingly.

So the publisher gambles. He knows that he'll at least get some income — and if a deal is "hot," he may wind up making more money than if he had sold the space outright!

Radio and TV stations are under pressure, not day by day like a newspaper, not weekly or monthly like a magazine — but minute by minute. The 60 seconds that just passed is gone forever. Unlike the publisher, who can cut his product cost by reducing the number of pages he prints, the broadcaster has a fixed commitment to stay on the air so many hours a day — and his overhead grinds on. That's why the majority of broadcasters will take on at least a few "P.I." or "Guaranteed" accounts — and why some subsist on very little else. In fact, at one time there was a big station in Texas that wouldn't take anything except "P.I.'s." They found that if they picked the cream of the crop of Direct Response offers, they could sometimes get more income from each "spot" than if they sold it to a "national" account or a retailer! And they eliminated the

Radio and TV stations are really under pressure — minute by minute. The 60 seconds that just passed is gone forever.

need for (and expense of) salesmen and were always "sold out." Not a commercial minute was wasted!

This "commission" arrangement is a great way to go if you have little or no capital.

You can use the "commission" arrangements to get started if you have little or even no capital. However, I have to be honest and say that I don't use these methods to "test" a new product or a new ad for an established product. Instead, I test in media that I've used for a long time and have extensive records on, so that I can judge the results objectively. "P.I.," "H.I.N.," and "Guaranteed" deals are in a sense "artificial" and don't allow me to make direct comparisons.

After I've tested, and I know that a product is "hot," I'll make a publisher or broadcaster my partner — but not until then. Because, if it's a "proven" product, and the results are poor, my "partner" knows that it's the weakness of his medium and won't find the fulfillment of his obligations as painful. If it's a run-away success, we're both happy. In either case, he'll call me again when he's in trouble.

There's one other circumstance in which I use these no-risk techniques. That's when someone is trying to sell me on advertising in his medium — and I have serious reservations. Perhaps I feel that the cost is too high for the number of readers, listeners, or viewers. Or I doubt that the audience composition (by sex, age, or interest) is suitable. If he thinks it is, I ask him to prove it — by taking a share of the profits. I know my offer "works." The only thing that's in question is whether his medium will or won't. If he's willing to gamble, fine; if not, I probably haven't missed much. You can dribble away a lot of money, a few dollars at a time. No medium is "cheap" if it doesn't produce results. No medium is "expensive" if you have a profit after paying the bill.

No medium is "cheap" if it doesn't produce results. And no medium is "expensive" if you show a profit after using it.

HOW TO PURCHASE MEDIA

Now, how do you go about buying media when you're

prepared to risk cold cash?

First, you take advantage of all the "discounts" that exist. Here are some tips:

TIP #1 You buy at "wholesale."

That means that you pay a rate that is far lower than the one that's printed on the rate card — the price that the medium quotes (and is being paid by the majority of "uneducated" advertisers).

Rate cards, particularly in the case of low circulation magazines, quote the "asking" price. If you know what you're doing, you can pay a lot less. I'd say that in many cases I pay 20 to 50 percent less than the "list price." In a few instances, my under-the-table discount is even more.

I'm not trying to imply that I'm getting any bargain. The price I'm paying is what the medium is really worth. At the price I'm paying, my ads will pay off. If I had to pay any more — anywhere near the "asking price" — the results would be marginal, and I could lose my shirt.

I recently asked one of the magazine sales representatives who, among his clients, paid the rate-card prices. He replied, "Almost everybody does. All of the 'national' advertisers and all the 'one-shot' mail order advertisers do."

"But," I said, "you know that a mail order advertiser can't pay those prices and make a profit."

"I know," he said, "but, if a man doesn't ask me for a lower price, am I going to volunteer it? Besides, most of the little guys don't know what they're doing anyway and wouldn't make out if they paid half of what you're paying. I'm doing them a favor, showing them that they ought to get out of the business.

"Once in awhile," he went on, "some little guy pays me top dollar and almost breaks even or maybe makes a little. Him, I'll help. I won't cut the price, because I'd be admitting I got to him the first time. But since I know that he's got the makings of a steady advertiser, I'll give him

Never, ever pay "rate card" rates for any advertising. I rarely consider any medium unless I'm getting a 20 to 50 percent discount.

some 'free' space every so often. That way he thinks I'm a hero, and he ends up paying what he should have been paying right along."

Incidentally, this sales representative is a very nice guy, and I've never caught him in a direct lie. Some omissions, perhaps, but never a direct lie. Which is more than I can say for a few of the "reps."

Now, the key words in that whole speech are "steady advertiser." And you can add to that the advertisers who buy big units of space — full pages — and lots of them. Because those are the guys, naturally, who get the deals.

TIP #2 If there's no discount off the rate card, here's what to ask about: "remnants." So many large magazines and newspaper supplements are putting out "regional" editions these days that there's an advantageous situation for the Direct Response advertiser. A large "national" advertiser buys one or more of these "regions" because he only has distribution in those areas. He pays a premium because he's only buying a selected part of the circulation. But you can pick up the unsold balance of the circulation at a substantial savings. However, these "remnants" are usually available only in space units of one-half page, three-fifths of a page, or full pages in the case of newspaper supplements like *Parade* and *USA Today* — or two-thirds of a page or full pages in the slick, big-circulation magazines. And even with the "remnant" discount, the amount you have to shell out can make you pucker a bit.

TIP #3 Buy through a bulk buyer.

There are a handful of people in this business who contract with magazines to buy a large number of pages throughout the year. There are others who trade something the magazine wants in the way of goods or services for their value in advertising pages. Their gimmick, of course, is that they acquired what they traded or bartered for a lot less. In effect, these Bulk Buyers guarantee that the magazine will

"Remnants" and "bulk buyers," two other ways to get substantial discounts (up to 50 percent and more) on your media purchases.

have a certain number of ad pages in every issue. In return, the magazine gives them a very attractive price per page. The Bulk Buyer fulfills his contract by running advertising for those products he owns or has a proprietary interest in — and sells off the rest for what he can get. What he can get may vary from a 10 percent discount to a 40 percent discount. Or whatever. The only rule is that he can't sell to advertisers who are already using the magazine.

TIP #4 If you handle your own advertising, form an advertising agency.

This is really a very complicated procedure. You will need a business license and some stationery. On second thought, you might not need the business license. As a result of this tremendous investment, you might get a 15 percent discount on any advertising you buy! (The only exception is your local newspaper. They will probably give you a much greater discount, but it will be in the form of the "retail rate" as opposed to the "national" or "general" rate they charge the out-of-town advertisers.)

Form your own ad agency and take 15 percent off the top of virtually all your advertising.

Your local radio station will give you a "retail" rate plus the advertising agency discount. True, some of the stuffier, old-line media may not "recognize" you as a bona fide advertising agency (there are certain criteria for financial stability and the number of accounts you service), but most of the smaller ones and many of the medium-sized ones will. Particularly if it's clear that that's the only way they're going to get your business.

TIP #5 There are still other ways to save money buying advertising. That's to make a deal with someone who's contracted to buy, say, 12 pages at a 20 percent discount (right off the rate card). But they've bitten off more than they can chew. So they'll sell you some of that space for less than you'd have to pay otherwise.

I said it before, and I'll say it again, never, ever, pay the published rate for any advertising you buy.

Instead of making a "P.I." deal with a broadcaster or publication directly, you can work through a broker. If you have a good product, with a proven track record, there are two or three people (generally, Bulk Buyers) who will act as a middleman.

However, they will want the mail directed to them, will open the orders, and keep all of the money 'til they've covered their costs. Which means that until income reaches that point (and it may never come) you don't get a dime. From that time forward, you only get a prearranged part of the income.

Even if you could live with the financial aspect of the deal, there's another (and in my mind, more serious) drawback. There's an unavoidable slowdown in the time it takes for the mail to go to them and then be forwarded to you. This is aggravated by the fact that they'll take anywhere from a week to a month to get around to processing it. So the longer the deal runs, the greater the percentage of complaint letters. The brokers couldn't care less. But you should.

Start out small — test your ads in your own home town — before attempting to slug it out in the "big leagues."

If you've gotten the impression that buying advertising is, for the novice, like walking through Central Park at midnight without a gun you're right. But at least I've given you a water pistol! Which is more than I had when I started. And believe me, I got mugged more than once.

But, really, I've told you more than you need to know at this stage of your career. Because you should test your ads right in your own home town before you try to slug it out in the Big Leagues.

When you're ready to make the move up, contact some — or all — of the people whose names I'll give you later.

However, for the moment, let's assume that you're going to start modestly, right in your own backyard. (I still do, on every project.) Here are some things you should know about it.

NEWSPAPERS

I prefer testing in newspapers. Production's easy and cheap (I've already gone into that). You can generally assess your results in two or three days (I covered that, too). And here are some tips:

TIP #1 Don't run your ad in the Mail Order Section, if the paper has one.

Readership is poor, and, generally, your ad has to conform to a restricted size and layout. The only person I can imagine poring over the Mail Order Section is someone hoping to find something — anything — to buy. Or maybe someone who's in the business and is curious about what competitors are doing. If you think those ads "must work," because there are so many of them, save a few issues. You'll see how few are repeated. The only ones I see, week in and week out, are the guys who invite you to "write for free information" and then try to sell you a correspondence course for several hundred dollars. And I'll bet that even this handful of successful advertisers would do better if they took this next tip.

Tip #2 Put your ad in the Main News Section.

I should note that recently I've found that the absolute best position, when you can afford it, is a full page, front (outside page) of a section. The further forward the section, the better. If you can't get a front outside page, try a back outside page of a section. You'll find that some back pages work and some don't.

For practical purposes, and in as much as a full page can be a very expensive way to go, I suggest you start out with something smaller and apply the following:

If there are two or more sections of Main News, try to get it in the first section. You might think that an ad directed primarily to women should be in the Women's Section or Society Section, or if you're looking for male customers that you'll find them in the Sports or Financial Section. You're wrong. Placement in the Main News Section gives you your best exposure to either or both sexes. The only exception to this rule that I've found in 16 years is Larry Voegele's book on Professional Handicapping.

When buying ad space in newspapers, your best position is in the main news section, far forward, right hand page, above the fold.

These ads do best on the "Race Entries" page. Presumably, the racing fan doesn't read anything else.

Most newspapers won't give you any static about getting into a particular section. Here's where you start running into trouble, because here's the rest of what you should have, in terms of "position," for your ad to succeed:

It should be on the right-hand page. It should be "above the fold" (the "fold" is the horizontal middle of the paper if it's a standard-sized newspaper). And, if possible, it should be on the "outside edge" or, as it's sometimes called, the "thumbnail position." You can see how it got its name if you'll notice where your hands are when you hold a newspaper.

Now, to the degree that the position of your ad follows this formula, it will increase your chance of success. To the degree it varies from this position, your likelihood of failure is multiplied.

I've spent millions, and my records show that it makes a whole world of difference where your ad appears.

Newspaper salesmen can show you all kinds of surveys to "prove" that it doesn't make any difference where your ad appears. I can only say that I've spent millions of dollars of my own money, making my own survey — and my records show it makes a lot of difference!

If it doesn't make any difference, why don't they put their front-page news in the middle of the paper and the Classified Section on the front page? Believe me — the closer you get to the front page, the more likely it is that people will read the "news" of your product.

Now, how do you try to insure that your ad will appear where you know it'll do the most good? Well, you could weigh the newspaper and whichever day of the week the newspaper is consistently the lightest (has the least number of pages), that's the day you want to schedule your ad. Because that's the day that the newspaper will doubly welcome your business. The paper's lighter because it has fewer ads. Therefore, it'll be easier for the makeup man to give you the position you request — and you will have less competition for the customer's dollar.

I avoid the hernia-inducing Sunday papers. Unless I put my ad in the Comics — yes, the Comics, or in the TV Magazine. (When I buy the TV Magazine, I request a right-hand page towards the back. That way, my ad hasn't been "lost" after the reader looked at the Sunday or Monday program listings — and I'll pick up some people who'll thumb through to see what's coming up.) And I've had some success with very large ads in the front page of the Classified Section.

TIP #3 Sign a contract — the smallest (the one that involves the least obligation) that's available. That's because newspapers have an "open rate" — which is their highest rate — and a series of "contract rates" which mean that the more advertising you run, the less it costs you per "line" or inch.

If you buy at the "open rate," you'll pay the same high price every time you run. (Although some newspapers will permit you to try one ad at the "open rate" and then backdate a contract when you run a second.)

The reason you want the smallest contract is that if you exceed it, you'll get a rebate at the end of the year on all the advertising you've bought — based on the contract level you reach. On the other hand, if you shot too high, you'll be "short-rated." If you are "short-rated," you'll be billed for the difference per line for the contract you signed and the rate you actually earned. This can be a tidy sum. For your second year, you'll have a better idea of how much space you expect to use and can sign a contract for that amount.

Don't sign a contract that guarantees you'll run every week. Instead, sign an annual "bulk space" contract (usually 500 to 1,000 "lines" or 36 to 72 inches).

TIP #4 Don't run an ad just before or during holiday weekends, or on any holiday that falls in the middle of the week, or just before Thanksgiving or Christmas.

Avoid "thick" paper days — there's a lot more competition for the reader to see your ad.

Avoid running an ad just before or on a holiday weekend. The customer's mind is probably somewhere else.

TIP #5 Don't buy "throw-aways" or "free circulation" newspapers. They don't work.

TIP #6 Be wary of newspapers with less than 100,000 circulation. Their "C.P.M." (cost per thousand) subscribers is ordinarily too high. But I know a few that pay out handsomely.

I have never found that repetition improves newspaper's results. If an ad falls flat the first time, it'll do worse the next.

TIP #7 Don't let anyone kid you that repetition improves results. In the Direct Response Business each ad has to stand on its own two feet. If your first ad lies down and dies, a second ad will only do worse. In fact, if your first ad's results are excellent, expect the returns to decline from then on. When you run an unprofitable ad or two after a series of winners, get out of the newspaper for awhile. Let the deal rest for at least a month or two — and then try it again. Sometimes a change of headline will perk it up.

The greatest thing about using newspapers — and radio and TV — in your town is that you can buy them for far less than I or any other out-of-town advertiser can. No matter how much money we spend, you have the advantage of a much lower cost. That's because these media, as I told you before, have a "national" or "general" rate for me, and a "local" or "retail" rate for you. Despite all the money I spend, and the advertising agency discount I'm allowed to take, you still have me beat. An ad that might be barely profitable for me could be a bonanza for you — due to your lower advertising cost. Do you remember my telling you that this is where being "small" is actually an advantage?

So, if you're ready, contact the newspaper's Retail Sales Department and talk to the salesman. And when you're ready to buy advertising in other towns' newspapers, your salesman can tell you how to go about that.

RADIO

Without further ado . . .

TIP #1 Stations that feature talk shows, all-news

formats, and country and western music are usually effective, and in about that order. Stations that program contemporary music, middle-of-the-road music, and classical music usually won't work unless your product is targeted towards that special audience, and even then they're doubtful.

The reason is that people listen to talk shows and news — that's why they tuned in, and they hang on to every word — even your commercial. They have what's called a "foreground" sound. I'm not sure why country and western formats are productive, but they sometimes are. Maybe because the fans have a loyalty to the announcers — have more confidence in them than those "fancy-talking dudes."

Contemporary, middle-of-the-road (those "good old songs"), and classical music stations usually aren't productive because they provide a "background" sound. There are some exceptions, but you can blow a lot of money finding out which ones they are. Unless you can get a "P.I." or buy on a "Guaranteed" basis.

If you're thinking about buying radio time, listen to the station. If you hear a lot of spots in which the "tag" of the commercial suggests calling a phone number, or there are some Direct Response advertisers, it might be worth a try. If these advertisers continue week after week, they know something. Because the phone calls must produce "leads" for salesmen, and the orders must be coming in to the Direct Response companies — or they wouldn't continue to advertise.

It doesn't matter whether you "like" the station or not. The only thing that counts is how productive it is.

If you do decide to buy some time, place your schedule where other advertisers who measure response are.

TIP #2 Run *enough* spots.
Unlike newspapers or magazines (where repetition

When buying time on radio, start with "talk show" or "all news" formats. People "listen" to these stations when tuned in.

Unlike newspapers and magazines, repetition helps build radio response.

often depreciates results), broadcast response builds. Maybe they tuned in on the middle of your commercial, or maybe they missed the address. They need another chance to get it all. Or maybe they just need convincing. Reading is active — they have to decide to do it. Listening is passive — they can just sit and let it happen.

But a one-week test is all you need to decide whether to continue or not. If I have enough orders at the end of the first week so that the total gross income is at least enough to pay for the advertising, I'll renew my contract. If it's a little less, I'll either gamble and renew — or take a week's hiatus to check it more carefully. If it's a lot less, I'll cancel for good. If I do continue, I'll do so for one week at a time — and stay on top of the results. But don't forget, as you go ahead, that the weekly results have to increase sharply (because most of the mail is coming from the previous week or weeks). If they level off, cancel.

TIP #3 If the station puts more than one commercial in a "break," make sure that yours is the first. That'll give your customer a chance to write down the address while the next commercial is on and before the program resumes.

TIP #4 Just because you go to bed early, don't forget that a lot of people don't. If you live in a metropolitan community, there's a whole army of people who don't get off work 'til midnight — and there are a lot of insomniacs, too. Some of your most effective commercial time is after midnight — and your costs are rock-bottom. You'll be surprised at the results if there's a personable, low-key host on the show. "Night people" are lonely, and they show their loyalty to the friendly host by buying what he sells.

TIP #5 If the station has some good "salesmen announcers," you'd be wise to submit a "fact sheet" instead of a cut-and-dried commercial. They'll ad-lib, covering your main sales points, and you'll probably end up with a "pitch" that's considerably longer than the 60 seconds you paid for. And the longer they talk, the more they sell.

If there are several "personalities" on the station, it doesn't hurt to set up a little competition. Make your mailing address "Send $3 to Widgets, care of Michael Silvertongue, KABC, Los Angeles 90004." I've never seen an announcer yet who didn't think he was the best of the lot — and was insecure enough to have to prove it.

TIP #6 Don't run a commercial directed at men during what the stations call the "traffic hours." True — there are a lot of them listening, but it's hard to write down an address when you have at least one hand on the steering wheel.

TIP #7 You, too, can be an advertising agency and save 15 percent!

To get started, just call the radio station and ask for the local sales department — and talk to the salesman.

TELEVISION

I spent 12 years in TV running an advertising agency and working as one of those salesmen announcers (do I hear someone saying "pitchmen?"). I made a lot of money — and blew it all, plus another $50,000, trying to produce my own TV show.

That debt was the best thing that ever happened to me. It made me desperate enough to try anything — and I found Dyna/Psyc.

I stopped working the 18-hour days, 7 days a week — a schedule that had literally paralyzed me three times. (The diagnosis was "exhaustion and nervous tension." The last time I was in the hospital, the doctor conducted a bunch of tests, including the one where they stick a tube in your scrotum and thread it through the arteries leading to your heart. After 10 days of delightful experiences like that, the doctor came to my bedside. "Well," he smiled, "I can tell you a lot of things that aren't wrong with you." When I got the bill for $2,000 [1970s prices] I knew why he

Your 15 percent ad agency discount applies to radio advertising, too.

You'll notice that there are a lot of similarities between radio and TV advertising. Not the least of which is that TV commercials will benefit from repetition.

was smiling.)

With Dyna/Psyc, I did a lot less work — and made a lot more money. (The other day a friend of mine said, "You're the only guy I know who retired first — and then got rich!")

The reason I've told you all this is partly self-indulgence, but mostly to establish my credentials as knowing something about TV.

Here are some of the things I know about buying TV time:

TIP #1 Buy "fringe" time — daytime until about 6 o'clock at night, or after 11 p.m. You're right — you don't get the big audiences that the prime-time shows deliver. But you don't pay nearly as much per person for the ones you do reach. And many stations will permit 90-second or even 2-minute spots in these fringe periods. And you need all the time you can get. You have to tell before you can sell.

TIP #2 Get your commercial within the program. Not at a "station break." Not just after opening credits (the name of the show). Not just before closing credits (the names of the technicians).

TIP #3 If there are two or more commercials in a break, fight to be first.

TIP #4 Before you buy time on a station, watch the programs. Buy time in those where you see other "lead" deals and Direct Response advertisers. There may be a waiting list. Good . . . wait.

TIP #5 Don't buy spots in half-hour programs unless you can nail down Tips #2 and #3. Old movies are your best bet. I love 'em myself, but the people who watch films from England or dubbed foreign films either don't buy enough or there aren't enough of them. Adventure, cowboy, and tear-jerker films work best. Comedies are so-so. Action programs, like Roller Games and wrestling can be a gold mine. Talk shows, particularly if they involve controversy, can be very productive.

TIP #6 Remember I said that, on radio, the all-news format can work. But don't buy news programs on TV. In the first place, they're terribly expensive — and that's all the places you need.

TIP #7 Like radio, and in contrast to publications, your commercial will benefit from repetition. But, for the purposes of testing, you don't need as many spots because you have both the customer's eyes and ears to absorb the ordering information. If there's a late movie five nights a week, you might try one spot in each of three nights. Since they know what movies they're going to show, pick the ones that fit the criteria I gave you in Tip #5. And if they're having a foreign film festival, watch and enjoy it — but don't buy any commercials in it. And don't sign a 4-week or a 13-week contract until you've completed your test.

TIP #8 One kind of late night program to avoid is the one where all of the advertisers are local merchants. These are usually the result of the station selling a block of time to a promoter. He, in turn, high pressures and sweet-talks the barber, the pool hall, and the pizza parlor into advertising on TV. The price is ridiculously low — but not worth it.

TIP #9 Remember that advertising agencies get a 15 percent discount and a few of them will earn you more than they cost. Darned few.

When you're ready to try TV, call the station and ask for the local sales representative.

MAGAZINES

I've already alerted you to the fact there are lots of "inside deals" in this area. A few magazines stick by the rate card, but you could put them all in one stack and get over them without jumping. To clarify, I don't mean that they play footsie with the "national" advertisers (although

As a rule, magazines normally give discounts to mail order advertisers.

The percentage of readers who respond to your offer is not what's important. Profit is important.

more and more of them are buying "bartered" space) but magazines normally give a discount to mail-order advertisers. And some, as I've indicated, go a lot further.

Here's a rule of thumb: if, based on the rate for a full page, the cost is about $4 per thousand of circulation, you're on pretty safe ground. I've paid a little more for a highly specialized audience I wanted to reach, and I frequently pay half that much — or less. To put that $4 figure in mathematical terms: a magazine with a paid, audited circulation of 1,000,000 should have a page rate of less than $4,000. Less 15 percent for the advertising agency. If you're, in fact, the advertising agency, your net cost should be $3,400. To the degree that you pay more than that $4-per-thousand figure, you're increasing your risk. To the degree that you pay less, you increase your chance to make a profit. And profit is the name of the game.

What percentage of the readers will respond to an offer? I don't know — and I don't care. All I watch is expense (what the advertising costs) and income (how many dollars it produced). For example, if an ad cost me $4,000 (the fictional rate for a magazine with a circulation of 1,000,000), I'd want to get at least $8,000 worth of orders. Or, to put it another way, my income should be double my cost. And if you're going to grade results, that would be somewhere between "good" and "excellent." If I've budgeted correctly, that dollar income should give me a fair profit. And I can drop down some, without losing any money. But every dollar that comes in over the $8,000 figure is half profit! Because, in a sense, I've already paid for the advertising — and the rest is free!

However, if you insist on reducing this to percentages, it might be instructive. You'll see how few people you can reasonably expect to respond. (And maybe I'll never have to listen again to the starry-eyed people who say, "The circulation of the *Times* is more than a million — and if only two or three percent send in orders . . . !")

So let's proceed with our conversion to percentages. Let's say that you have a $30 offer. You need 267 orders to produce that $8,000 income. And 267 is two-hundred-sixty-seven-hundredths of one percent! If it's a $50 offer, you'd need 160 orders, or sixteen-hundredths of one per cent. Or if it's a $20 offer, you'd need 400 orders, or twenty-three-hundredths of one per cent.

Now, these percentage figures are not what you can "expect" to get — they're what you can hope to get — IF the ad is successful.

Why is it so low if you're selling something that "everyone" should want? Because: (1) Some of the people who get the magazine won't read it. (2) Some of them will read only part of it — and your ad may not be in that section. (3) If they do read that section, some will not "see" your ad. (4) Out of those who see it, many will not read it. (5) Out of those who read it, some will not believe it. (6) Of those who do believe it — and mean to act on it — some will forget or never follow through.

Pretty discouraging, isn't it? Not at all — if you're prepared for it and set your sights accordingly. In other words, if you're not like those people who say, "The circulation of the *Times* is more than a million — and if only . . ."

So what percentage of people will respond? Enough — if you're lucky.

Buying magazine advertising requires a lot bigger nest egg than any other media. Because, if you haven't established a credit rating with them (and they're tough), you have to pay in advance. That means 60 to 90 days before your ad appears, if it's a monthly publication. If they have extended you credit, you have to pay within 10 days after the magazine comes out to get a "cash discount" of 2 percent — and no later than 30 days if they're ever going to extend credit again.

Remember that I told you the "average" monthly

magazine will, in 6 months, double the number of orders it pulls in the first 30 days? Well, that's O.K. for projecting income and making a decision as to whether to buy the magazine again. But it also means that you're going to wait quite awhile to get your advertising money back — and pay for the product, packaging, postage, and overhead — before you get into the black.

One of the main benefits of magazine advertising is that you can pinpoint your market.

What's good about magazines is that you can pinpoint your market. Men, boys, women, girls, psychology freaks, sexual deviates, motorcycle nuts — they all have their own little magazines, and some of the magazines can deliver combinations of these groups.

So when you've tested your ad in the newspapers (which is what I recommend) and you're ready to take a whack at the magazines, here are some tips:

TIP #1 Try to get a right-hand page. If your ad appears on a left hand page, results will be drastically diminished.

TIP #2 Try to buy enough space so you can be the only ad on the page. A full page insures it (in which case you want to request "editorial only" on the left-hand page). A two-thirds page in a "standard size" magazine, if the other column is editorial, is a good buy. A vertical half page in a "big size" magazine (like the *Ladies Home Journal*) will do the same job. I've bought a couple of horizontal half-pages — to my regret. People are conditioned to look first (and sometimes only) at the top of the page.

"Edits" can be a great way to get started in business, even if you have no money for advertising.

TIP #3 If you buy enough space, ask that there be "no backing coupon." Because if there's a competitive coupon on the "back" of yours — and it's cut out — you've lost a possible sale.

TIP #4 Ask if you can get a "free edit." Many magazines will give you one or more "edits" (small "articles" in their "Shoppers Guide Section") when you buy an ad. They won't produce a whole lot of orders (about the best I've done is $800), but every little bit helps. Other magazines, particularly the magazines directed at "Salesmen," may give you a good-sized article.

Incidentally, these "edits" can help you get started in business even if you have no money for advertising. Get a good 8 x 10 photo of your product at work, write a short, punchy ad — and send both out to all the magazines that have "Shoppers Guide Sections." If your product's new and exciting, quite a few may print it — and you'll be on your way! Dozens of magazines have these "Sections." If you want to know which they are, visit a newsstand, pick out the magazines that would appeal to your prospects and look for it in the "Mail Order Section." The magazine's address will be there or, if not, somewhere in the first few pages of the magazine.

TIP #5 Base your advertising buying on circulation, not "readership." The "readership" will be three to four times as high as the circulation, and small circulation magazines often quote that figure because it's so much more impressive. But your $4-per-thousand "rule of thumb" is based on circulation.

TIP #6 Another thing to check is "newsstand sales" as opposed to "subscriptions." (That information should be given to you along with a rate card.) For the Direct Response Business, a high percentage of newsstand sales is desirable. It means the purchaser of the magazine went to a little trouble to get it — and may read it more thoroughly.

TIP #7 Have you formed your own advertising agency yet?

When you're ready to get started on your magazine advertising, go to your local library and pick up a copy of the most current SRDS (Standard Rates and Data Service, 5201 Old Orchard Road, Skokie, Illinois 60077) publication entitled, *Consumer Magazine and Farm Publication Rate and Data.* In it you'll find a listing of every magazine you've ever heard of — and then some. The listings include such

Get your hands on a copy of the standard rates and data service publication titled "Consumer Magazine and Farm Publications Rate and Data." In it you will find a listing of virtually every magazine you've every heard about.

information as the publisher's editorial profile, ad rates, circulation, discounts available, addresses of reps and/or branch offices — virtually everything you'll need to know about a specific publication. You may also want to contact the person listed below. He can get your ad placed in most of the magazines now being published. You'll need to tell him what you are selling or show him a copy of your ad so he'll be able to suggest which magazines might be best suited for your offer. He is currently my only recommendation because, aside from the fact that he is scrupulously honest, he also happens to handle all of my ad placements. He's a good man and, unlike some others in the business, he won't steer you wrong.

MEGA MEDIA ASSOCIATES, INC.
STUART A. COGAN
603 EAST BALBOA BLVD., THIRD FLOOR
NEWPORT BEACH, CALIFORNIA 92661
(714) 673-2290

DIRECT MAIL

There's very little I can add here, because in terms of "how to buy it," it's a fairly simple medium. The only caution is to "shop" for printing prices because they can vary widely, and, of course, you can effect great savings by ordering large quantities. But don't step up your order until you've had a chance to test the "pull" of your letter.

To whom do you mail your letters? Well, what's the "profile" of your prospect? Man? Woman? Skiing enthusiast? Overweight? Earns $60,000 a year?

Mailing list brokers have hundreds of lists and millions of names and a lot of information about the people on those lists. You'll certainly want to contact them when you want to "rent" out the names of the customers you've acquired; and if you want to do a mailing of your own, a conscientious mailing list broker can be a lot of help in "zeroing in" on your target.

There are dozens of mailing list brokers listed in *Direct*

Direct Mail — the favorite of many a novice in this business — allows you to focus your advertising efforts on only those prospects who are most likely to be interested in your offer.

Marketing Magazine. I'm sure there are many other fine ones, but here are four I've done business with:

Dependable List, Inc.
950 South 25th Ave.
Bellwood, IL 60104
(708) 544-1000

JAMI Marketing Services
Two Blue Hill Drive
Pearl River, NY 10965
(914) 620-0700

Hank Marshall Marketing
P.O. Box 2729
Laguna Hills, CA 92653
(714) 581-5856

Mega Media Associates,Inc.
P.O. Box 4259
Newport Beach, CA 92661
(714) 673-2290

(Yes, I also use Stuart Cogan as my mailing list broker.)

Or you might check the Yellow Pages for someone nearby. You'll also find "Direct Marketing" for "Co-op Mailings." These are mailings made to specific groups (such as expectant mothers). You can participate with your particular offer — if it's pertinent — for a fraction of what it would cost you to make a mailing on your own.

Also, the broker you select will be able to put you in touch with people in this business who, for about three to five cents per piece, will include your advertising in their package or follow-up mailing. (These are called co-op mailings and package insert programs.) I heard about one large direct-selling luggage company who saved its business from bankruptcy using this advertising technique.

If the company you're "piggy-backing" with has customers who should be interested in your product, you'll probably do all right.

If you're curious about the various mailing lists and package insert programs that are available to you — just as with magazine advertising — you'll want to take a trip to your public library and pick up a copy of the most current

It's now up to you. Just don't be too busy earning a living to make any money.

Standard Rates and Data Services title, *Direct Mail List Rates and Data.* In it you will find that there is a mailing list (and package insert program) for just about every group imaginable. From Aircraft Owners to Zenith Book Buyers — quite literally "A to Z!"

So now you know how to "think up" a product (and a product can be a thing or a service), how to set your selling price and control your costs, you know the business procedures, how to write and produce your ad, and how to buy media.

Are you still too busy working for a living to make any money?

EPILOGUE: WHERE DO YOU GO FROM HERE?

Welcome to the first day of the **Best** of your life! Sound familiar? That's how I started the book and now here you are at the end. Only this is not the end at all, only the beginning. The beginning of the future that can be everything you choose to make it. I and those who have written and shared with me have gone through quite a lot together, and we have come to know each other pretty well. When you started out reading this book you were looking for something, and you thought enough of yourself to invest in your future. Now you know a great deal more about you. The fact that you have worked through all the steps of *The Lazy Man's Way* says you are serious about changing your life and you are willing to work at it. The tools you have started to use should already be working for you — giving you direction and energy, expanding your awareness, and heading you toward balance and fulfillment in every aspect of your life. So where do you go from here? That's easy. Start over, read it again. "What? I thought I was finished?" Finished, hardly! On *The Lazy Man's Way* you are never finished. There is always a new dimension unfolding, a new challenge to be met, a newly discovered glass wall between you and something you want to remove. No, you are not finished, but you are well on your way.

But why start over? Joe and I have given you a condensed form of the insights and knowledge gained from a lifetime of experience. There is no way that you can absorb everything that you have read and done in this book in one sitting. The second time through you will be amazed by how much you did not remember and, if you don't remember it, you can't use it. There is another important reason for going through it again. You are not the same person you were when you started. The changes that have taken place in you will give you a whole new

Every exit is an entry somewhere else.

TOM STOPPARD (B. 1937)
English playwright, novelist

The reward of a thing well done, is to have done it.

RALPH WALDO EMERSON (1803–1882)
American poet, essayist, philosopher

Nothing great is created suddenly, any more than a bunch of grapes or a fig. If you tell me that you desire a fig, I answer you that there must be time. Let it first blossom then bear fruit, then ripen.

EPICTETUS (55–135)
Greek Stoic philosopher

Perseverance is more prevailing than violence; and many things which cannot be overcome when they are together, yield themselves up when taken little by little.

PLUTARCH (A.D. 46–120)
Greek biographer, essayist

perspective. And, if anything, you will get far *more* out of this book the second time than you did the first. You have just completed your first graduate course in human attitude engineering, and you have been given quite a tool kit to use; and like any tool, unless it is used, nothing happens. And after a while, you forget how to use it. Don't let that happen to you. Keep working on your attitudes. Don't let a day go by without carefully studying your affirmations. Don't forget to practice self-awareness. Stay on top of your self-talk. Don't let that voice in your head drag you back into old self-limiting attitudes and failure habits. And keep on using the power of Super Suggestion. When you have totally absorbed the positive suggestions, try writing and recording your own, dealing with specific problems.

When you have finished your second time through *The Lazy Man's Way to Riches*, you can continue to use this material as is needed for a refresher or a guide to handle a specific problem. You have Joe Karbo and Richard Gilly Nixon as your personal advisors anytime you want. Periodically, go over the whole book again. Some signals that it is time to go back through the book are nagging problems you can't get rid of, feelings of frustration in some area of your life, stagnation in any area of your life, a decline in your physical or emotional well-being, or a lack of financial progress. Any one of these is a sign that you are not fully using your tool kit and it is time to go back and re-train yourself.

Consider the postage stamp, my son. It secures success through its ability to stick to one thing till it gets there.

JOSH BILLINGS (1818–1885)
American humorist

Remember back in Part 1, Chapter 1, I told you about Linda and how she read and re-read *The Lazy Man's Way to Riches* and highlighted it each time in a different color? The next time you go through the book you will find yourself highlighting things you didn't see the first time, or now see differently. Each time you re-read the book you will do it in less time and will see more and learn more. Interestingly enough you will learn more about *you*, and you will be pleasantly surprised at how you have grown and how your views have changed and matured.

And now it is time to warn you about one obstacle that can still keep you from the Riches you desire. You have been working on changing yourself and changing the attitudes and behaviors that have been a part of you for years. And if you have been using your tools, you are definitely changing those attitudes. But beware! Those old attitudes are like deep ruts. Stop using your tools and you will slip right back into those ruts. And you know where they lead! It is a little decision to spend 10 or 15 minutes everyday using these tools that will get you everything you desire out of life. That little decision can now be a major turning point in your life.

I think it is about time I told you about Joe's reasons for going to the trouble of putting this program together. I know he would like me to pass them on to you. So here are his words:

> Obviously, I will make money from this project but there are lots of ways I can do that — that don't involve quite as much work for me. This program is part of an overall campaign. A campaign to attack what I see to be one of the most serious problems our society faces.

> There is sickness in our country that is eating away at our fiber. It is the disease of apathy and fear and lack of personal responsibility. It destroys human beings by destroying their hopes and dreams and our governments and schools can do nothing to halt its spread.

> But, each individual can do something given the right tools, the right encouragement, and under-standing of the real problems and a realization that they are not alone in this fight.

> I know that the principles of The Lazy Man's Way are an antidote to this sickness and I am

Practice yourself, for heaven's sake, in little things; and thence proceed to greater.

EPICTETUS (55–135)
Greek Stoic philosopher

There is one quality more important than "know-how" and we cannot accuse the United States of any undue amount of it. This is "know-what" by which we determine not only how to accomplish our purpose, but what our purposes are to be.

NORMAN WIENER (1894–1964)
American mathematician, educator

Society of Partners has local ▶
chapters throughout the United
States. These local chapters are
formed to bring people together
for mutual assistance based on
the principles of "The Lazy
Man's Way To Riches." To join
a chapter, form a chapter, or
subscribe to the Society's
newsletter, contact The Society
through Nixon • Karbo
Publishing Company,
1 (800) 800-7707

*Only the consciousness of a
purpose that is mightier than any
man and worthy of all men can
fortify and inspirit and compose
the souls of men.*

WALTER LIPPMANN (1889–1974)
American teacher, editor, journalist

*Until we meet again, may the
good Lord take a liking to you.*

ROY ROGERS (B. 1912)
American actor, singer
"King of the Cowboys"

*determined to spread them as widely as I can. My
book was a start, but I have come to realize that we
need constant reinforcement to continue to thrive
and grow. That is the real reason for my personal
consultation program. That is the reason I founded
the Society of Partners and that is why I want to get
the seminars going around the country, and in
many other countries as well. To expand on the
ideas of my book and to provide a springboard for
the formation of local chapters. To provide that
encouragement and support and continued contact
with positive, like minded, people. It is not that I
think of myself as some kind of Messiah come to
save the world. I am simply one man doing the best
he knows how. Success has been defined as
making steady progress toward a worthwhile goal,
and I have always been hooked on success so I will
be continuing on this path.*

Joe had a way of inspiring others to follow his lead so
you can bet that Betty and the family and those of us that
had the good fortune to know him, or to be touched by
him, carry on this campaign. I waited until now to share
Joe's purpose with you because now that you have been
through the program you are more likely to understand
what Joe was working toward. And what those of us who
are involved in this project are determined to continue.

I would enjoy hearing from you. What you did with
your tools. Which ones were the most useful to you? And
how you feel about Joe's campaign. You are certainly
welcome to join in and help spread these ideas. We need
all the help we can get. So here we are. Not at the end but
at the beginning. I won't say goodbye because I am not
leaving. I will be right there with you every step of *The
Lazy Man's Way to Riches.*

Where do you go from here? I suggest you start at
Page 1.

AFTERWORD

This expanded, revised, and updated version of *The Lazy Man's Way to Riches* was done out of a deep-felt belief that the lessons of this fine work should be kept in print and made available for another 20 years for a new generation.

There comes a point at which the old adage, "If it ain't broke, don't fix it . . . " no longer applies. The fact that the first edition of this program sold more than three million copies internationally — mostly by word-of-mouth — is a wonderful testament to the effectiveness of this program. The prestigious 20 year history of this program and the rewards it offers are evidenced by the thousands of testimonial letters the readers have sent confirming that, "This program has permanently changed my life for the better!"

Of course, growth and your personal development are never-ending processes. Therefore, as our knowledge deepens from our own experiences, and as we obtained valuable feedback from our readers, this program was updated, revised, and expanded and shall be again and again.

We wanted to produce a comprehensive program that involves you, excites you, makes you think and, most importantly, helps you on the journey from where you are to where *your* ideal life awaits — the destiny you envision for yourself. In writing and revising the program, neither Joe nor I have withheld anything as our "secret;" we've shared it all here.

We would be delighted to hear from you, our readers, for future editions. Your input can help us "flesh out" chapters; add favorite quotes or meaningful stories. Please share your success with us. Tell us what chapters or steps were particularly helpful in gaining that success. Offer your suggestions for improvement. Let us know what still perplexes you.

We would especially appreciate your thoughts on extensions to any one of the principles or ideas that you would like to see explored further. That is what our seminar program focuses on — expanding, amplifying, and extending the principles and lessons of this program. Only you can help make both this program and the seminars more rewarding with your input.

Although I can't guarantee your success, the principles offered here are tried and proven. They work for those who use them. I do extend this word of caution, however: Be careful . . . if you follow the principles and steps set forth in this program, you *will* get your Riches. So choose them carefully. Good luck!

Richard Gilly Nixon
El Morro Beach, CA   February, 1994

To help me help others achieve their true Riches,
write to me at:

c/o F. P. Publishing Co., Inc.
16560 Harbor Blvd. Suite "O"
Fountain Valley, California 92708

Thumbs Up!

BIBLIOGRAPHY/REFERENCE MATERIAL

TITLE

    Barnes & Nobles Book of Quotations
    Best Quotations for All Occasions
    The Concise Columbia Dictionary of Quotations
* *The International Thesaurus of Quotations*
    The Magic of Believing
* *Speakers Sourcebook*
    21st Century Dictionary of Quotations

AUTHOR

Fitzhenry, Robert I.
Henry, Lewis C.
Andrews, Robert
Tripp, Rhoda Thomas
Bristor, Claude
Van Ekeren, Glenn
Princeton Language Institute

* denotes our favorites

TITLE	AUTHOR
As a Man Thinketh	Allen, James
Breakthrough Advertising	Schwarz, Eugene
Building a Small Business That Works	Gerber, Michael
Building a Mail Order Business	Cohen, Dr. William A.
The Complete Guide to Self Publishing	Ross, Tom & Marylyn
Confessions of an Advertising Man	Ogilvy, David
Critical Path	Fuller, R. Buckminster
Dare to Win	Hansen, Mark Victor
Direct Marketing	Nash, Ed
Dollars in Your Mailbox	Weckesser, Ph.D., Ernest P.
The "E" Myth	Gerber, Michael E.
Even Eagles Need a Push	McNally, David
Full Esteem Ahead	Timmons, Tim
Future Life	Chapin, M.D., Donald
How I Made $1,000,000 In Mail Order	Cossman, E. Joseph
How to Make Big Money in the Next 30 Days	Carter, David
How to Make It Big in the Seminar Business	Karasik, Paul
How to Win Friends and Influence People	Carnegie, Dale
How to Write, Speak and Think More Effectively	Flesch, Rudolf
Killer Advertising	Halbert, Greg
Live Your Dreams	Brown, Les
Mail Order Success Secrets	Hicks, Tyler G.
Man's Search for Meaning	Frankl, Viktor E.
My Life in Advertising/Scientific Advertising	Hopkins, Claude
A New Guide to Rational Living	Ellis, Ph.D., Albert and Harper, Ph.D., Robert A.
The Path of Least Resistance	Fritz, Robert
The Power of Positive Thinking	Peale, Norman Vincent
Profitable Direct Marketing	Kobs, Jim
* *Psycho-Cybernetics*	Maltz, M.D., Maxwell
* *The Richest Man in Babylon*	Clason, George S.
The Robert Collier Letter Book	Collier, Robert
The Selling Power of a Woman	Walters, Dottie
The Seven Habits of Highly Effective People	Covey, Stephen R.
Speak & Grow Rich	Walters, Dottie

SUGGESTED READING (CONT)

Speakers Sourcebook   Van Ekeren, Glenn
The Stress of Life   Selye, Hans
Successful Direct Marketing Methods   Stone, Bob
Tested Advertising Methods   Caples, John
Think and Grow Rich   Hill, Napoleon
The True Believer   Hoffer, Eric
Your Marketing Genius at Work   Abrahan, Jay

* denotes our favorites

SUGGESTED AUDIO CASSETTE PROGRAMS

CASSETTE PROGRAM   **SPEAKER**

The Awakened Life   Dyer, Ph.D., Wayne
The Best of the Best Series   Hansen, Mark Victor
* Challenge to Succeed in the '90s   Rohn, E. James
Goals   Ziglar, Zig
* How Do You Face the Day?   Foreman, Ed
How to Be a No Limit Person   Dyer, Ph.D., Wayne
How to Build Your Self Esteem   Canfield, Jack
* The Lazy Man's Way to Riches   Nixon, Richard Gilly
Lead the Field   Nightingale, Earl
The Millionaire Mind Set   Abbott, Chuck
Overcome Fear in Public Speaking   Foreman, Ed
Path of Least Resistance   Fritz, Robert
Psychology of Winning   Waitley, Ph.D., Denis
Relationship Strategies   Alessandra, Tony
See You at the Top   Ziglar, Zig
* Self-Talk & Mind-Controlled Relaxation   Foreman, Ed
The Seven Strategies for Wealth and Happiness Rohn, E. James
Speak & Grow Rich   Walters, Dottie
* Take Charge of Your Life   Rohn, E. James
Turn Teen Years into Terrific Years   Foreman, Ed
Unlimited Power   Robbins, Anthony
Vibrant Health   Foreman, Ed
Yes, You Can Overcome Any Challenge   Foreman, Ed

RECOMMENDED SEMINAR LEADERS/SPEAKERS

A seminar by any of the following people is a wonderful investment in yourself.

SPEAKER

Abbott, Chuck
Allesandra, Tony
Bedley, Gene
Boe, Anne
Brown, Les
Canfield, Jack
DeJong, Hans
Dyer, Wayne

Foreman, Ed
Fripp, Patricia
Hansen, Mark Victor
Hayes, Ira
Merritt, Connie
Nicholas, Ted
* Nixon, Richard Gilly
Pippert, Becky

Robbins, Tony
Robert, Cavett
* Rohn, Jim
* Timmons, Tim
Waitley, Denis
Walters, Dottie
Ziglar, Zig

* denotes our favorites

There are others out there who have written great books, produced audio cassette programs, and deliver stunning seminars. Please tell us your favorites — those who have made an impact on your life. We will try to include them on our list.

QUOTE AUTHOR INDEX

FOR YOU!
A FREE COPY OF THE GAME PLAN FOR SUCCESS,
THE LAZY MAN'S WAY TO RICHES NEWSLETTER!

Why would you want our newsletter? Because school is never out for the professional. Physicians, lawyers, realtors, athletes, C.P.A.'s, policemen, pilots . . . practically everyone who needs to keep sharp, stay up, pull ahead, grow and do better, gets continuing education in as many ways as possible. That's what Game Plan for Success is — continuous education. Brain food, smarts, answers to your questions (both asked and unasked – known and unknown). It's insight. Awareness. A resource. A key. A microscope and a telescope.

Game Plan for Success takes up where Lazy Man left off. It continues to give you guidance, mentoring and so much more. And it's all yours for only $60 a year — all 10 issues, if you decide to become a subscriber. However, if you order now, using the order form on the back of this page, it's only **$29.95** with this one time offer!

Order a two year subscription now and it's still half price and you'll receive Richard Gilly Nixon's audio tape, "How to Have Your Best Month Ever" or a copy of the original 1973 edition of The Lazy Man's Way to Riches– FREE! And you get 20 issues of success for your brain.

Not sure? Timid? Broke? Well, we'll make it easy for you to be introduced to the newsletter. Just supply us some information about yourself by filling out the form on the back of this page, and you'll receive the premiere issue of the Game Plan for Success newsletter absolutely **free**!

Do it now and be on your way to a future of success and Riches.

If you're looking for . . .

. . . services that will help guide you down the road to Riches, Mr. Nixon, this book's co-author, offers a variety of essential services for today's businesses as well as individuals wishing to succeed. Just a few of the services offered include:

Business Consulting	*Audio Tapes*	*Keynote Speaking*
One-to-Three Day Public Seminars	*Mini-Workshops*	*Private Seminars*
Learning Annex Seminars	*Special Reports*	*Small Business Evaluation*

For more information regarding these programs or customized programs that would more suit your needs, please contact Mr. Nixon at:

F. P. Publishing Co., Inc, • 16560 Harbor Blvd. Suite "O" • Fountain Valley, CA   92708
(800) 800-7707   (714) 775-8199   Fax: (714) 531-6332
E-Mail FPNixon@AOL.com

- -

We're looking for information about you

For your FREE copy of the Game Plan For Success newsletter, please fill in the following:

Name: ❏ Mr. ❏ Ms. ❏ Mrs. _____

Address:_____ City_____ State_____ Zip _____

Phone: (   ) _____ Age ❏Under 25 ❏25-35 ❏35-45 ❏45-55 ❏Over 55 ❏No way!

How did you learn about this program?
- ❏ Magazine_____
- ❏ TV Commercial
- ❏ Newspaper Ad
- ❏ Radio Commercial
- ❏ Other_____
- ❏ Bookstore
- ❏ TV Infomercial
- ❏ Radio Interview
- ❏ Direct Mail

What Is Your Highest Educational Level?
- ❏ High School Graduate ❏ GED
- ❏ College Graduate ❏ Graduate School
- ❏Other_____

My Goals Are: ❏ Business ❏ Personal ❏ Both

Occupation:
- ❏ Professional
  (C.P.A. Dr., Attny., etc.)
- ❏ Therapist/Phychologist
- ❏ Executive
- ❏ Large Corporate Employee
- ❏ Small Business Employee
- ❏ Self Employed
- ❏ Sales/Marketing
- ❏ Retailer
- ❏ Wholesaler
- ❏ Other_____

Yearly Household Income:
- ❏ Under $25,000 ❏ $25,000-$60,000
- ❏ $60,000-$100,000 ❏ $100,000-$250,000
- ❏ Over $250,000

❏**YES!** I'm ready to save 50% right now! The Game Plan for Success newsletter is just what I need. Please enter my ❏one year ($29.95) or ❏two year ($59.90) subscription. For my two year subscription I choose ❏"How to Have the Best Month Ever" tape or ❏The original 1973 *The Lazy Man's Way to Riches* book. Enclosed is my check or money order for _____. Or simply bill my credit card.

Please charge to my: ❏ Visa ❏ MasterCard ❏ American Express ❏ Discover

Acct. No. |__|__|__|__|__|__|__|__|__|__|__|__|__|__|__| Exp. |__|__|__| Daytime Phone _____

Name:_____ Address:_____

City_____ State_____ Zip _____ Signature _____

(Offer expires 7/1/96 and may be withdrawn at any time)